THE
LORD'S
TABLE

THE LORD'S TABLE

THE MEANING OF FOOD IN EARLY JUDAISM AND CHRISTIANITY

GILLIAN FEELEY-HARNIK

SMITHSONIAN INSTITUTION PRESS

WASHINGTON AND LONDON

Library of Congress Cataloging-in-Publication Data
Feeley-Harnik, Gillian, 1940–
    The Lord's table : the meaning of food in early Judaism and
Christianity / Gillian Feeley-Harnik.
        p.   cm.
    Includes bibliographical references and index.
    ISBN 1-56098-338-8 (alk. paper)
        1. Food—Religious aspects—Christianity.   2. Food—Religious
aspects—Judaism.   3. Lord's Supper—History—Early church, ca.
30-600.   4. Judaism—History—Post-exilic period, 586 B.C.–210 A.D.
I. Title.
BR115.N87F44   1994   93-41414
234′ 163′09015—dc20   CIP

British Cataloguing-in-Publication Data available

Manufactured in the United States of America

99 98 97 96 95 94   5 4 3 2 1

⊗ The paper used in this publication meets the minimum requirements of the
American National Standard for Performance of Paper for Printed Library Materials
Z39.48-1984.

Permission to quote the lines from "Passover," by Linda Pastan, originally published in
1982 in her volume *PM/AM: New and Selected Poems,* has been granted by W. W.
Norton, New York; for the lines from "Cuisine Bourgeoise," copyright 1954 by Wallace
Stevens, published in *The Collected Poems of Wallace Stevens,* permission is granted by
Alfred A. Knopf, Inc., and by Faber and Faber Ltd., London.

The essay, lacking poetry extracts, preface with associated references cited, and other
front matter, was published with the subtitle "Eucharist and Passover in Early
Christianity" in 1981.

To Alan

Down the long table, past fresh shoots of a root
they have been hacking at for centuries,
you hold up the unleavened bread—a baked scroll
whose wavy lines are indecipherable.

Linda Pastan, "Passover"

. . . Who, then, are they, seated here?
Is the table a mirror in which they sit and look?
Are they men eating reflections of themselves?

Wallace Stevens, "Cuisine Bourgeoise"

CONTENTS

vii

CONTENTS

ACKNOWLEDGMENTS

I am grateful to Jon W. Anderson, Sidney W. Mintz, and Michael Silverstein for their thoughtful comments on the preface to this book.

The essay benefited from the contribution of many of my colleagues in anthropological and biblical studies. I am especially grateful to Professor T. O. Beidelman for introducing me to the anthropological study of the Bible, for critiquing innumerable drafts, and for teaching the graduate seminar on the anthropology of Christianity for which the essay was originally written; to Professors J. David Sapir, J. Christopher Crocker, Peter Metcalf, Michelle Zimbalist Rosaldo, and Renato Rosaldo for their very useful advice on revision; and to Professor Peter Metcalf for his painstaking editorial assistance and his encouragement.

Being uncomfortably well acquainted with the biblical maxim "he that diggeth a pit shall fall into it," I am grateful to my colleagues in the history of religion for doing their best to guide me to Professors Anne Matter and Norman Petersen for their critical reading of early drafts of the manuscript and for long hours discussing topics related to biblical scholarship, and to Professors Phyllis Ann Bird and Robert A. Kraft for their assistance. I take full responsibility for the way I have used their advice and for any errors that still remain.

I also thank Rosemary Lane, Donna Chenall, and Blair Jackson for their assistance in typing and proofreading, and Jane Barry and Eileen D'Araujo for their skill in editing.

I am grateful to Williams College for granting me a leave in 1979–80, and to the Bunting Institute of Radcliffe College for providing ideal circumstances in which to write.

PREFACE

"Noshing is sacred." In three words, Israel Shenker evokes two contrary views of food—of life—and all possible variations between. Shenker (1979) speaks to contemporary patterns of religious pluralism, to the latter-day Corinthians among us, within us, our coexistence now made possible by ceaseless separations of "church" and "state." Religious pluralism also characterized the Mediterranean world in biblical times, when noshing was sacred (or maybe not) but differently from now. "Meats for the belly and the belly for meats" (I Corinthians 6:13) still sounds familiar, yet the popular "Page-a-Day" astrology calendar does not just echo Paul's letter to the Corinthians (I Corinthians 6:19) in advising Pisceans on July 13, 1993: "Treat your body like a sacred temple. Eat more fruits, vegetables and vitamin-rich foods." All the more reason to wonder how food and eating keep confounding our every effort to sort the complexities of life into neat categories, indeed encourage us to keep rethinking what we live by as participants and observers.

As an anthropologist, I have taken a relational approach to these issues, focusing on the diversities of early Judaism from which multiple Christianities first emerged and gradually redefined themselves as different. Since Christianity became a state orthodoxy in the early fourth century C.E., Judaism and eventually Islam have continued to be the explicit, but also hidden, ghettoized, or suppressed streams against or through which mainstreams have been defined even after the disestablishment of religion in some places. Not surprisingly, given the social dynamics of opposition and oppression, the critical connections that all parties have drawn on to create their mutual identities are the first to be forgotten. The resulting amnesia is perpetuated in denominational divisions of labor that biblical scholars are now beginning to cross, but that elsewhere remain common. This book was and is an effort to understand the early and persistent connections, disentangled from later separations. Given increasing evidence of the influence of biblical scholarship on the formation of Euro-American social theory in the nineteenth and twentieth centuries (Eilberg-Schwartz 1990:31-112; Tambiah 1990), I begin this brief preface with questions about anthropological approaches to the Bible, then go on to other questions that recent studies might raise.

New historical research has expanded our knowledge of the extraordinary flourishing of religious pluralism during the intertestamental period (Goodman 1987 is an outstanding example), and several major works have documented the central significance of food and eating in a wide range of Jewish, Christian, and Islamic contexts (e.g., Brumberg 1988; Buitelaar 1993; Bynum 1987; Curran 1989; Fredman 1981; Jeanneret 1991; Mintz 1985; Neville 1987), including the ancient Mediterranean (e.g., Brown 1982; Eilberg-Schwartz 1990; Garnsey 1988; Gowers 1993; Segal 1991:224-53). Most comparative research still focuses on structures of classification (e.g., Aycock 1992; Bulmer 1989; Carroll 1985; Leach and Aycock 1983), limited, in matters of food, to the prohibitions of Leviticus and Deuteronomy. As Bulmer (1989:305) rightly observes, "Leviticus and Deuteronomy are a *locus classicus* referred to again and again in anthropological writing." Why should this be so?

Now I would argue that the "abominations" (the standard English translation of four Hebrew words) owe their classic position in theoretical debates about "superstition" and "rationality" to the persistence of ongoing controversies about peoplehood that I tried to outline in this book. In effect replicating major controversies about law in the intertestamental period, the prohibitions are seen as canons of adherence to "tradition" or "custom," thus substantiating rational choice theories based on the "freedom" of "modern" social actors. In anthropology, this approach culminates in theories of negation as the elementary form of political life.

Obviously prohibitions may serve domination, but the most careful contemporary studies (e.g., Browning 1992) suggest that individual rational free choice is one of the major ideologies of our time. Mintz's (1985) work indicates the ways that the contemporary food industry, linked to an economic system based on steadily increasing consumption, hawks new products by claiming they widen individuals' freedoms of choice when in fact they homogenize and narrow them. Contrary to

our mythologies, freely choosing is still a rare, heroic act. Indeed, the
paradoxical "freedom" of people "redeemed" from "slavery" in Egypt to
be God's "slaves," serving the hardest moral ideals, is one of the most
distinctive common preoccupations of writers in the Hebrew Bible and
New Testament, and a recurrent theme over the past several centuries
(Feeley-Harnik 1982; Walzer 1985).

The Lord's Table focuses on why and how sectarians in the
intertestamental period used dietary rules and other eating practices to
address major ethical questions of identity and affiliation in radically
changing circumstances. The study combines comparative research on
the semiotics of food with the arguments of biblical scholars Renée
Bloch and Geza Vermès that we should look first to participants' own
modes of analysis—notably *midrash.* I argue that food, articulated in
feeding, eating, starving, and fasting, provided a powerfully concentrated
"language" for debating moral-legal issues and transforming social
relations, for people who would have no graven images. Midrashic
studies have since become widespread in religious studies (e.g., Bruns
1987; Fishbane 1989), and the work of Eilberg-Schwartz (1990) shows
the value of close research on root metaphors. Ironically, given the
historicity of midrashic forms of interpretation and the materiality of
metaphor, the influence of literary approaches has widened rather than
narrowed the gap between textual and social-historical studies.

As an anthropologist, I would still argue for an integrated approach,
grounded even more deeply in participants' modes of analysis, to gain
some critical perspective on those modes we can no longer assume to
be neutral or universal. It now seems to me that French, British, and
American semiotic theories on foods as "signs" and "symbols" achieve
explanations of socialization through habituation, naturalization, or
embodiment, by projecting the insights and convictions of biblical and
classical writers, disconnected from their social-historical roots, onto a
nature-culture divide natural mainly to Europeans and Americans. How
is it possible to escape from such seamless unities to further our
understanding of particular and general patterns of human behavior,
while doing justice to social pluralism?

The work of Bakhtin (1968) on "heteroglossia" and Heilman (1987)
on "interlanguages" suggests one approach. Bakhtin (1968) focuses
especially on heteroglossia arising out of political oppression, in which
people ostensibly speaking the same dominant language expand its
capacities for multiple meaning through punning, irony, satire, allusion,

and ambiguity, thus freeing themselves to say the unsayable. In his study of Rabelais's fantastic critiques of churchly states, he focuses especially on the powerful capacities of feasting and drinking to liberate speech. Bakhtin's approach would illuminate scriptural writers' ambivalence about human polities that could reproduce Egypt in Canaan, the actualities of political pluralism in the intertestamental period, and also the ontological impossibilities of naming and knowing.

Heilman analyzes how Modern Orthodox Jewish men read the Talmud in the contemporary United States and Israel. He shows how the reader-speakers create new "interlanguages" by combining linguistic registers—Yiddish, biblical Hebrew, Israeli (Sephardic) Hebrew, English, and sometimes Aramaic and Greek—intimately connected to the pluralities of their lives. Speaking interlanguages is one of the major ways they integrate their different worlds, even if only fleetingly. Heilman shows how ancient words and books come alive again in the mouths and bodies of their speakers. His work helps to explain how the books themselves acquire in these relations a generational life, a social personhood with fleshly attributes of age, gender, and class (see also Goldberg 1987; Kirshenblatt-Gimblett 1982).

Talmud-*lerners* celebrate their fellowship by concluding each tractate with a meal (*siyum*), prepared by their wives. Heilman does not explore the eating of the speaking or its gendered dimensions, yet some of the most creative recent work on eating, feeding, and meaning focuses on the close association of women and food (e.g., Brumberg 1988; Bynum 1987). The gendered approaches to interpretation that Bynum (1987:277-96) finds characteristic of medieval women have striking analogues in biblical texts, conveyed in clothing as well as feeding (see Feeley-Harnik 1990). We need further historical research on the various and changing bodies of fleshly spirits whom a God (with no body, Eilberg-Schwartz 1990) could consume or devour in a moment.

One clear feature of biblical controversies about bodies is their common focus on *faces*, or, more exactly, seeing face to face. Biblical meals draw their sustenance from the paradox of how to see/know "face to face" the ineffable, imageless presence of God in life, in another person (e.g., Exodus 33:11; Deuteronomy 34:10; I Corinthians 13:12); how to "see/recognize" (Heb. *akenaa*) or "discern, evaluate, recognize" (Gk. *diakrinein* in the New Testament) what is deep, hidden, buried, ultimately unknowable. The quandry is epitomized in relations with beings in burning bushes; on clouded mountaintops; under furry skins,

Preface

veils, skirts, cloaks; on tablets; at tables; in scrolls—shining, clouding, devouring, protecting, deflecting encounters, thwarting complete understanding, yet through which life-giving words, meals, emerge.

The intense mutuality of these relations, in which neither could "stand for" another, is not adequately conveyed by signifier-signified distinctions, organized hierarchically on mind-body lines. "A mirror dimly . . ." (I Corinthians 13:12) plainly refutes this approach, looking two-sided, but reflecting only one. "Mouth to mouth" (Numbers 12:7-8) is the most direct statement of this mutuality, drawing its force from biblical writers' repeated observations of the substantiality of speech in the mouth. Indeed, "the mouth" of God is a whole human being, even as the "face" is the whole presence of a being, thus inextricably "historical" in our own terms.

How are we to understand the generative union of eating-speaking, the mouth-to-mouth presences created in their relations, celebrated in heavenly wedding feasts, the capacities of meals to achieve complete "mergings" (as in the later talmudic tractate *Eruvin*)? Or, if we stood outside all this, we might ask: How do people come to attribute meaning to food or words, eating or speaking? How do these acts acquire social value?

The most common answer to this question lies in the unexamined metaphor of a market place central to the varieties of linguistic theory from which contemporary theories of culture and semiotics have come. The metaphor compares the social processes by which people create, acquire, convert, and incorporate the meanings and values of signs to the processes of production, exchange, and consumption through which goods acquire values and prices in a commoditized—abstracted—free-market economy. Although this metaphor might be widespread, evidence of long-standing connections between words and money in European and American literature (Shell 1982) suggests that it arose out of particular social-historical relations worthy of closer study before universalizing econocentric explanations of significance.

Like slavery in the Bible, "miraculous feeding" calls for the reintegration of economic with other analytical approaches (see Brown 1982; Garnsey 1988). But the central image of "God's slave"—as radically severed, yet as wholly connected as a living human could be—suggests an additional kind of political economic phenomenology involved in placing and displacing persons, and thus perhaps especially relevant to the spatial politics so central to later Jewish-Christian relations as well.

memory + stomach

THE LORD'S TABLE

Across major differences, from *yada* to *gnosis*, the biblical writers emphatically insist on the mutuality of eating-speaking and remembering, a profoundly historical view most explicitly stated in God's command to the Israelites to tell their children about the passover sacrifice (Exodus 12:26-27) and in Jesus's command to "Eat . . . drink . . . Do this in remembrance of me" (Luke 22:19). Yet despite the prominence of this theme in the arts, the hints of similar connections in ethnographic monographs (Trobriand Islanders locate memory in the stomach), and some attention to the memory-enhancing effects of acetylcholine and glucose in rats and elderly humans, there is surprisingly little research on this topic.

Even as the imagery of slavery speaks powerfully to social processes of abstracting people from known places, so feeding speaks to processes of *re*-grounding people in relation to one another through complex sensory memories of experiences anchored in places—tables, tablets, houses, homelands. Gastronomy is geography; foods are intimately linked to the place-times of their growing, making, and eating. In our age of mass factory production, it is mainly connoisseurs of luxury foods—coffee, tea, wines, spices, merging into perfumes and bodily aromas—that possess what now seem such mysterious skills of determining the single place and time on earth where a precious food originated, a significant place-time critical to its value. Ours may well be an age when nothing seems "sacred"—"set apart and forbidden" (!) in Durkheim's famous phrase—precisely because of radical political-economic strategies, akin to enslavement, in which some humans have been rendered relatively, even absolutely, groundless compared with others; where privilege is synonymous with *place* in the deepest phenomenological sense, and must be challenged in every meal.

References Cited

Aycock, A. 1992. Potiphar's wife: Prelude to a structural exegesis. *Man*, n.s. 27:479–94.

Bakhtin, M. 1968 (1965). *Rabelais and his world*. Translated by Helen Iswolsky. Cambridge, Mass.: M.I.T. Press.

Brown, P. 1982. The problem of miraculous feeding in the Graeco-Roman world. In *Center for Hermeneutical Studies: Colloquy 42*, pp. 16–24. Berkeley, Calif.: Graduate Theological Union.

Browning, C. R. 1992. *Ordinary men: Reserve Police Battalion 101 and the final solution in Poland*. New York: HarperCollins.

Preface

Brumberg, J. J. 1988. 'Fasting girls': The history of anorexia nervosa. Cambridge, Mass.: Harvard University Press (New American Library).

Bruns, G. L. 1987. Midrash and allegory: The beginnings of scriptural interpretation. In R. Alter and F. Kermode, eds., The literary guide to the Bible, pp. 625–46. Cambridge, Mass.: Harvard University Press (Belknap Press).

Buitelaar, M. 1993. On fasting and feasting: An ethnographic study of Ramadan in Morocco. New York: St. Martin's (Berg).

Bulmer, R. 1989. The uncleanness of the birds of Leviticus and Deuteronomy. Man, n.s. 24:304–21.

Bynum, C. W. 1987. Holy feast and holy fast: The religious significance of food to medieval women. Berkeley: University of California Press.

Carroll, M. P. l985. A structuralist exercise: The problem of Moses' name. American Ethnologist 12:775–8.

Curran, P. 1989. Grace before meals: Food ritual and body discipline in convent culture. Urbana: University of Illinois Press.

Eilberg-Schwartz, H. 1990. The savage in Judaism: An anthropology of Israelite religion and ancient Judaism. Bloomington: Indiana University Press.

Feeley-Harnik, G. l982. Is historical anthropology possible? The case of the runaway slave. In G. M. Tucker and D. A. Knight, eds., Humanizing America's iconic book, pp. 95–126. Chico, Calif.: Scholars Press.

———. 1990. Naomi and Ruth: Building up the house of David. In S. Niditch, ed., Text and tradition: The Hebrew Bible and folklore, pp. 163–84. Atlanta: Scholars Press.

Fishbane, M. 1989. The garments of Torah: Essays in biblical hermeneutics. Bloomington: Indiana University Press.

Fredman, R. G. 1981. The Passover seder: Afikoman in exile. Philadelphia: University of Pennsylvania Press.

Garnsey, P. 1988. Famine and food-supply in the Graeco-Roman world. Cambridge: Cambridge University Press.

Goldberg, H. E. 1987. Torah and children: Symbolic aspects of the reproduction of Jews and Judaism. In H. E. Goldberg, ed., Judaism viewed from within and from without: Anthropological studies, pp. 107–30. Albany: State University of New York Press.

Goodman, M. 1987. The ruling class of Judaea: The origins of the Jewish revolt against Rome A.D. 66–70. Cambridge: Cambridge University Press.

Gowers, E. 1993. The loaded table: Representations of food in Roman literature. Oxford: Clarendon Press.

Heilman, S. C. 1987 (1983). The people of the book: Drama, fellowship, and religion. With a new preface. Chicago: University of Chicago Press.

Jeanneret, M. 1991. A feast of words: Banquets and table talk in the Renaissance. Translated by J. Whiteley and E. Hughes. Chicago: University of Chicago Press.

Kirshenblatt-Gimblett, B. 1982. The cut that binds: The western Ashkenazic Torah binder as nexus between circumcision and Torah. In V. Turner, ed., Celebration: Studies in festivity and ritual, pp. 136–146. Washington: Smithsonian Institution Press.

Leach, E., and D. A. Aycock. 1983. *Structuralist interpretations of biblical myth.* Cambridge: Cambridge University Press and the Royal Anthropological Institute.

Mintz, S. W. 1985. *Sweetness and power: The place of sugar in modern history.* New York: Viking Penguin.

Neville, G. K. 1987. *Kinship and pilgrimage: Rituals of reunion in American Protestant culture.* New York: Oxford University Press.

Segal, A. F. 1991. *Paul the convert: The apostolate and apostasy of Saul the Pharisee.* New Haven, Conn.: Yale University Press.

Shell, M. 1982. *Money, language, and thought: Literary and philosophic economies from the medieval to the modern era.* Berkeley: University of California Press.

Shenker, I. 1979. *Noshing is sacred.* Indianapolis: Bobbs-Merrill. [S.J. Perelman suggested the title.]

Tambiah, S. J. 1990. *Magic, science, religion, and the scope of rationality.* Cambridge: Cambridge University Press.

Walzer, M. 1985. *Exodus and revolution.* New York: Basic Books.

1

ANTHROPOLOGY AND THE BIBLE

> I supplied this world with unfailing
> food and a mysterious law; but those
> whom I created turned to a life of cor-
> ruption.
>
> 2 Esdras 9:19, *NEB*[1]

The eucharist, the meal of bread and wine that commemorates
the death and resurrection of Jesus Christ, is one of the central
sacraments of Christianity. Also known as the Lord's Supper
(Caena Domini), the Lord's Table *(Mensa Domini),* and the
Lord's Body *(Corpus Domini),* it derives from the descriptions of
the last supper of Jesus Christ with his disciples collected in the
gospels and in the letters of Paul, in which thanksgiving, *eucharistia* in the Greek of the New Testament, played a large
part.

The eucharist has changed considerably over the centuries,
as any history of its ideology and practice will show. The purpose of this work is to analyze the nature and significance of the
meal during the time in which it originated as one of the central
symbols of a Jewish sect—that is, during the time of Christ, to
whom the injunctions "eat my flesh" and "drink my blood" are
attributed—and the somewhat later time of Paul and other New
Testament writers, on whom we are primarily dependent for

---

1. This quotation is from *The New English Bible with the Apocrypha* (1970),
hereafter cited as *NEB.* Unless so noted, biblical quotations in this work are from
the *New Oxford Annotated Bible with the Apocrypha* (May and Metzger 1977).

I

information concerning the origins and development of early Christianity.

The eucharist is familiar to us now, but it was unusual, even shocking, to participants and observers at the time of Christ. Why did early Christians choose to represent their beliefs in such an extraordinary meal? The answer must be sought in the larger context, in the eating habits of contemporary Jews and gentiles as exhibited in documents written or in use during the Greco-Roman period in Palestine and the diaspora.

Meals, I will argue, symbolize proper behavior among social groups in relation to one another and in relation to God. Who may eat what with whom is a direct expression of social, political, and religious relations. The eating behavior described by early Christian symbolists—the feeding miracles, the fasting, the dietary indiscretions, and especially the last supper—was intended to contrast their more universalistic politico-religious beliefs, attributed to Jesus Christ, with the more nationalistic conceptions of other Jewish sects, symbolized above all by the passover meal.

The purpose of this chapter is to discuss some of the anthropological work on food and the Bible out of which this argument developed and to describe the approach to these subjects that will be taken here.

Anthropology and Biblical Scholarship

Although anthropologists have always been interested in religion, they have rarely analyzed the Bible from an anthropological perspective. Edmund Leach is one of the outstanding exceptions. In the fourth of five articles on Old and New Testament themes published between 1961 and 1973, Leach castigates anthropologists from Frazer to the present for their conspicuous avoidance of biblical material, which he attributes to an "extraordinary squeamishness about the analysis of Christianity and Judaism, religions in which they themselves or their close friends are deeply involved." In his view, "If anthropologists are to justify their claim to be students of comparative religion, they need to be less polite" (1967:46).

2

Anthropology and the Bible

We could, with Geertz (1968:22), argue that anthropologists have been studying their own religions all along, disguised as the religions of "exotic others." Nevertheless, in fairness to Frazer, we must also acknowledge that if he did not deal adequately with virgin birth or any other New Testament topic, he did tackle the Old Testament, notably in his three-volume work on *Folk-Lore in the Old Testament* (1918), written for the purpose of "detecting the savagery under civilization" (1:viii). Furthermore, his influence on biblical scholarship, through his own work and through the work of William Robertson Smith, his teacher and close friend, was considerable (Beidelman 1974; Hahn 1966:44–82; Rogerson 1978).

Indeed, it is largely owing to the treatment of biblical themes by Frazer and his contemporaries that the comparative, or "anthropological," approach to biblical studies has fallen into disrepute, not only among anthropologists, but also among biblical scholars (Wilson 1977:13–14). Biblical scholars came to attack anthropological analyses of the Bible for many of the same reasons anthropologists came to criticize the methods of evolutionists and diffusionists generally. They depended too often on data of poor quality, snatched from context and forced into speculative evolutionary designs that purported to be about time and change while remaining remarkably static and normative. Commenting on the dangers of imposing anthropological theory at the cost of Old Testament realities, as illustrated in Hubert and Mauss's study of sacrifice (1899), Hahn summarizes issues that are still problematic in anthropological analyses of biblical subjects:

> In order to fit the data into their scheme of interpretation, they treated the Old Testament as all of a piece, ignoring the possibility of variation in viewpoint or of historical growth in the ideas expressed. Declaring that their purpose was to make a general analysis of sacrifice, not a historical study of its forms, they took the whole Pentateuch as their base, disregarding the critical analysis of its parts and paying little or no attention to the data which criticism had amassed regarding the historical development of sacrificial customs among the Israelites. More confidence in the validity of their conclusions would have been possible if they had

3

taken into account the results of other approaches to the Old Testament. [1966:63]

Except for Schapera, in his Frazer Lecture on "The sin of Cain" (1955), anthropologists avoided biblical studies until the 1960s, when Edmund Leach, then Mary Douglas, began writing on the subject. Their example has inspired many, if not all, of the more recent studies, including the present one.[2] The methods of these efforts range from structuralism to cultural ecology. Nevertheless, they share a common interest in justifying our claim to be students of comparative religion and in broadening our cross-cultural understanding by including archeological and historical as well as ethnographic data.

Some of these authors use anthropological theory and methodology to explicate the Bible, just as Frazer sought an explanation of the mark of Cain in comparative ethnography because the meaning of the mark was not stated in the biblical text (1918, 1:78–103). Others are more interested in using biblical material to explain the religious behavior of other people. Thus Schapera (1955) uses the Old Testament accounts of Cain and Abel to analyze the distinctions made in African societies between the killing of kin and the killing of non-kin. Leach (1967) deliberately includes Christian material in explaining alleged beliefs in virgin birth among Australian aborigines and Trobrianders. Likewise, Bourdillon (1977) examines divination and politics in ancient Israel in order to contribute to our understanding of contemporary Shona oracles.

Similar motives seem to account for the renewed interest of biblical scholars in anthropological analysis. This is particularly true of New Testament specialists, who had never shared their Old Testament colleagues' interest in anthropology (Derrett 1973:100; Gager 1975:14–15).

Gager, as a biblical scholar, wonders, like Leach, why "the study of early Christianity, as normally practiced, seems so different from the study of more exotic religions in Africa, Australia, and Melanesia?" (1975:xi), and suggests that theological,

---

2. Leach 1961, 1962, 1966, 1967, 1973a, 1973b; Douglas 1966a, 1971, 1973; Andriolo 1973; Beidelman 1963; Bourdillon 1977; Bourdillon and Fortes 1980; Carroll 1977; Derrett 1971, 1973, 1979; M. Harris 1974a, 1974b; Keyser 1975; Marshall 1979; Pamment 1972, 1973; Pitt-Rivers 1977; Pocock 1975.

cultural, and historical factors, afflicting even the ostensibly more objective historical-critical school, are responsible. New Testament scholarship in particular has been so overwhelmed by theological and related concerns that he regards his own treatment of early Christianity as "a social world in the making" as "a paradigm-shift in a highly traditional field of scholarship" (ibid.: 2, 3).

Gager argues that one of the most fruitful ways of dealing with the limits imposed by "woefully incomplete" data is to move away from the historical and sometimes theological particularism that has characterized New Testament scholarship toward a more comparative and theoretical approach. The value of such an approach lies in the external controls and additional data concerning human behavior in similar situations that models drawn from the study of other cultures may provide (1975:xi, 3–4).

Other scholars, arguing that Gager's efforts at broad cross-cultural comparison are premature, have nevertheless been inspired by the possibilities to create a study group on "The Social World of Early Christianity," jointly sponsored by the American Academy of Religion and the Society of Biblical Literature, for the purpose of collecting the basic historical data they feel are essential to such an enterprise (Meeks 1975a; J. Z. Smith 1975, 1978a).

These scholars are not alone in advocating a more anthropological or sociological approach to the analysis of biblical and related material. Especially notable are the studies of Gottwald (1979) on the political economy and ideology of early Israel; Neusner (1973a) on the concept of purity in Talmudic Judaism, to which Mary Douglas has contributed a "critique and commentary"; Theissen (1978) on the community organization of the "Jesus movement"; and Wilson on genealogy and history in the biblical world (1977) and on Israelite prophecy (1980). To these might be added a variety of other works reflecting the kind of multicultural approach that seems to be increasingly characteristic of the field.[3]

3. See, for example, Bauer 1971; Davies 1977; Isenberg 1975; Isenberg and Owen 1977; Kee 1977, 1980; Kelber 1976b; R. A. Kraft 1975; Malherbe 1977; Meeks 1972; Meeks and Wilken 1978; J. Z. Smith 1978b and M. Smith 1971a. See also the review articles of Harrington 1980; Scroggs 1980; and Worgul 1979.

This monograph is intended as a contribution to the cooperative, interdisciplinary research of colleagues in anthropological and biblical studies. Anthropologists stand to benefit especially from the richness and historical depth of the data on food symbolism in Israel and among Jews of the diaspora during the Greco-Roman period. An anthropological understanding of the cultural and social significance of food symbolism elsewhere and in other times may help to clarify some of the more enigmatic culinary issues in scripture as well.

The Anthropology of Food

Food is the subject of a vast anthropological literature. The problem of who eats what with whom and why has been approached from a variety of perspectives, ranging from the ecological to the symbolic.

It is my own conviction that nutritional and other utilitarian considerations do not adequately explain the ideology and behavior involved in the production, preparation, and consumption of food. People classify as "food" only a small portion of the wide range of edible and nourishing materials available to them in their environments. Moreover, attitudes toward the plants, animals, and other things characterized as edible, edible under certain circumstances, or inedible appear to be related by means of complex systems of classification to other ways in which they conceptualize their worlds.[4] Before expanding on this theme, it might be useful to examine some of the alternative explanations as they have been applied to Jewish dietary laws.

The prominence in both the theory and practice of Judaism of rules concerning food has long posed a problem to anthropologists as well as biblical scholars. Frazer could not neglect what he regarded as "relics of ruder times . . . preserved like fossils in the Old Testament" (1918, 1:vii). He begins his chapter "Not to Seethe a Kid in its Mother's Milk" by saying:

4. See, for example, Bulmer 1967; Douglas 1957, 1966, 1971, 1973; Leach 1964; Lévi-Strauss 1962, 1964–71; McKnight 1973; Middleton 1961; Panoff 1970; Tambiah 1969; Verdier 1966; Wijeyewardene 1968; and Yalman 1969.

A modern reader is naturally startled when among the solemn commandments professedly given by God to ancient Israel he finds the precept, "Thou shalt not seethe a kid in its mother's milk". And his surprise is not lessened but greatly increased by an attentive study of one of the three passages in which the command is recorded; for the context of the passage seems to show, as some eminent critics, from Goethe downwards, have pointed out, that the injunction not to seethe a kid in its mother's milk was actually one of the √ original Ten Commandments. [1918, 3:111]

Neusner, a contemporary scholar, finds it likewise necessary to explain why he spends so much time on dietary rules in a book about the Talmud: "Anyone familiar with Jewish religious observance will notice that food plays a considerable part throughout" (1973b:18).

Dietary laws are classified in the Pentateuch as *ḥukkim,* " 'divine statutes,' which by definition are not explained in the text" (*Encyclopaedia Judaica,* 6:42). Scholars of Judaism have tried to account for the laws in a variety of ways, classified by the *Encyclopaedia* (6:42) as hygienic and sanitary, aesthetic and folkloric, or ethical and psychological. The entry concludes with a summary of the diametrically opposed positions on food of the contemporary Reform and Conservative parties.

Conservative Judaism, exemplified in the work of Dresner (1966) and Siegel (1966) on the contemporary significance of the dietary rules and their proper observance, goes back to the rabbinic pronouncements of the Mishnah, assembled circa 200 C.E.[5] The purpose of the dietary laws is holiness: their observance hallows the individual and sets him and the group to which he belongs apart from others. In contrast, the Reform Movement resolved at the Pittsburg Conference of 16–18 November 1885 that the dietary rules were simply the product of particular and now foreign historical circumstances: "their observance in our days is apt rather to obstruct than to further modern spiritual elevation" (*Encyclopaedia Judaica,* 6:44). It is up to the individual to decide whether or not he wants to observe them. "After all,"

---

5. B.C.E. (Before the Common Era) and C.E. (Common Era) are alternatives to B.C. and A.D. in studies of the inter-Testamental period.

according to J. D. Rayner of the London Liberal Synagogue, "religion is not primarily concerned with eating habits. To create the impression that this is one of Judaism's chief preoccupations is to debase it in the eyes of Jews and non-Jews" (1968:12).

The explanations that anthropologists have devised to account for Jewish dietary laws are similar to those the participants have devised for themselves. M. Harris, for example, rejects as inconsistent the traditional hygienic explanations that, from Maimonides to the present, have stated that pork is prohibited as a health hazard (1974a). Pigs are no dirtier than cows, dogs, and chickens, and may even be cleaner, depending on the circumstances. Nor are pigs the only domestic animal to harbor parasites. Anthrax, known in biblical times to affect animals and human beings, is carried by cattle, sheep, goats, horses, and mules, but not pigs. In addition, cattle may have tapeworms; sheep and goats may have brucellosis. These diseases can be more severe than trichinosis—anthrax may even be fatal, while trichinosis rarely is—and yet their animal carriers are not tabooed (ibid.:36–39). Nevertheless, Harris would agree that "definite mundane and practical forces were at work" (ibid.:40).

In Harris's view, the Israelite prohibition on pork constituted "sound ecological strategy" (1974a:41). Nomadic Israelites could not raise pigs because, apart from being maladapted to an arid habitat, pigs are not herd animals (ibid.:42). Pigs could have been raised in semisedentary or village communities, but given their physiology, they were "more of a threat than an asset," requiring too much human effort to compensate for essentially unfavorable ecological conditions. Small-scale production would only increase the natural temptation for succulent pork: "hence, Jahweh was heard to say that swine were unclean, not only as food but to the touch as well" (ibid.:44).

Harris recognizes that his theory does not explain why several other kinds of animals should be included in the same taboo, nor why Jews should continue to observe ancient laws on food when they no longer live in the Middle East. He discounts the first problem by arguing that other animals covered in the rules—for example, osprey, vulture, hawk, and shellfish—would

never have been significant sources of food. The second he explains sociologically. The rules help people "to think of themselves as a distinctive community" (1974a:45).

Douglas (1966a) takes a classificatory approach to "the
abominations of Leviticus" that tries to account for the rules as
a whole. Explanations suggesting that the rules are meaningless
or arbitrary, that they are allegories of virtues and vices, or that
they are designed to protect the Israelites from foreign influence, are rejected as too piecemeal or as simply "expressing
bafflement in a learned way" (ibid.:43–49). Douglas argues instead that the distinctions made between clean and unclean animals in the fourth and fifth books of the Torah are explicable in
terms of the classification system implied in the creation story
in the first chapter of the first book, Genesis, where the world is
divided into earth, waters, and firmament. Certain creatures are
proper to each realm. Earth creatures are those with four legs
that hop, jump, or walk. Water creatures are scaly and swim
with fins. Sky creatures are two-legged fowl that fly with wings.
Categorically proper animals are clean. Unclean animals are
the anomalies: the four-legged creatures that fly, creatures with
two hands and two legs that go on all fours, creatures that creep,
crawl, or swarm upon the earth or in the waters. Swine, then, are
simply one case among many. They are anomalous and hence
unclean because they have cloven hooves but do not chew the
cud like a properly ruminant ungulate (ibid.:54–55).

In addition to their classificatory function, Douglas argues
that the rules "develop the metaphor of holiness on the same
lines" as other negative rules and positive commandments in
the Old Testament. Holiness, according to scripture, is exemplified by completeness and conformance to the proper categories; "holiness requires that different classes of things shall not
be confused" (1966a:53):

> If the proposed interpretation of the forbidden animals is
> correct, the dietary laws would have been like signs which
> at every turn inspired meditation on the oneness, purity and
> completeness of God. By rules of avoidance, holiness was
> given a physical expression in every encounter with the ani-
> mal kingdom and at every meal. Observance of the dietary
> rules would thus have been a meaningful part of the great

liturgical act of recognition and worship which culminated in the sacrifice in the Temple. [ibid.:57]

Douglas's arguments echo those of the early rabbis, who held that the laws had a symbolic rather than naturalistic function; as aids to moral conduct, their purpose was "to refine man" (*Encyclopaedia Judaica,* 6:42). She is also close to Philo, a Jewish contemporary of Jesus. According to Philo, "If we keep and observe these [commandments], we shall gain a clearer conception of those things of which these are the symbols" (*The Migration of Abraham,* 93). But he is also interested in the human consequences of observing the law and adds, laconically, "And besides that we shall not incur the censure of the many and the charges they are sure to bring against us."

Recently, Douglas has refined her approach to the dietary rules, benefiting from the research of Bulmer in New Guinea and Tambiah in Thailand, both of whom followed the more sociological approach to cultural categories that is evident elsewhere in Douglas's work. Bulmer (1967) and Tambiah (1969) did not simply analyze the formal properties of the systems of animal classifications they were studying. They examined the way in which order in animals was related to the orders that people discerned in other areas of life: persons, houses, land, vegetable resources, supernatural beings, and so on. Having demonstrated the complex interrelationship of different systems of classification, they attempted to relate them to actual human behavior.

The work of Bulmer, Tambiah, and others has proved that edibility is not merely an empty "stressmarker" without further significance, as Lévi-Strauss once claimed (1966:96–108). It is owing precisely to the complex interrelationship of cultural categories that food is commonly one of the principal ways in which differences among social groups are marked. Persons undergoing rites of passage are usually prohibited from eating those highly valued foods that would identify them as full members of society (Middleton 1961:4). Men are distinguished from women by means of food, children from adults, gods from demons, kin from non-kin (e.g., McKnight 1973). Various categories of kinship, with their associated rights and duties, may be differentiated on the basis of dietary rules, as well as various categories of adulthood such as age-grades. Subtle differences in social class—real or aspired to—may be marked by differences in food (Middleton 1961). Castes, occupational and religious groups, even whole nations, are distinguished by the food they eat (e.g., Dumont 1970:130–51).

Commensality, expressed in ordinary meals or wedding feasts or commemorative meals like the jaBirisi ceremony among the Gururumba of New Guinea (Newman 1965) or the passover and eucharist that figure in this essay, can be understood only in terms of interrelated cultural systems and associated behavior. Indeed, some meals like the passover and eucharist *require* a simultaneous translation to spell out the associations as the meal is eaten. In establishing precisely who eats what with whom, commensality is one of the most powerful ways of defining and differentiating social groups. It may be used to represent kinship or connubium. It may also be used to establish a community of interests, marking close relationship, among those who are neither kin nor affines (see, for example, Arnott 1976; Dumont 1970; Firth 1973; Greenewalt 1977; G. Harris 1978; Ortner 1978; Richards 1932, 1939; Smith 1885, 1889; and Young 1971).

William Robertson Smith, in *Kinship and Marriage in Early Arabia* (1885), was one of the first scholars to emphasize the importance of food and eating in defining and maintaining kinship and marriage bonds. He developed this idea in his analysis of religious sacrifice among Arabs and Israelites (1889:251–93):

> The very act of eating and drinking with a man was a symbol and a confirmation of fellowship and mutual social obligations. The one thing directly expressed in the sacrificial meal is that the god and his worshippers are *commensals* [Smith's emphasis], but every other point in their mutual relations is included in what this involves. Those who sit at meat together are united for all social effects, those who do not eat together are aliens to one another, without fellowship in religion and without reciprocal social duties. [1889: 251]

This is the basis of G. Harris's discussion of Taita religion in *Casting Out Anger* (1978). Harris argues that the association between eating, sexuality, and conquest that is so widespread in

Africa is not prominent in Taita society, where eating together is the primary means of achieving peace. Commensalism is part of every Taita religious ritual. Human beings eat the gifts of food they use to placate angry mystical agents, an act that draws them together in mutual good will. Religious ritual thus resembles Taita life, in which commensality and the exchange of gifts, especially of food, are the principal means of creating and maintaining good fellowship (ibid.:151–55).

Young's *Fighting with Food* (1971) elaborates on the comparable set of ideas found in Melanesia, where food is "used everywhere to create, maintain and manipulate social relationships" (ibid.:146). The sociopolitical value of food is, in his view, "the organizing ethic of the social system. Other values such as those vitalizing prestige, individualism, egalitarianism, kinship and community, are made commensurate through and by reference to food" (ibid.). Food is not merely the idiom of social relationships; it has an exalted value of its own, especially evident in the context of politics (ibid.:146–70). Contrasting two communities and referring constantly to the extensive ethnography concerning pig festivals and food exchange among Melanesian people, Young demonstrates how Goodenough Islanders fight with food as a means of acquiring prestige and maintaining control over one another. He suggests that their marked interest in food-getting, food-keeping, and food-giving may have developed as an adaptive ecological response to the periodic drought and famine characteristic of life on small tropical islands (ibid.:171–88). But these activities and associated beliefs have also been cultivated as "political resources" in the process by which groups accommodate themselves to one another (ibid.:185).

Considering how much is known about the significance of food in the association and segregation of groups, it is curious that so little work has been done on the manipulation of dietary rules—as metaphorical statements of proper relationships—for political and economic purposes in western society. Eldridge Cleaver provides one interesting example in a discussion of soul food and Elijah Muhammad's prohibition of pork to Black Muslims that reflects the influence of the Bible on black political language:

You hear a lot of jazz about Soul Food. Take chitter-lings: the ghetto blacks eat them from necessity while the black bourgeoisie has turned it into a mocking slogan. Eating chitterlings is like going slumming to them. Now that they have the price of a steak, here they come prattling about Soul Food. The people in the ghetto want steaks. *Beef Steaks.* I wish I had the power to see to it that the bourgeoisie really *did* have to make it on Soul Food.

The emphasis on Soul Food is counter-revolutionary black bourgeois ideology. The main reason Elijah Muhammad outlawed pork for Negroes had nothing to do with dietary laws. The point is that when you get all those blacks cooped up in the ghetto with beef steaks on their minds—with the weight of religious fervor behind the desire to chuck—then something's got to give. The system has made allowances for the ghettoites to obtain a little pig, *but there are no provisions for the elite to give up any beef.* The walls come tumbling down. [Cleaver 1968:29–30; emphasis in original]

It is not irrelevant that the lunch counter was an important focus of the civil rights movement of the 1960's. Malcolm X also uses the political symbolism of food in summarizing the larger issues involved in race relations in America:

I'm not going to sit at your table and watch you eat, with nothing on my plate, and call myself a diner. Sitting at the table doesn't make you a diner, unless you eat some of what's on that plate. Being here in America doesn't make you an American. [Malcolm X 1965:26]

These arguments, like those I have just described, attempt to link the structural properties of symbol systems to their consequences for human behavior, to explain not only how they are thought but how they are lived. Thus Bulmer and Tambiah criticized Douglas's (1966a) analysis of the abominations of Leviticus for neglecting to explain the complex ways in which these systems of animal classification were related to other aspects of Jewish thought and behavior, specifically the close association they had observed between food prohibitions and relations of sex and marriage.

Douglas has responded in "Deciphering a Meal" (1971) by arguing that there is a strong association between table and altar, individual Israelite and nation of Israel that relates boundaries at meals, as in the distinctions between clean and unclean animals, to political boundaries. Although Israelites do not recognize the association between bed and board that is found in New Guinea and Thailand, nevertheless, exogamy and endogamy are politically significant issues in ancient Judaism, as Leach (1966) has shown. Sex, therefore, cannot be omitted from the meaning of common meals. The emphasis, however, is not on rules about exchanging women, but on rules about not exchanging them. The purpose of Douglas's article is to demonstrate that the apparent trivialities of the domestic table may be as significant as poetry or other exalted forms of communication in ordering thought and experience. She is careful, therefore, to emphasize that she is not reducing the dietary rules to politics by clarifying the association between table and temple, individual and nation. She is simply "showing how they are consistently celebrating a theme that has been celebrated in the temple cult and in the whole history of Israel since the first Covenant with Abraham and the first sacrifice of Noah" (ibid.:77).

Two other contributions to the study of Jewish dietary rules have appeared since then: Soler's "Sémiotique de la nourriture dans la Bible (1973) and Alter's "New theory of *kashrut*" (1979). Soler, a French diplomat, wrote his essay while working as consul for cultural affairs at the French embassy in Tel Aviv between 1968 and 1973. He argues that food, like any language, has a structure that can be analyzed; and further that biblical food regulations can be analyzed without regard to history. Different dietary regimes are associated with different biblical covenants: the first with Adam and Eve at creation; the second with Noah and his progeny following the flood; the third with the Israelites following the appearance of Moses. The third covenant is recognized by signs, all of which involve some kind of cut or separation—circumcision, the sabbath (a cut in time), and the dietary rules (a cut in the continuum of animals). All of them represent God's selection of Israel, which cut it off from the nations.

Soler finds the meaning of the dietary prohibitions not in the food itself, but in its relation to other foods in the system and in the relationship of the system to other systems in the cosmology. His discussion of meats and vegetables, carnivores and herbivores, is reminiscent of Frazer's argument concerning Israelite food prohibitions, which he felt might have originated in the manner he attributed to pastoralists in Africa that apparently ate only game resembling cattle (1918, 3:160–61). Frazer admitted that the Hebrew system was too "liberal" to be explained so simply. Soler, faced with the same problem, introduces the concept of blemish in an argument that is, as he says, "strikingly similar" to Douglas's reasoning in *Purity and Danger,* although he did not see her work until after he had completed his own.

Alter's approach to the liberality of the dietary rules is worth reviewing in some detail because it so clearly reflects recent thinking in biblical scholarship. Alter is a professor of Hebrew and comparative literature and a contributing editor of *Commentary,* where his essay appeared in 1979. He starts by rejecting "pragmatic" explanations of the dietary rules, in which he includes medical, ecological, and sociological arguments concerning idolatry or separatism.

Alter agrees with Philo, Douglas (1966a), and Soler that the dietary rules are probably allegorical. He accepts Douglas's and Soler's arguments for the importance of purity in ancient Hebrew cosmology, which he finds amply confirmed in the emphasis on separation and separating devices in the postbiblical rabbinic dietary code. But he would not take the next step and argue that the rules have implications for social relations.

Alter finds little concern with the potentially separatist consequences of dietary regulations either in the Bible, where it is the Egyptians in the Joseph story who refuse to eat with the Hebrews, or among the early rabbis. The well-known statement of the third-century sage Rav—"the [dietary] commandments were given only to *(ṣrp)"*—may mean either that they were intended "to bind (people) together" or "to purify (people)." The rabbis have interpreted it both ways, suggesting that they "fully appreciated the socially isolating effect of the dietary laws." In fact, dietary law in the diaspora has been "a powerful agency of Jewish solidarity and of separation from the circumambient Gentile world." Nevertheless, "there is not much evidence that this was the chief conscious purpose of the prohibitions, or the chief initial purpose" (1979:46, 47).

Alter also objects to the image of the Hebrew mind that emerges from structuralist analysis: a mind "utterly inexorable and automatic in its adherence to the principle of preserving sharp distinctions" (1979:49). No human mind, no cultural system, he argues, is so perfectly uniform. Inconsistencies, chance elements, anomalies, and contradictions are equally characteristic of human thought. Therefore, they should not be forced into the system rhetorically, as in Soler's interpretation of "cut" to mean the separation of the Israelites from the nations, or by small factual distortions. Alter cites the elaborate narrative techniques devised by biblical authors for "suggesting the multiplicity and ambiguity of motives and feelings" (see Alter 1978), the Talmud's "commitment to subtle dialectical analysis," and the kabbalistic tradition, "enamoured . . . of paradox and multiple meanings" (1979:49–50).

God's acts as depicted in the Bible may be orderly and progressive, but they are contrasted with human acts that are "repeatedly characterized by uncertainty, unpredictable reversals, ambiguity, imponderability." To the static qualities of unity, integrity, and generic perfection that Douglas attributes to holiness, Alter would add "vitalism" in God and human beings: "God is a living God and His commandments, as the Bible tells us again and again, confer life on those who observe them" (ibid.:51). It would be wrong, in Alter's view, to assume that the legal system through which this creative holiness is achieved should be perfectly clear and consistent. To join these two vital spheres, the human and the divine, the Law "must be in many respects enigmatic, proceeding with a logic that is often hidden and sometimes ungraspable." Nearly three and a half millennia of Jewish history have surely demonstrated more than one consistent strategy for ordering reality: "indeed, the persistent polyphony of Jewish culture may ultimately be one of the secrets of this peculiar people's survival" (ibid.:52).

I agree wholeheartedly with Alter's critique of structuralist analysis. It seems absurd, in any case, to have to argue that any kind of complex human behavior should have just one explanation. In fact, one reason the dietary laws interest such a wide variety of scholars is precisely because they bring together so many areas of life we are accustomed to separating: the fleshly, the spiritual, the environmental, and the social, in all their historical variability. No one theoretical framework as yet contains them.

The analysis that follows is thus not intended to supplant or destroy the arguments of my predecessors, but rather to add to them by putting the dietary rules in a larger cultural, social, and historical context. The abominations of Leviticus did not exist in a cultural vacuum but were part of a large body of other rules pertaining to the cultivation, organization, composition, preparation, timing, location, and company appropriate to the consumption of different kinds of meals. This body of rules has increased steadily in complexity and scope since the banishment from Paradise, as Shenker's (1979) interviews with four contemporary rabbinical specialists show. The social context must be considered in more detail because the rules had consequences for social relations that participants clearly recognized and took into account in their behavior, as is (*contra* Alter) amply documented by biblical and extrabiblical sources. A historical perspective, finally, is required to overcome the image of the timeless Israelite that seems to haunt the literature and to help us get down to specifics.

Alter is right to remind us of the complexity and ambiguity of human thought, especially thought about fundamentals like food. Ironically, the term "stiff-necked" that Soler applies to Mosaic logic is the term God uses at precisely those moments when the Israelites are stubbornly hankering after foreign wine, women, song, and supernaturals, which they are wont to do at least as often as they long for Yahweh and Israel. What is obvious from a historical perspective is not the rigidity of the law, but its flexibility, the unending process of interpretation and redefinition in which the only constants seem to be the questions: what is Judaism, what is Jewish, who is a Jew?[6]

6. A good contemporary example is the letter of the Israeli Sephardic writer A. B. Yehoshua to the *New York Times*, 5 May 1974, in the wake of the Yom Kippur War:
> Our stiff-neckedness and arrogance derive from a lack of confidence in the world. It's a terrible irony that our fears create our own traps. Masada is far more today than just a national symbol. It is like a self-fulfilling metaphor that colors our every-day life. Every Israeli carries that hill around inside him; and the obsession only serves to bring the reality closer. The only way to shed our fatalism is to break our preoccupation with the past and learn to improvise. We must create a new Jew. [Cited in Feldman 1975:248]

The point is that the creation is recurrent.

The discussion has reached the point where we can stop talking about the intellectual and social significance for archetypical Israelites of a monolithic law. It is the purpose of this work to examine the nature of this law and how it worked out in a particular case: how and why Jews and gentiles living in Palestine and the diaspora around the time of Christ conceived of, manipulated, and transformed dietary rules for their own political, social, and religious purposes. They created many different meals in the process, including the eucharist, which will be our primary focus.

Argument and Methods

The argument in summary is as follows. Chapter 2 establishes the diversity of Judaism during the Greco-Roman period, when Christianity was just one among many sects of Judaism. Diversity of belief and practice, especially concerning Israel and its relation to outsiders, had always been a feature of Judaism. During this period, however, the controversy came to center increasingly on the law that was codified during and after the Babylonian exile. The law came to be the means whereby the true Israelite and true Israelite custom should be defined. Sectarians were united in their adherence to the law, but deeply divided in their interpretation. Most of the Jewish sects that we know of from the time of Christ were fairly nationalistic. Early Christians differed in advocating a more universalist approach to politico-religious relations within Israel and between Israel and surrounding peoples.

Chapter 3 focuses on the interpretation of the law. Jesus Christ and his followers tried to communicate their beliefs in forms that would be comprehensible to their contemporaries, but those forms, for that very reason, already had other connotations attached to them, some of which they opposed. They expressed their dilemma repeatedly in parables telling of old cloaks and new patches, water and wine. The law, as expressed above all in scripture, constituted the tradition they had to work with. Early Christians transformed the law by means of a process of interpretation known as *midrash* that was developed in

Judaism after the law was codified. They created new relations among texts that in some cases totally reversed the significance of the old order. The last supper, a familiar meal with a shocking conclusion, is the most outstanding example. But in fact it was only the last in a long series of culinary disorders. The true Israelite created by early Christians was a "glutton," a man who ate indiscriminately, like an animal, and was eaten.

Chapter 4 deals with the question of why food was so controversial in Judaism, why it was such a powerful means of both condemnation and exaltation. The evidence suggests that food was one of the most important languages in which Jews expressed relations among human beings and between human beings and God. Food was identified with God's word as the foundation of the covenant relationship in scripture and in sectarianism. During the inter-Testamental period, when God's word became increasingly identified with the law, food law came to represent the whole law. The violation of dietary rules became equivalent to apostasy.

Early Christians used the language of food to establish the legitimacy of Jesus and the novelty of his message. The last supper, discussed in chapter 5, establishes binding relations between human beings and God, but relations of a very different order from those established in scripture or by other sectarians. The meal is a redefinition of sacrifice. Of all sacrificial meals, it most closely resembles the passover, but every critical element in the passover is reversed: the time, the place, the community, the sacrifice, and ultimately the significance of the meal. The passover is a feast that celebrates kinship and nationhood. Jesus' sacrifice symbolizes the death of family and polity. His new covenant includes all humanity.

Chapter 6 examines the same meal, transformed in Peter's vision. The passover and the eucharist, as complex symbols of salvation in food, deal with a wide variety of issues, using the highly charged substances of wine and blood. Peter's vision transforms the wine back into water. His meal simplifies the message, isolating the issues of kinship and nationhood and spelling them out unmistakably by demonstrating the relationship of the new passover to the abominations of Leviticus.

Finally, a word on methodology. Leach may be right in suspecting anthropologists of squeamishness or timidity where biblical studies are concerned, especially considering the enthusiasm with which less salient aspects of western culture have been welcomed back into the cross-cultural fold. But there are good reasons for being cautious about such an undertaking.

Language is one stumbling block. Few anthropologists, myself included, have the command of the vernaculars—at least Hebrew, Aramaic, and Greek in this case—they would normally require of themselves for fieldwork. I have used the following English translations: *The New Oxford Annotated Bible with the Apocrypha* (May and Metzger 1977; Metzger 1977) and *The New English Bible with the Apocrypha* (1970); Charles's edition of the Pseudepigrapha (1913); Charlesworth's edition of the Odes of Solomon (1973); Dupont-Sommer's edition of the Dead Sea Scrolls (1961); the Loeb Classical Library editions of Philo (1929–62) and Josephus (1926–65); Danby's (1933) and Blackman's (1951-56) editions of the Mishnah; and the Soncino edition of the Talmud (Epstein 1935–52).[7]

7. The Apocrypha are documents written in Hebrew, Aramaic, and Greek by Jews living in Palestine and the diaspora from about 200 B.C.E. to 100 C.E. They were probably not excluded from writings that Jews recognized as scripture until late in the first century C.E., when Christians formally accepted the Septuagint or Greek version of the Old Testament that included them, and Jews accepted a Hebrew version of the Old Testament that did not. The Pseudepigrapha, including the Odes of Solomon, are documents written in Hebrew, Aramaic, and Greek, dating from about 200 B.C.E. to 200 C.E. In contrast to the Apocrypha, they were accepted as scripture by some groups but not by others, although they were never canonized by either Jews or Christians (Rost 1976:30).

The Dead Sea Scrolls are a collection of manuscripts, primarily in Old Testament Hebrew, including fragments of scriptural, apocryphal, and pseudepigraphic writings, commentaries on scripture, and books by and about a religious community of Jews, probably Essenes. Most of them were found in the area of Qumran on the Dead Sea. They were probably associated with a monastery in the vicinity that was occupied between 150 B.C.E. and 70 C.E.

The Mishnah is a body of oral tradition, developed primarily by Pharisees during the inter-Testamental period and promulgated under the leadership of Rabbi Judah, Patriarch of the Jewish community of Palestine circa 200 C.E. The Mishnah, the Tosefta (traditions from circa 70-200 C.E., supplementary to the Mishnah and published circa 250 C.E.), and the Gemara (commentary on the Mishnah and other traditions transmitted in Palestinian and Babylonian rabbinic academies) together constitute the Palestinian (completed circa 400–425 C.E.) and Babylonian (completed circa 500 C.E.) Talmuds (Neusner 1973c:97–141).

The very richness of the primary and secondary source material poses additional problems. It is very difficult, as Bourdillon points out (1977:124), for an outsider to become familiar with all the relevant literature in a field that has been the object of intense scholarly interest for millennia. Even biblical scholars acknowledge the problem (see, for example, Hengel 1974, 1:4). Other limits are inherent in the material itself. Biblical scholars no longer espouse the normative nineteenth-century view of early Christianity as a monolithic doctrine gradually corrupted by pagan practice. They recognize that early Christianity was not merely one among many varieties of Judaism, but was itself divided into several competing sects. Paul's view is not the same as the views of the evangelists, who differ among themselves. None of their views may be identical with those of Jesus Christ. Koester summarizes the situation:

> Christianity did not begin with a particular belief, dogma or creed; nor can one understand the heretical diversifications of early Christianity as aberrations from one original, true and orthodox formulation of faith. Rather, Christianity started with a particular historical person, his works and words, his life and death: Jesus of Nazareth. Creed and faith, symbol and dogma are merely the expressions of response to this Jesus of history. [1971b:205]

The historical Jesus remains elusive. Few subjects have inspired such prodigious effort leading to such inconclusive results (Gager 1974, 1975:7; Koch 1972:10). The relevant documents contain material from a variety of sources, some from Jesus' own lifetime, some from Paul, some from the evangelists, some from still later periods. Some material may even have been interpolated into the text by the persons who put some of the books together to be canonized. Biblical scholars recognize each document as influenced by the time and place in which it was written. But one of the most difficult problems in biblical criticism is to decipher the exact nature of those circumstances.

Biblical scholars disagree about the traditional material available to each writer and the nature of his personal contributions as author and editor. Jesus Christ is known only from secondary sources about which no strong consensus yet exists concerning where, when, by whom, and for whom they were written, although most were probably composed between ten and one hundred years after his death. These books, only some of which were gathered together as the "New Testament" about 150 years after Christ's death (von Campenhausen 1972), are biased in support of his cause. Although he was a Jew, there are no Jewish sources of any value that refer to him (Sandmel 1978: 397). The surviving Jewish sources—the late writings of the Old Testament canon, the apocryphal and apocalyptic works and such extrabiblical fragments as those found at Qumran—are biased in a different direction, having been collected and preserved by circles that sought to repudiate alien Hellenistic influence (Hengel 1974, 1:108).

Historical and theological limitations in the material make it so difficult to relate ideology to the actual behavior of human beings in particular times and places that some biblical scholars insist on separating "sociology" from "history" altogether. Thus, according to Koester,

> form criticism seeks to identify basic patterns in the history of the tradition and to determine their *Sitz im Leben,* i.e., to determine the function of traditional material in the life of people and communities. This, however, is a sociological and theological question, and the determination of the *Sitz im Leben* must not be identified with the determination of the place, time, and situation in which Jesus said or did one thing or another. [1971a:159–60; see also Gager 1975:22]

Anthropologists would not confuse, for example, Mark's version of what Jesus Christ did with what Jesus Christ actually did. Nevertheless, recognizing that history too is a cultural artifact, they might find it more difficult to dissociate history from ideology, theology, or myth, or, to use the terms of biblical scholarship, tradition from redaction. The purpose of this monograph is to analyze the significance of the eucharist not according to Jesus Christ, about whom we know almost nothing directly, but according to the way in which his beliefs and actions, his history, were represented by Paul and the gospel writers, about whom we know somewhat more. It is therefore a sociological study of redaction. But since redaction is meaningful only in a temporal context, the monograph is also historical. Its purpose is to trace transformations in tradition, in the structure of belief as it is related to changing social circumstances through time, by focusing on a problem in Judaism that existed long before the inter-Testamental period and has persisted long after it.

Frazer's comments on the pitfalls involved in combining structural with historical analysis in biblical studies have not lost their relevance:

> A candid inquirer in the realm of folk-lore at the present time will state his inferences with a degree of diffidence and reserve corresponding to the difficulty and uncertainty of the matter in hand. This I have always endeavoured to do. If anywhere I have forgotten the caution which I recommend to others, and have expressed myself with an appearance of dogmatism which the evidence does not warrant, I would request the reader to correct all such particular statements by this general and sincere profession of scepticism. [1918, 1:ix–x]

2

JEWISH SECTARIANISM IN THE GRECO-ROMAN PERIOD

Set on the pot, set it on,
  pour in water also;
put in it the pieces of flesh,
  all the good pieces, the thigh and
    the shoulder;
    fill it with choice bones.
Take the choicest one of the flock,
  pile the logs under it;
boil its pieces,
  seethe also its bones in it.
                    Ezekiel 24:3–5

In order to place the Christian symbolism of the last supper in context, we must first understand the nature of Jewish sectarianism as it developed during the period following the Babylonian exile. Some of the critical events of that period will be outlined very briefly in the following pages. Readers interested in more detail should consult the excellent histories of Widengren (1977) on the Persian period; Hengel (1974) and Schäfer (1977) on the Hellenistic and Maccabean periods; Grant (1973), Leaney (1977), Neusner (1977), Safrai and Stern (1974), and Smallwood (1976) on the Roman period.

History after the Babylonian Exile

Our knowledge of the Persian period comes mainly from the Old Testament books of Chronicles 1 and 2, Ezra, and Nehemiah.

Although much about the period is still obscure, partly because the circumstances under which these books were written are still disputed (Widengren 1977:503–9; Williamson 1977:5–88), certain facts can nevertheless be established.

The Babylonians conquered Jerusalem in 597 B.C.E. They destroyed the temple there in 587 and exiled the king, the court, and the upper classes to Babylon. Cyrus the Persian conquered Babylonia in 539. He permitted the exiles to return to Judea under the governorship of a Jewish noble he appointed, who was probably not of Davidic ancestry (Widengren 1977:520), despite the efforts of the Chronicler to prove the contrary (1 Chronicles 3:18). Many Jews did return, though others, because of the poverty in Judea, went elsewhere. The end of the exile is dated to around 520. Cyrus also ordered the Jerusalem temple rebuilt; it was completed in 516/515 B.C.E., mainly owing to the exhortations of the prophets Haggai and Zechariah (Widengren 1977: 519–22).

It was during this period that Jews began to use Aramaic, the official language of the Persian empire, in everyday speech, reserving Hebrew for scripture. Passages in Ezra (7:10) and Nehemiah (8:1–9; 18:3, 9) suggest public reading of scripture, followed by explanation, probably including translation (Bloch 1957:1269). It was probably during this same period, between about 450 and 375 B.C.E., that the Torah assumed its present form with the incorporation of the Priestly Code. The Torah may have been intended to support the power of the newly reorganized temple and priesthood. But it also seems to have contributed to a growing division between the Jerusalem temple, organized around sacrifice and controlled by the priests, and the synagogue, organized around scripture and its interpretation by laymen.

The Greeks conquered the Persian empire, including Judea, in 323 B.C.E. Alexander the Great died the same year, and the empire was divided among his generals, Judea falling to the Ptolemies of Egypt. Previous conquerors—Assyrians in 722, Babylonians in 597, Persians in 539—had exiled Jews but had done almost nothing to their homeland, to which, eventually, they were allowed to return. The Greek conquest was different. The Greeks colonized their empire, founding numerous cities and establishing an extensive international trade network, using local groups like Phoenicians and Idumeans as middle-men (Hengel 1974, 1:12–55).

The influence of Greek military, political, and economic organization is obvious from contemporary documents. But even deeper and longer-lasting, in Hengel's view, was the influence of Greek culture, mediated above all through the *koine,* the variety of Attic Greek that developed among peoples of the eastern Mediterranean during the Hellenistic period. Greek held the empire together despite the political and economic fragmentation that began with Alexander's death (Hengel 1974, 1:56). Its influence went far beyond that of Aramaic. It was the language of commerce, law, diplomacy, letters: "anyone who sought social respect or even the reputation of being an educated man had to have an impeccable command of it" (ibid.).

Already established in aristocratic and military circles in Palestine between 260 and 250 B.C.E., Greek was so widespread in the time of Antiochus IV Epiphanes that even the Maccabean revolt did not eradicate it, nor would the Maccabees have wanted it to, since it was their primary means of communicating with the Jews of the diaspora. In the New Testament period, between the reign of Herod and the destruction of the temple in 70 C.E., there was probably a "considerable minority" of Jews in Palestine who spoke Greek as their mother tongue, besides large numbers who were bilingual: "we can ask whether some of the immediate circle of Jesus' disciples were not themselves bilingual" (Hengel 1974, 1:104–5). Certainly the books of the New Testament were written in the Greek *koine.*

As Hengel points out, it is fruitless, given the evidence of Hellenism in Jewish Palestine, to continue to maintain the traditional distinction between "Palestinian" and "Hellenistic" Judaism. From the mid-third century on, *"all Judaism must really be designated 'Hellenistic Judaism'* in the strict sense" (Hengel 1974, 1:104; italics in original).

Hellenization did not mean, however, the total assimilation of Jews to Greek culture. A good example of the complexity of the Jewish response to Hellenistic culture is the Letter of Aristeas, which, although extremely conciliatory to Greeks and their representatives in the empire, nevertheless communicates the view that different peoples should be allowed to preserve their own customs. The letter purports to be a contemporary account by an Alexandrian Greek in the service of Ptolemy II Philadelphus (285–246 B.C.E.) of the translation of the Torah from Hebrew into Greek by seventy-two Jewish scholars in seventy-two days. Although the book of Esther, which expresses a similar view, may well date from the early Hellenistic period (Rost 1976:199), the author of the letter was most likely an Alexandrian Jew writing around 130 B.C.E. (ibid.: 101–2).

The account is a fiction. Yet it probably derives from the historical reality that it was politically advantageous for the Ptolemies, perhaps as early as the reign of Ptolemy II, to promote an approved Greek translation of the Torah for the Jewish community, a codification of the "laws handed down by the fathers," which they could declare binding on both the Jews and the state (Rost 1976:104; this is also Rost's interpretation of the composition of the Torah under Persian domination, as reported in Ezra). The Greek Torah may have been a kind of Magna Charta for the Jews, making it possible for them to be recognized as a distinctive ethnic group with their own legitimate religion, a *religio licita,* to use the term the Romans later applied to this status (Smallwood 1976:539).

There was no portion of the Jewish population that was not influenced by Greek culture, even the most militantly anti-Hellenist (Hengel 1974, 1:102, 108, 252, 311, 312). But it was probably a relatively small, though rich and powerful, upper class that actually benefited from Hellenism and sought to promote it (ibid., 1:47–57). The Book of Judith, composed early in the period, is evidence for strong nationalist feelings, which became stronger and more widespread under the Seleucid conquerors of Judea in 200 B.C.E., who seem to have been considerably more repressive than their Ptolemaic predecessors. The Wisdom of Jesus the Son of Sirach, portions of the Ethiopian Enoch, and other books express the growing nationalism of the time.

It was during the reign of Antiochus IV Epiphanes (175–164 B.C.E.) that the worst events took place, as we know from Daniel, passages in the Ethiopian Enoch, the Qumran War Scroll, and other documents thought to have been composed around 170 B.C.E. (Rost 1976:199–200), and also from such later reports of the period as books 1, 2, and 4 of the Maccabees and the histories of

Josephus. Whether Antiochus IV or the Jews made the first move —that is, whether the sudden escalation of events in 167 B.C.E. was the result of developments within the Jewish community or a political measure initiated by the Syrians, or both—is still "extremely controversial" (Schäfer 1977:562). Both Syrians and Jews were eventually involved in the program of Hellenization, including Antiochus IV, who brought in his own troops, and Jason, whom Antiochus had appointed as High Priest, who brought other pro-Hellenist Jews into the government. Jason was a representative of the economically and politically powerful Tobiad family and one of the leaders of the "Hellenistic reform party," in which the Tobiads were prominently involved. The main goal of the reform was to transform Jerusalem from a Jewish temple state into a Greek *polis,* in Hengel's words, "to do away with the result of five hundred years of Jewish and Israelite history" (Hengel 1974, 1:73).

Jerusalem was renamed Antiochia. The Torah was abrogated as the city's constitution. Jason bought the authority to enroll men of Jerusalem as citizens of the new *polis,* essentially depriving the urban and rural poor of their rights. A gymnasium, closely associated with the cult of Heracles and Hermes, was built near the temple. Jewish participants in the games, which were carried out naked according to Greek custom, removed the marks of their circumcision by epispasm (*Encyclopaedia Judaica,* 5:968).

Internecine quarrels between Jason and a rival Hellenist, Menelaus, provided Antiochus with the opportunity for military intervention. He attacked Jerusalem in 169 B.C.E., murdering its inhabitants and plundering the temple. He attacked again in 168 or 167 B.C.E., with armies led by his mysarch Apollonius, who captured the city by treachery on a sabbath, murdered indiscriminately, tore down the city walls, and constructed in the City of David, the religious heart of Jerusalem, a military fortress that he peopled with a gentile garrison. According to Schäfer (1977:584), the temple itself became the common property of all citizens of the *polis,* including gentiles.

Antiochus's edict, intended for the entire Seleucid kingdom, "that should be one people and that each should give up his customs", was promulgated with a special edict intended for Jerusalem and Judea:

He directed them to follow customs strange to the land, to forbid burnt offerings and sacrifices and drink offerings in the sanctuary, to profane sabbaths and feasts, to defile the sanctuary and the priests, to build altars and sacred precincts and shrines for idols, to sacrifice swine and unclean animals, and to leave their sons uncircumcised. They were to make themselves abominable by everything unclean and profane, so that they should forget the law and change all the ordinances. "And whoever does not obey the command of the king shall die." [1 Maccabees 1:41–42, 44–50]

A pagan altar was constructed on top of the great altar of sacrifice in the temple in December of 167 B.C.E. The Book of Daniel refers to it as "the abomination of desolation" (Daniel 11:31; 12:11). The temple itself was dedicated to Zeus Olympios (Schäfer 1977: 580–85; Hengel 1974, 1:267–314).

The result was the Maccabean revolt, described in books 1, 2, and 4 of the Maccabees and two works of Josephus, *The Jewish War* and *The Jewish Antiquities*, by which political independence was achieved, the temple was purified and rededicated, and the Hasmonean dynasty (c. 135–63 B.C.E.) was established. The revolt returned Jews to political power, but it did not unify them. The history of the Hasmoneans is one of almost constant civil and religious strife, ending only when Rome, stepping in ostensibly to aid one of two warring Hasmonean brothers, took Judea for itself. Representatives of various Jewish factions continued to serve intermittently as High Priest, until the last of them, Archelaus, was deposed in 6 C.E., following the complaints of a Jewish delegation. Judea was ruled subsequently by Roman procurators.

Roman rule in Judea has had an odious reputation, owing less to deliberate cruelty than to the incompetence of Roman rulers, their poor judgment, and the difficulty of governing a people for whom religion was inseparable from nationalism (Smallwood 1976). Smallwood argues that the Romans could keep religion and politics separate despite the imperial cult. They were able to follow a policy of religious toleration throughout all of the empire, except Palestine, where it was more realistic to view Judaism as a subversive political movement.

Uprising and repression succeeded one another, culminating in the destruction of the temple in 70 C.E. during the First

Jewish Revolt (66–74 C.E.) and more thorough Romanization in the wake of the second, the Bar Cochba rebellion (132–35 C.E.). Jerusalem was turned into a Roman city and renamed Aelia Capitolina, temples to Jupiter and Hadrian (as Olympius) were constructed on the site of the temple to Yahweh, and Judea was turned into a Roman province, Syria Palaestina.

With the destruction of the temple, the power within Judaism shifted from the sacrificial system in the hands of the priests to scripture and its interpreters. A rabbinical "academy-government," founded at Yavneh in 70 C.E., exercised those powers of self-government left to the Jews. A new one was founded at Usha in Galilee, following the second revolt against Rome. It was these bodies and their successors in Palestine and Babylonia that developed the elaborations on the Torah that make up the Talmud.

Who Is the True Israelite?

The vicissitudes of Jewish history after the return from Babylon might be summarized in the words cited at the head of this chapter, which God dictated to Ezekiel as an "allegory" of the impending Babylonian conquest. But they also bring to mind the remarks of Amos Oz, the Israeli novelist, commenting on the fact that news of the Knesset vote of 28 September 1978 approving the Camp David accords spread among Israelis together with the false rumor that Golda Meir had died:

> "Israel is making peace in a hysterical mood. Opinion swings from the messianic to the apocalyptic, with nothing in between. Many intellectuals are exhilarated, elated. They say, 'We have arrived.' For my own part, I don't think we have arrived. First we have to make peace with the Egyptians, then with the other Arabs—the Palestinians, the Syrians, and the Jordanians. Then we have to confront the unresolved existential problem of Zionism. We have to decide who we are, what the content of being an Israeli is." [Quoted in J. Kraft 1979:93]

The question was raised as soon as Jews left the wilderness and entered the land of Canaan, the holy patrimony filled with pagan strangers among whom they were a minority: Who is the true "Israelite" and who is the foreign usurper? The prophets, as politicians and moralists, had always claimed to find the true Israel within their own various circles (Pedersen 1926, 4:542, 555). But as Pedersen (1926, 3:131) points out, their vehement reaction against mixing with foreigners developed—"as is usually the case with reactions"—only when the mixing was almost completed and had set its stamp even on the reactionaries.[1] Thus the distinction between "true Israelite" or "true Israelite custom" and "foreign usurper" or "foreign custom" was hardly clear. On the contrary, it was an area of extreme ambiguity on which Jews held a very wide variety of opinions.

Nineteenth-century translations into European languages of Jewish books like Enoch and Jubilees that had been preserved only by the Ethiopians and other Eastern Christian churches suggested something of the variety of Jewish religious expression during the inter-Testamental period. But it was the discoveries of the Gnostic codices of Nag Hammadi in Egypt in 1945 and, especially, of the Dead Sea Scrolls at Qumran in 1947–56 that, as Vermès has said, "opened a new era in the study of Jewish biblical exegesis" (1961:4), with consequences for both methodology and theory.

The antiquity of these manuscripts, written in Coptic, Hebrew, and Aramaic, reawakened interest in the noncanonical books of the Apocrypha and Pseudepigrapha, known only in Greek or translations from the Greek. Old texts were republished, and new ones found buried in libraries. Pseudo-Philo's *Biblical Antiquities,* for example, was originally published in Europe in 1527. It began to receive renewed scholarly attention toward the end of the nineteenth century; the Latin edition was republished in 1949 by Notre Dame University Press. Several organizations have been established recently to facilitate the discovery, analysis, and publication or republication of such texts, including the International Organization for Septuagint and Cognate Studies, founded in 1968 (R. A. Kraft 1970); the Pseudepigrapha Project of the Society of Biblical Literature,

1. See also Bourdillon 1977; Hengel 1974; Keyser 1975; Leach 1966, 1973a; Pamment 1972, 1973; M. Smith 1971a; Williamson 1977.

founded in 1969 (Charlesworth 1971); and the International Center of Christian Origins, founded at Duke University in 1973 (Vecsey 1978).

The revised view of postexilic Judaism that has resulted from this research is summarized in Hengel's argument that the most significant feature of Jewish literature in the Persian and early Greek periods is not the uniform and deadening influence of "Hellenistic" literary forms, but "the tendency . . . towards *development, . . . richness and pluriformity,"* which he finds "atonishing," given the small size, the poverty, and the political insignificance of the Jews at the time (Hengel 1974, 1:112, 113, 107; italics in original). This diversity was probably much greater than the surviving fragments suggest, owing in part to the destruction of manuscripts by parties with opposing views (ibid., 1:102, 108), in part to the complex organization of the groups themselves (M. Smith 1961:347–48). Creative literary activity flourished more than ever under the Ptolemies and during the later Greek and Roman periods (Hengel 1974, 1:107; Stone 1973).

The diversity of postexilic Judaism is evident not only in the documents that have survived from the period, but in what they imply about social organization. The discovery of the Dead Sea Scrolls focused attention on the sectarian side of Judaism, suggested by the number and variety of groups named in the literature—Pharisees, Herodians, Sadducees, Essenes, Zealots, Therapeutae, Sicarii, Nazarenes, and so on. Because of fragmentary evidence and problems of dating, it is rarely possible to associate groups with documents, and it is therefore difficult to determine their exact nature (R. A. Kraft 1975:190). Nevertheless, like the manuscripts, they probably do not represent the full range of variation, since the sources in which the groups are named are for the most part limited geographically to Palestine, and, moreover, "ignore the great masses of the people who do not seem to have been 'card-carrying members of any formal group' " (ibid.: 189).

Josephus, for example, takes pains to distinguish himself from precisely those masses in explaining his own introduction to the Jewish sects of his time. Noting his precocious "love of letters," he writes:

At about the age of sixteen [53–54 C.E.] I determined to gain personal experience of the several sects into which our nation is divided. These, as I have frequently mentioned, are three in number—the first that of the Pharisees, the second that of the Sadducees, and the third that of the Essenes. I thought that, after a thorough investigation, I should be in a position to select the best. So I submitted myself to hard training and laborious exercises and passed through the three courses. Not content, however, with the experience thus gained, on hearing of one named Bannus, who dwelt in the wilderness, wearing only such clothing as trees provided, feeding on such things as grew of themselves, and using frequent ablutions of cold water, by day and night, for purity's sake, I became his devoted disciple. With him I lived for three years and, having accomplished my purpose, returned to the city. Being now in my nineteenth year I began to govern my life by the rules of the Pharisees, a sect having points of resemblance to that which the Greeks call the Stoic school. [*The Life,* 7–12]

Josephus's comments illustrate a feature of Judaism that seems to have been fundamentally involved in the formation of sects: the value attributed to the individual. Smith (1961, 1971a) argues that the diversity characteristic of the inter-Testamental period is rooted in prophetic tradition, which honored the right of the individual to dispute established religious authority on matters concerning worship.[2] He points out that the books of Kings and most of the Prophets, in contrast to contemporary non-Jewish documents, are concerned primarily with such religious conflicts, associated closely with political and economic problems. Prophets such as Amos, "the preacher of justice," Jeremiah, and Nehemiah, who advocated a return to Yahweh, were constantly castigating the priests and nobility for exploiting the poor and enslaved. The same theme is evident in the polemics of the Pharisees, Qumran Essenes, and Christians

2. A tradition that dissension is good for the community is reflected in Paul's remarks to the Corinthians: "When you assemble as a church, I hear that there are divisions among you; and I partly believe it, for there must be factions among you in order that those who are genuine among you may be recognized" (1 Corinthians 11:18–19).

against the politico-religious aristocracy (M. Smith 1961:350–51).

The years immediately preceding the Babylonian exile saw the temporary triumph of parties advocating a polytheistic approach to worship that included, but was not limited to, the worship of Yahweh. At the same time, prophetic teaching was combined with other material and codified as law in the Book of Deuteronomy, and that law became the rallying-point of a group of scholars and pietists focused on Yahweh and the chosen people. They rewrote the history of Israel to accord with their concept of the pious life as "the life devoted to the repetition, interpretation and practice of the sacred law" (M. Smith 1961:351).

The Babylonian exile did not destroy the power of the temple. The Torah must be seen as the embodiment of both Deuteronomic and priestly traditions, a product of compromise (Smith 1961:355). Nevertheless, the exile considerably strengthened the power of the Deuteronomists and led to even further developments, owing to the identity they had established between Yahweh and the nation of Israel, which required that sacrifices to Yahweh could be held only at the Jerusalem temple. The proponents of Deuteronomy in exile had to reinterpret scripture in a way that permitted them either to sacrifice outside Jerusalem or to develop a nonsacrificial form of worship. The Samaritan acceptance of the Pentateuch, the foundation of the temple at Leontopolis, the possible evidence of sacrifice at Qumran and sacrificial as well as legal aspects of early Christianity suggest that different groups at different times did both (ibid. 1961:351). Nevertheless, it is the essentials of nonsacrificial worship—the institution of the synagogue based on prayer and the ceremonial reading of the law—that are associated with Ezra, who probably brought them back to Palestine from Babylonia. This kind of worship leads inevitably to sectarianism, according to Smith, "because it facilitates the formation of small, private cult-groups which even the poor can afford to maintain." This is essentially what synagogues are: They require no expensive buildings, no sacrifices, no elaborate ritual. Strabo believed that the simple, inexpensive character of Jewish worship was the main reason for its success (cited in ibid.: 351–52).

The identification of piety with knowledge of the law, its interpretation and practice, and the identification of the individual learned in the law as the final religious authority, both of which derived from the prophetic tradition codified in the Torah, are thus linked inseparably with Jewish sectarianism: "touch the Law and the sect will split" (M. Smith 1961:359).

Hengel's (1974) analysis of the Hellenist period supports the view that the divisions of postexilic Judaism derived increasingly from different approaches to the law. He portrays the Maccabean revolt as a "struggle over the law" between those with a "zeal for the law" (quoting the phrase used in 1 Maccabees 2:26), regarded as the embodiment of wisdom, and those with a "zeal against the law" (his own phrase, ibid., 1:305), regarded as the embodiment of superstition and folly. The revolt made zeal "an essential feature of Jewish piety" (ibid., 1:114), but its success did nothing to reduce the diversity of opinion concerning the fundamental questions. On the contrary, diversity increased precisely because of the increasing prominence of the law. The assimilationists were temporarily checked. The validity of the Torah was upheld. Indeed, "from now on, any movement which criticized the Torah in a fundamental way was doomed to failure" (ibid., 1:252). But zeal for the law only intensified the bitterness of the disputes concerning its interpretation.

Different groups clearly continued to hold very different opinions, derived from their own interpretations of the law, concerning the nature of Judaism and the politico-religious and social obligations of Jews to the "circumambient Gentile world," to use Alter's suggestive phrase. Kee (1977:97–99), speaking of Palestine before the first revolt of 66–73 C.E., distinguishes them in terms of four options. One was to collaborate with foreign rulers by conforming to the way of life they sought to impose on the Jews. This was the approach of the Hellenists and to some extent of the Herodians and Sadducees during the Roman era. The first Book of the Maccabees (1:11) describes such people as "lawless men [who] came forth from Israel, and misled many, saying, 'Let us go and make a covenant with the Gentiles round about us, for since we separated from them many evils have come upon us.'" A second option was to collaborate to the extent of accepting their political and economic control, but maintain religious and domestic independence. This was the solution of the Pharisees, according to Neusner (1971, 1973c). A third, the solution of such groups as the Essenes and Therapeutae, was to withdraw from the world, including fellow Jews, in the hope that divine intervention would establish God's rule under drastically changed circumstances. A fourth option was to revolt, destroy the foreign oppressors, and re-establish Israel's independence, the goal of such groups as the Hasidim (to a limited extent: see Hengel 1974, 1:175–76), the Maccabees, and the Zealots and Sicarii described by Josephus in the second and third books of *The Jewish War* (Smith 1971b). This was not a very popular solution, according to Neusner (1973c:147), who argues that most Jews wanted some sort of accommodation with the Romans that preserved their identity as a people. To these four might be added a fifth option: to include gentiles in the salvation that God had promised for his chosen people. This was the early Christian solution, although Christians too disagreed among themselves.

Each of these groups considered its own ideas and practices to represent the only legitimate solution according to the law. The Hasidim, to judge from Daniel, seem to have regarded themselves as the faithful remnant to whom a special understanding of God's plans had been revealed. The Qumran Essenes, who probably broke off from the Hasidim around 150 B.C.E. following the appointment of the Maccabean High Priest Jonathan (Hengel 1974, 1:224; Vermès 1975:13, 57, 61–65), represented themselves, "the Community of the New Covenant," as the only legitimate Israel (DuPont-Sommer 1961: 73, 76, 82-84, 91, 127, 132).

The Pharisees, another splinter group from the Hasidim (Hengel 1974, 1:176), also claimed to represent the holy community, the true people of God. The word *periša* 'separatist', from which their name is derived, is a synonym for *qaddiša* 'holy one' (Jeremias 1963:223). Although both the Pharisees and the Essenes derived their teaching from the Hasidim and consequently had much in common, they were bitter rivals (Hengel 1974, 1: 254). The Essenes criticized the Pharisees for "toning down and dissolving the law" (ibid., 2:167, n. 889), whereas the Pharisees, according to Josephus, argued with the Sadducees concerning the legitimacy of the oral law (*The Jewish Antiquities,* 13:296–98; 18:16–17).[3]

This was the enduring consequence of the Maccabean revolt. It did not unify the Jews politically, but it focused even more attention on the law as the source of their diversity. In Hengel's words, "the failure of the Hellenistic reformers to abolish the Torah by force in effect *fixed* intellectual development *on the*

---

3. The bitter dispute between the Samaritans and the Jews, savagely perpetuated from the Restoration into New Testament times, concerned precisely which of the two was the true ancient Israel, the guardian of the true law and inheritance, and which was the foreigner and usurper. The Samaritans have long called themselves the Shamerim, i.e., "keepers" or "observers" of the truth *(al ha-amet);* both names are constantly used in their chronicles (*Encyclopaedia Judaica,* 14:728; S. Talmon 1977; Widengren 1977:511–14, 537–38).

The hostilities of the Belz and Satmar Hasidim are an interesting contemporary example of the close connection between sectarianism, ultimate questions of identity, and the law in Judaism. Although both are ultra-Orthodox and very similiar in dress and deportment, they are divided by profound differences in political and religious belief, including sharply divergent views on Israel. The Satmar are strongly anti-Zionist. Although they maintain a community in Israel, they will not cooperate with the secular government or accept money from it. The Belzer Hasidim have their headquarters in Israel, have good relations with the government, and accept government funds for their schools and institutions. The two are also at odds over the courts and slaughterhouses of the ultra-Orthodox in Israel. Although these institutions are currently controlled by the Satmar Hasidim, the Belz group recently tried to set up a court and a kosher slaughterhouse of its own. Fights related to the dispute broke out between the groups in Williamsburg, Brooklyn. As a reporter investigating the fights pointed out: "The Jewish courts, under Israeli law, have the last word on marriage and divorce matters and are the final arbiters on the thorny question of 'who is a Jew' (Goldman 1979:B7).

The Synagogue Organization of Reform Judaism, an American group, is currently challenging the Israeli government policy that recognizes only Orthodox practices as legitimate Judaism and prohibits non-Orthodox rabbis from performing weddings, funerals, conversions, and other ceremonies. According to the resolution presented at the fifty-fifth convention of the Union of American Hebrew Congregations, "Reform Judaism continues to suffer second class status in Israel. . . . Converts accepted by Reform rabbis in Israel are not registered as Jews. Unlike Orthodox institutions which are supported almost totally by Government funds, [Reform] synagogues and programs receive almost no public assistance, although the major portion of funds contributed to it by Jews throughout the world come from non-Orthodox Jews" (Briggs 1979:A5). Representatives of the group call for "recognition of all streams of Judaism in Israel" and for the allocation of funds to "religious institutions of all movements within Judaism," and say that if the government does not respond to their demands, they will take the matter to the Israeli Supreme Court.

Torah" (1974,1: italics in original). Despite hopeless disputes concerning its right interpretation, the law was the means whereby they could establish their right to exist as a community distinct from every other, the law that expressed their unity. The law came to have absolute authority, to be regarded as the only authentic medium of revelation from which all other forms of revelation (regarded as interpretations of the law) were derived; it came to cover every aspect of life; it came increasingly to distinguish Jew from gentile.

Hengel (1974, 1:169–75) describes the process by which the early Pharisees identified the law with the cosmos. The Torah became "the mediator of creation and revelation between God and the world," with "manifold and far-reaching" consequences:

> In this way . . . its six hundred and thirteen individual commandments and prohibitions received a "cosmic" significance going beyond the realm of the individual; they were "materialized forms of expression" of the divine ordinance of creation and salvation. Each individual commandment, indeed each individual consonant possessed absolute importance; each deliberate or unintentional transgression of a commandment, each omission of a letter in copying the Torah meant in principle an attack on the divine structure of the world, formed by the Torah, for "the Torah is indivisible.". . . From this there followed with logical consistency both the casuistic securing of the commandments by the oral Torah, the hedge around the law, and the scrupulous fixation of the text. [Ibid., 1:172]

Having cosmic significance, the Torah, through the oral Torah, came to cover every aspect of life, as the Mishnah and Gemara, the products of this process, clearly indicate. Although it distinguished between the sacred and the "common," as between the sabbath and the other days of the week, no formal distinction was made between sacred and secular law, private and public. The Torah gradually became the final arbiter in every area of life, the sum of all wisdom. Thus when sectarians disputed points of religious law, they were debating important political, social, and economic issues.

38

As the law was applied increasingly to every aspect of Jewish life, it increasingly singled out Jew from gentile. Earlier literature had made God's wisdom available to all the nations, even if they usually rejected it. This theme tended to recur in the Judaism of the diaspora because of "its more exposed position and consequent missionary tendency" (Hengel 1974, 1:174). The more nationalistic literature written during the years preceding the Maccabean revolt—for example, Baruch and The Wisdom of Jesus the Son of Sirach—argues that the Torah was revealed exclusively to Israel as God's gift to ensure her salvation and should be safeguarded from aliens (ibid., 1:131–53).

The nationalization of wisdom accounts for the goal of the Hasidim and, later, the Pharisees of educating the whole people in the Torah, which Hengel regards as "probably unique in the ancient world" (ibid., 1:78–83, 174). The Torah was God's gift not to the learned but to all Israelites. Paul, who was a Pharisee, describes their mission scornfully only because he is making the argument, familiar in Judaism, that it is "not by hearing the law but by doing it that men will be justified before God" (Romans 2:13):

> you may bear the name of Jew; you rely upon the law and are proud of your God; you know his will; instructed by the law, you know right from wrong; you are confident that you are the one to guide the blind, to enlighten the benighted, to train the stupid, and to teach the immature, because in the law you see the very shape of knowledge and truth. You, then, who teach your fellow-man, do you fail to teach yourself? [Romans 2:17–21, *NEB*]

When the Pharisees withdrew their support from the Hasmonean dynasty in the reign of Hyrcanus (135/4–104 B.C.E.), whom they saw as having moved too far from the goals of the Maccabean revolt (Schäfer 1977:598), large numbers of the people followed them precisely because, as their teachers in the synagogue, the Pharisees had instilled in the people the same "zeal for the law" (Hengel 1974, 1:294). Hengel (ibid., 1:175) attributes the survival of Judaism and the Jewish community through all national catastrophes to the education of the people in the Torah, coupled with their growing isolation from outsiders. When the nation was destroyed, the law was internalized (Neusner 1971, 1973c). According to Falk,

> Talmudic law is based on the principle of personality, i.e., rights and duties depend upon the traditional law of a man's father rather than upon the norms of the state in which he lives. The law is part of the divine covenant with the people of Israel and stress is put upon the distinction between the "Sons of the Covenant" and gentiles. Therefore, personal law is particularly important in the Jewish legal system. [1974:505]

Jerusalem at the Time of Jesus

The social consequences of this struggle for the law were complex. Following the return from exile in Babylon, when those who considered themselves "pure" are said to have separated themselves from those who had mixed with gentiles (Ezra 6:21; 9; 10), legitimate descent became one of the leading principles of Jewish social organization. The prophet Jeremiah had already posed the essential question: "Yet I planted you a choice vine, wholly of pure seed. How then have you turned degenerate and become a wild vine?" (2:21). Ezra's final chapter (10) enforced the dissolution of existing mixed marriages, noting that the process of examination took three months and listing each offending male by name. The detailed genealogical tables laid down in the books of Ezra, Nehemiah, and 1 Chronicles (1–9) are a further reflection of interest in descent.

The Chronicles, however, express a more tolerant view than Ezra or Nehemiah, according to Williamson (1977), who argues against the traditional theory that the books were originally part of a single work. Williamson acknowledges that the definition of the community was "the primary centre of debate" following the exile (ibid.:136). The separatist and assimilationist parties had become equally extreme and rigid in their views during the fourth century B.C.E., when the Chronicles were probably written, and no contemporary writer concerned with guiding his people could have ignored these issues (ibid.:83–86, 139). But the

Chronicler responded not by condemning mixed marriages, which he actually seems to have condoned (ibid.:60–61), but by providing a different definition of Israel organized around a faithful nucleus that would not exclude errant children of Israel who wished to return.

The continuing interest in descent is seen in books like Jubilees, the Genesis Apocryphon, and Pseudo-Philo. In Jubilees (30:7–17), probably written circa 109–105 B.C.E. by a member of the Qumran Essenes (Rost 1976:132), intermarriage is threatened with death. The Genesis Apocryphon, another strong polemic against mixed marriage, was written in Aramaic about the time of Christ. The language suggests that this was the work of a lay pastor to the *am ha-arez,* the poor and uneducated mass of the population (Rost 1976:184). Pseudo-Philo, probably written by a Palestinian Jew, perhaps in Palestine, shortly after the fall of the temple in 70 C.E. (ibid.: 197), is comparable to 1 Chronicles (1–9), Ezra, and Nehemiah in the importance it attaches to genealogical relationships.

Jeremias (1969:270) argues that Palestinian Jewish society at the time of Jesus, particularly in Jerusalem, was organized by law according to purity of descent. Carefully arranged marriages were the means of political as well as religious salvation. Only families of pure ancestry, as traced in the genealogies of Ezra, Nehemiah, and the Chronicles were assured of messianic salvation, the rest having to rely on their own merit (ibid.:270, 275, 301, 317, 328; Black 1961). Only pure Israelites had full civil and political rights. The most important honors and offices were reserved for Israelites who could prove legitimate descent from Abraham (Jeremias 1969:297–302). Foreign ancestry disqualified a person not only from certain redemption for his sins, but also from seats on courts and tribunals and other positions of honor (ibid.:317, 297–300). Israelites of unknown lineage were prohibited even from becoming members of the assembly of the Lord (Deuteronomy 23:2).

The Essenes prohibited intermarriage, commensalism, or any close contact with all other Jews, and they were probably not the only such group that did so (Weber 1952:415). Black (1961:124) thinks the kind of exclusive legalistic perfectionism exhibited by the Essenes was probably even more pronounced among related sects such as the Therapeutae. He says of the Qumran Essenes:

> One further and important consequence of this extreme Torah radicalism of Qumran was its exclusiveness. The aloofness of the Pharisee and his distance from the ʿam ha ʾareṣ [Jews ignorant of the law] is a relatively mild tolerance contrasted with the intolerant hatred of the sect for outsiders; the sectarians were 'sons of light', all others, especially foreigners, were the 'sons of darkness'. When ethical parallels with the Gospels are cited from the *Manual of Discipline,* such as sectarian teaching on anger and hatred, it should be remembered that such high standards did not apply outside the Qumran fraternity. [Ibid.; see also 42, 97–98, 129, 168, 170]

Despite the concern with descent, however, there were many categories of people in Jewish society who deliberately, by nature, or through ignorance did not conform to the ideal of the law. In addition to Jews of mixed or illegitimate origin, these included the "sinners," the members of despised trades such as tax collectors, herdsmen, peddlers, or tanners, the physically deformed, the am ha-areẓ or mass of the population, Samaritans, and, to a certain extent, women.

Sinners were comparable to gentiles in their lack of observance of the law, as Paul suggests when he speaks of "we . . . who are Jews by birth, not Gentile sinners" (Galatians 2:14). Tax gatherers or publicans were Jews who bought tax-collecting concessions from the Romans, thus earning the hatred of other Jews for being in the service of the foreign oppressor and for enriching themselves by extortion into the bargain (Smallwood 1976:151–52). Their occupation could be nothing less than dishonest and immoral. The Pharisee in Luke (18:11–12) relies on that assumption when he prays: "God, I thank thee that I am not like other men, extortioners, unjust, adulterers, or even like this tax collector. I fast twice a week, I give tithes on all that I get." Herdsmen were similarly condemned: "'One does not rescue from pits gōyīm [gentiles] and those who breed and pasture small cattle' (because they often also bred swine)" (Jeremias 1969:311, n. 43). Jews belonging to despised trades forfeited civil and political rights to which even Israelites of mixed ancestry were entitled, and were thus put on the same footing as gentile slaves, another highly anomalous category within Jewish society (ibid.:310, 311, 345–51).

Defects of conduct were equated with physical deformities (Deuteronomy 32:5; Proverbs 9:7; Job 11:15). Physical blemishes—blindness, broken limbs, skin diseases, birth defects of various sorts, deformities caused by accidents—could exclude a man from full participation in the priesthood (Leviticus 21:16–23). A blemished priest was forbidden to approach the veil or the altar because "he shall not profane these places sacred to Me" (Leviticus 21:23). The Essenes were even more strict on this issue (see Dupont-Sommer 1961:107–8, 161, 181).

Am ha-arez were unobservant of the law because they were ignorant. The term originally referred to "the countrymen" or Jews outside of Jerusalem. During the restoration following the exile, when the Torah was made the constitution of Judea, it became a technical term for those ignorant of the law. Although it was their mission to educate the *am ha-arez,* strictly observant Jews like the Pharisees would have denied them connubium as well as commensalism, just as they would a sinner, tax collector, or gentile. According to the Pharisees in John (7:49), "this crowd, who do not know the law, are accursed."

The worst of these groups were the Samaritans. According to scripture (1 Kings 17), the Samaritans were once Israelites of the former northern kingdom of Israel. Because they despised the Lord's covenant, they were exiled in Assyria, where they "went after false idols and became false. . . . Their children likewise, and their children's children as their fathers did, so they do to this day" (1 Kings 17:15, 41). Therefore they were no longer Israelites. The Greek word for Samaritan in Luke (17:18) means "stranger in the land," "no blood kin" (Jeremias 1969:355). Samaritans were considered unclean. Marriage with them was prohibited. It was said in connection with the prohibition on marriage: "He who eats the bread of a Samaritan is like one that eats the flesh of swine" (ibid.: 256–57, n. 19).

Women seem to have occupied an extremely anomalous status with respect to the law. On the one hand, there were beautiful but pious heroines like Esther and Judith, credited with saving entire Jewish populations from destruction at the hands of the gentiles. On the other hand, women tended to be relegated to a subordinate position that was explicitly compared in some instances to the position of gentile slaves (see Jeremias 1969:359–76; Loewe 1966; MacDonald 1931).

It is not surprising that social relations between Jews and gentiles reflect the complexity of social relations within the Jewish community. To some Jews, gentiles were the standard of evil kinlessness and godlessness against which even the lowest Israelite was measured (e.g., Leviticus 18; 20). As the relationship of Yahweh to Israel was conceived as a true marriage, so images of whoring and adultery were used continually of gentile cults and thus also of faithless Israelites who worshiped foreign gods. These themes are especially prominent in Ezekiel (16) and throughout the Book of Hosea and the Song of Songs, but they recur again and again in the Torah, the Prophets, and the other writings of the Old Testament (e.g., Exodus 34:14–16; Leviticus 7:7; 20:5; Deuteronomy 31:16; Isaiah 54:6–8; Jeremiah 3:1–20).

Ignorant of the wisdom of the law, gentiles were sinners by definition: "The enemy have no Rock like ours, in themselves they are mere fools" (Deuteronomy 32:31, *NEB*). "God's enemies" (Colossians 1:21), they were profane, unclean (Isaiah 52:1; Joshua 22:19; Hosea 9:3; Amos 7:17). Josephus echoes this opinion in *The Jewish Antiquities* (14:285; 18:93–94). Social contact with gentiles, their bodies, clothes, beds, or cooking vessels, was avoided as defiling.

Eating with gentiles was particularly polluting, for they ate unclean food that was furthermore likely to have been offered to idols. They ate "swine's flesh and broth of abominable things is their vessels" (Isaiah 65:4; see also 66:3, 17). The Book of Jubilees, composed between 109 and 105 B.C.E., is emphatic:

> Separate thyself from the nations, and eat not with them. And do not according to their works, and become not their associate. For their works are unclean, and all their ways are a pollution and an abomination and uncleanness. They offer their sacrifices to the dead and they worship evil spirits, and they eat over the graves, and all their works are vanity and nothingness. [Jubilees 22:16–17]

Peter reiterates the same sentiments in Acts (10:28): "You yourselves know how unlawful it is for a Jew to associate with or to

visit any one of another nation." Intermarriage was utterly prohibited (Exodus 23:31–33; 34:11–16; Deuteronomy 7:3–4; 20:10–17;
Joshua; Ezra; Nehemiah; Jubilees 30:1–17).

Gentiles represented all the wild insensate things held separate from the Israelites solely by the grace of God. When John the
Baptist responded to the familiar excuse of the Pharisees and
Sadducees—"We have Abraham as our father" (Matthew 3:9;
Luke 3:8)—by saying, "I tell you God is able from these stones to
raise up children to Abraham," he was not testifying haphaz-
ardly to the almighty power of the divine creator. The gentiles
were those stones, as they were the weeds, brambles, thorn
bushes, and wild beasts that recur repeatedly in scripture. God's
covenant with Israel alone kept them at bay:

> You will laugh at violence and starvation
> and have no need to fear wild beasts;
> for you have a covenant with the stones
> to spare your fields,
> and the weeds have been constrained
> to leave you at peace.
> [Job 5:22–23, *NEB*]

Only faithless Israel, worshiper of foreign gods, is ever described as wild (Isaiah 5:1–7; Jeremiah 2:21; Hosea 2:16). So
Abimelech is compared in his evilness to a thorn bush and contrasted with the good cultivated plants, the olive, fig, and grape-
vine, which were frequently used to represent the true Israel
(e.g., Judges 9:8–15; Psalms 92:13–15; Jeremiah 17:8). And God can
ask rhetorically of his rebellious people: "Have I been a wilderness to Israel, or a land of thick darkness?" (Jeremiah 2:31).
When he turns his people over to their enemies, Israel shall be
named "No Kingdom There. . . ."

> Thorns shall grow over its strongholds,
> nettles and thistles in its fortresses.
> It shall be the haunt of jackals,
> an abode for ostriches. [Isaiah 34:12–13]

Jeremias (1958:40) describes the prevailing attitude of Jews
toward gentiles during the Greco-Roman period as "uncompro-
misingly severe." Nevertheless, there was apparently more interest and more success in making converts to Judaism during

the Greco-Roman period than at any other period in Jewish history (Daniel 1979:63). The success of Jews at proselytizing seems to have been one of the major reasons for the official reprisals against them (ibid.: 62–64; Smallwood 1976:130, 305–7, 376–85). Gentiles who were willing to abandon paganism and observe certain Jewish practices—recognize the God of Israel, the sabbath and other holy days, certain laws of the covenant—might be permitted to attend the synagogue. But such "God-fearers," as they were known, were still legally regarded as gentiles and therefore unclean (Jeremias 1969:320). They were strictly prohibited from straying any further into the temple than the so-called Court of the Gentiles (Harvey 1970:174; see also Deuteronomy 23:3; Nehemiah 13:1–3; Lamentations 1:10; Ezekiel 44:7–9). Nor were they permitted to marry, eat with, or otherwise associate with members of the Jewish community (Harvey 1970: 600).

Gentiles who submitted to circumcision and baptism and presented a sacrificial offering at the temple were acceptably "naturalized" Jews (Isaiah 56:3, 6–8). They were called "proselytes of righteousness." Although they did not possess the civil and political rights of full Israelites, they were permitted to make alliances of marriage with Israelites of pure descent except for the priestly families. The Herodian royal family belonged to the proselyte sector of the population, although Herod tried to conceal the fact by burning Jewish genealogical records and by having his court historian write that he was descended from the first Jews who returned from Babylon (Jeremias 1969: 281–83, 331).

Jesus' first contact with a gentile, according to Matthew (8: 5–13) and Luke (7:1–10), was with a gentile proselyte, a Roman soldier. The meeting occurred immediately after his statement of the new law. Peter's first contact with a gentile was also with a Roman centurion who had become a convert to Judaism (Acts 10). The parallel in Luke and Acts is probably intentional (Harvey 1970:436).

The proselyte in the Roman period was classified as *ger,* the term used in biblical times to refer to the "resident alien" or the stranger dwelling permanently among the Israelites, totally dependent upon them for his welfare (*Encyclopaedia Judaica,*

15:419–20). The vast majority of *ger* were the original inhabitants of Canaan, many of whom had been neither slain nor enslaved as commanded in the Torah. Although some social differences remained, intermarriage occurred and the *gerim* were gradually assimilated culturally and religiously (*Encyclopaedia Judaica,* 15:420–21). According to the *Eycylopaedia* (7:410), it was only following the reforms of Ezra that "a sharp distinction and a barrier of separation" was erected between the Jew and the gentile *(goi, akkum),* although, as discussed earlier, the Chronicler presents an alternative view, suggesting that neither theory nor practice was invariant.

The existence of proselytes indicates a continuation among some Jews of the receptive spirit of early Israel into the post-exilic period that is confirmed in the books of Ruth and Jonah and in passages of Jeremiah and Isaiah (40–66) that were probably written during this period. As before, not all Jews approved of the practice of assimilating foreigners (Weber 1952:423). The success of the Maccabees tended only to polarize the situation. On the one hand, greater national self-awareness and the active political and economic policies of the early Hasmoneans promoted even closer ties with the rapidly expanding diaspora. The missionary outlook of many Jews in the diaspora combined with the interest of the Greeks in this nation of "philosophers," as they viewed the Jews, put Judaism in the second half of the second century B.C.E. "well on the way towards becoming a world religion" (Hengel 1974, 1:255–61, 313). On the other hand, the success of the Maccabees also led to an even greater emphasis on the letter of the law, which was not conducive to proselytism and which, in Hengel's view, was associated with the antisemitic movement that arose at the end of the second century B.C.E. (Hengel 1974, 1:255, 261–67).

The destruction of the temple had more negative consequences. Palestinian teachers lost interest in proselytes after 70 C.E. (Hengel 1974, 2:115, n. 450), and the position of Judaism itself was weakened. Still the practice did not die out. The emperor Hadrian tried to stop it with a ban on circumcision. It is unclear whether the ban preceded or followed the Bar Cochba rebellion (132–35 C.E.) and therefore whether it was cause or consequence (Smallwood 1976:429–31). Antoninus Pius altered the law a few years later only to exempt the Jews (ibid.:469–73). The costly efforts of the Romans to prevent citizens from converting to Judaism were bound to fail because, as Smallwood points out, the weapon was ineffective. A ban on circumcision prevented neither women nor God-fearers of either sex from becoming Jews. Furthermore the rabbis continued to sanction the ritual bath, which had been substituted for circumcision during the rebellion as the symbol of a convert's reception into the faith. There were enough other ambiguities in the ban that it was finally disregarded. Proselytism was later prohibited in its own name, to no greater effect (ibid.:500–502).

Many Jews around the time of Christ expected a messiah who would reverse the current political and moral situation, in which they sinned and suffered, scattered like chaff across the nations, contaminated and oppressed by foreigners. The messiah would deliver God's chosen people from foreign domination and establish his kingdom on earth with Israel at its center. Yet there were other Jews who interpreted the more universalistic conceptions of Jeremiah (31) and Deutero-Isaiah (55) as representing the true will of God. It is to those Jews and proselytes of Judaism who became followers of Jesus Christ that we now turn.

And Who Is My Neighbor?

The disagreements about the law and the prophets expressed in early Christian writings reflect serious political differences, particularly concerning social relations within the Jewish community and between Jews and gentiles. The belief, enforced by the law, in the pre-eminence of pure descent was not held by John the Baptist, who exhorted even the legitimate descendants of Abraham to repentance as an indispensable condition of participation in the Kingdom of God (Matthew 3:9; Luke 3:8), nor was it the view that Paul, the evangelists, and the authors of other early Christian documents attributed to Jesus Christ.

Paul was a Jew, possibly a Pharisee (Acts 23:6; 26:5), converted around 31/32 C.E. and martyred probably around 55 C.E., in Nero's reign. He wrote the letters to the Romans, Corinthians (1 and 2), Galatians, Thessalonians (1), Philippians, and to Philemon during the middle and end of his missionary activity, although the order in which they were written is still unclear. The authorship of other letters attributed to Paul is debated (Kümmel 1975:250–51). The congregations of the churches were diverse, including both Jews and gentiles. Their quarrels among themselves seem to have been one of the main reasons why the letters were written (ibid.:247–403).

The author of the gospel bearing Mark's name is unknown. Kümmel (1975:97–98) argues that he was probably writing for a gentile community in the East, but Kee believes, because of his attention to purity laws and other Jewish concerns, that "the base of the covenant community . . . was in contact with a Jewish milieu" (1977:148). Mark's gospel, which is the earliest of the four, is dated to about 70 C.E. (Kümmel ibid.), but scholars disagree about whether it was written before or after the destruction of the temple.

The author of the gospel attributed to Matthew may have been a Greek-speaking Jewish Christian writing for Greek-speakers, most of whom were Jewish, probably not in Palestine, but perhaps in Antioch or Syria (Kümmel 1975:119). He may have had some rabbinic training. He emphasizes that Jesus is a lawgiver greater than Moses, who has come "not to abolish the law and the prophets . . . but rather to fulfill them" (Matthew 5:17–20). If Matthew used Mark as one source (the alternative hypothesis has not been ruled out), then Matthew was probably written circa 80–100 C.E.

Luke and Acts were written by the same person. From his ignorance of Palestinian geography, his avoidance of semiticisms, and other characteristics of his writing, it has been inferred that he was probably a gentile Christian writing for gentile Christians, somewhere outside Palestine, sometime between 70 and 90 C.E. (Kümmel 1975:149–51). Nevertheless, the most striking feature of Luke-Acts is its insistence that Christianity developed directly out of Judaism, that Christianity is in fact the only true Judaism and Christians are the only true Jews.

The gospels of Matthew, Mark, and Luke are called the "synoptic gospels" because they are so closely related. But the nature of their relationship, historically, socially and theologically, is a matter of ongoing debate (Kümmel 1975:38–80). In some ways Luke is much less controversial than Mark (the presumed gentile) or Matthew (the presumed Jew) on the subject of Jesus' relations with other Jews. The variations in their treatment of the centurion from Capernaum, in which Matthew (8:5-13) is more polemical, Luke (7:1-10) more conciliatory, are a good example.

In other ways, however, Luke phrases Jesus' opinions on Jewish-gentile relations even more sharply. Mark and Matthew both avoid using Samaritans to make their points. They even have Jesus avoid gentiles, as in Matthew (10:5-6; directly contradicted by Matthew 28:19), or treat them badly, as in Matthew (5:47; 6:7-8) or in the parable of the Syrophoenician woman, which is included in both Mark (7:24-30) and Matthew (15:21-28). Luke omits this parable. Furthermore, when Jesus' disciples in Luke (9:52-56) ask his permission to call down fire to consume the Samaritans for refusing to allow him to rest in their village, he rebukes them. Samaritans are treated well elsewhere in Luke's gospel and in Acts. Other parables found only in Luke, such as the parable of the prodigal son, make similarly strong statements about relations between Jews and non-Jews.

It is unknown who wrote the gospel of John or whether he was a Jew or a gentile. He was probably a Greek-speaker in a Jewish environment, perhaps in Syria, who composed the gospel sometime between 90 and 100 C.E. Luke-Acts appears to have been one source, and Mark was possibly another, although some biblical scholars argue that he did not rely on any one source but took different elements from a wide variety of synoptic traditions (Kümmel 1975:246; Kelber 1976a:158-59; Parker 1975). In any case, "an impressively broad consensus exists today that . . . the major ideas and symbols of Johannine Christianity derived from Judaism" (Meeks 1975:167).

John's gospel is very different from the synoptic gospels. He spends no time on the parables. He concentrates on controversies over Jesus' physical and spiritual nature staged between Jesus and "the Jews" or "the Judeans." He seems to be dealing particularly with Jews who had once been Christians, but then renounced the faith (John 8:31-32), and Jews who pressured fellow Jews, through expulsion from the synagogue, for example, not to become Christians, at least not openly (John 9:22, 12:42, 16:2).

All of these writers, and others whom we will encounter

later in this book, had very different views concerning Jesus; the relationship of his law to Mosaic law, and its proper application, given the diversity of his followers; the implications of the new covenant for the organization of the community; appropriate relations between Jews and gentiles; and so on. Nevertheless, it does seem fair to say that one of the most important ideas that distinguished them as Christians within Judaism was the idea that the community should contain Jews and gentiles together.

According to the synoptic gospels, Jesus states his universalistic doctrine in response to a question from a lawyer about which of the Lord's commandments is "the first of all" (Mark 12:28). He answers:

"The first is, 'Hear, O Israel:
The Lord our God, the Lord is one;
and you shall love the Lord your God with all your heart,
and with all your soul, and with all your mind, and with
all your strength.'
The second is this, 'You shall love your neighbor as
yourself.'
There is no other commandment greater than these."
[Mark 12:29–31]

Matthew (22:40) adds: "On these two commandments depend all the law and the prophets."

The first commandment is not surprising. Jesus' command to monotheism is the beginning of the *shema* (Deuteronomy 6:4), the declaration of monotheism that was a basic part of Jewish worship, recited by every Jew twice daily in his prayers. There was general agreement that it did in fact sum up the essentials of Jewish faith and Jewish life (Harvey 1970:183).

The second commandment is not unusual either. In this case too Jesus quotes the letter of the law:

"You shall not take vengeance or bear any grudge against the sons of your own people, but you shall love your neighbor as yourself: I am the Lord." [Leviticus 19:18]

A comparable summary of the Torah is ascribed to the rabbi Hillel, a contemporary of Jesus. A gentile approached his rival, Shammai, offering to convert if he could be taught the Torah in a minute (literally, "while standing on one foot"). When Shammai refused, he went to Hillel, who accepted him as a convert, saying: "Do not do to others what you would not have them do to you. That is the essence of Torah. All the rest is explanation of it. Go, learn it" (Shabbat 31a, cited by Sandmel 1978:471, n. 67). The Rabbi Akiva (circa 51–132 C.E.) is also said to have called Leviticus 19:18 the epitome of the Torah (*Encyclopaedia Judaica,* 11:530).

It is precisely in his interpretation of the term "neighbor," radically different from traditional interpretation, that Jesus' commandment is a "new commandment," which is how he introduces it to his disciples at the last supper in John (13:34). As the passage from Leviticus illustrates, "neighbor" in scripture was a term expressing certain reciprocal rights and obligations that were generally restricted to fellow Jews, members of the covenant people. The commandment to love one's neighbor as oneself is immediately followed by a statement that, as we shall see, is the conventional formula for expressing nationalistic Jewish separatism:

> "You shall keep my statutes. You shall not let your cattle breed with a different kind; you shall not sow your field with two kinds of seed; nor shall there come upon you a garment of cloth made of two kinds of stuff." [Leviticus 19:19]

Still, there was considerable disagreement about the exceptions within the Jewish community. As Jeremias (1963:202) points out, Pharisees would have excluded the *am ha-arez*; the Essenes required members of the "Community of the New Covenent" to "hate all the sons of darkness"; a rabbinical saying ruled that heretics, informers, and renegades "should be pushed [into the ditch] and not pulled out"; and a widespread popular saying excepted personal enemies—"You have heard that it was said, 'You shall love your neighbor and hate your enemy' " (Matthew 5:43).

Matthew's Jesus responds unequivocally: "But I say to you, Love your enemies and pray for those who persecute you" (Matthew 5:44). His handling of the traditional imagery of Leviticus (19:19) conveys the same message. Nurture rather than nature will determine who is wheat and who is weeds, who will be edible at harvest time and who will not (Matthew 13:24–30, 47–50).

Luke's version must nevertheless have come as a shock to a Jewish audience. In Luke, the lawyer, "to vindicate himself," is made to ask Jesus the critical question explicitly: "And who is my neighbor?" (Luke 10:29). According to Jeremias (1963:204), Jesus' listeners would have expected an Israelite layman as the third party and therefore an anti-clerical point to the story. Jesus answers with the parable of the good Samaritan, in which the lawyer's neighbor proves to be his worst enemy, and his worst enemies, who would leave him lying half dead in the road, prove to be the most nationalistic of his own countrymen, a priest and a Levite (Luke 10:30–37).

The Levites, assistants to the priests in the temple, stood for the first-born Israelites whom the Lord hallowed on the first Passover when he struck down every first-born in Egypt (Numbers 8:5–19). They acquired their temple office from Moses for having slain the "brothers," "companions," and "neighbors" who had worshiped the golden calf (Leviticus 32:26–29). Relations between Jews and Samaritans were particularly bad during the first century C.E., Samaritans in Jesus' lifetime (probably circa 6 C.E.) having defiled the temple court at Passover by strewing it with human bones (Josephus, *The Jewish Antiquities*, 18: 30; Smallwood 1976:157–58).[4]

Paul interprets the first commandment to monotheism in universalistic terms in one of the earliest of his extant letters, taking the opportunity at the same time to emphasize his fidelity to the law:

> Is God the God of Jews only? Is he not the God of Gentiles also? Yes, of Gentiles also, since God is one; and he will justify the circumcised on the ground of their faith and the

4. It should be noted that later rabbis acknowledged the ambiguity in the term "neighbor" and the possibility of interpreting it to include gentiles. According to a passage in the Talmud on compensation for damages, the Roman government once sent two officials to learn Jewish law. They reported: "We have scrutinized all your laws and found them just *(emet)*, except for the following instance. You say that if a Jew's ox gores that of a gentile, the owner is free from damages, while if a gentile's ox gores that of a Jew, he is obliged to pay damages. But if, as you say, "neighbor" (in Exodus 21:35) excludes the gentile, then he should be free even when his ox gores that of a Jew. And if, on the other hand "neighbor" includes the gentile, then the Jew should have to pay damages when his ox gores that of a gentile" (*Baba Kamma* 38a, cited in the *Encyclopaedia Judaica*, 7:412). The *Encyclopaedia* (11:529–30) points out that the commandment in Leviticus to love one's neighbor, although originally nationalistic in significance, has become progressively universalized in Jewish thought.

uncircumcised through their faith. Do we then overthrow the law by this faith? By no means! On the contrary, we uphold the law. [Romans 3:29–31]

But he claims repeatedly that "love is the fulfilling of the law" (Romans 13:10), as in the letter to the Galatians:

the whole law is fulfilled in one word, "You shall love your neighbor as yourself." But if you bite and devour one another take heed that you are not consumed by one another. [Galatians 5:14–15]

The two commandments are reiterated throughout early Christian writing: in Matthew (7:12; 19:19; 20:35–40; 22:34–40), Luke (6:27–36; 10:25–37), John (3:16; 13:34–35; 15:7–17; 17:20–26), Romans (8:32; 13:8–10), the first book of Timothy (1:4–5), James (2:8), throughout the two books of John, and elsewhere. But the letter to the Ephesians, among whom Paul spent the longest period of his missionary work (Harvey 1970:617), contains the clearest statement of the covenant to be established by Jesus' sacrifice:

remember that you [gentiles] were at that time separated from Christ, alienated from the commonwealth of Israel, and strangers to the covenants of promise, having no hope and without God in the world. But now in Christ Jesus you who once were far off have been brought near in the blood of Christ. For he is our peace, who has made us both one, and has broken down the dividing wall of hostility, by abolishing in his flesh the law of commandments and ordinances, that he might create in himself one new man in place of the two, so making peace, and might reconcile us both to God in one body through the cross, thereby bringing the hostility to an end. [Ephesians 2:12–16]

Although the letter to the Ephesians has sometimes been taken as a summary of Pauline doctrine, it is probably best interpreted, according to Kümmel (1975:364–66), as the letter of a Jewish Christian thoroughly familiar with some of Paul's letters, particularly the letter to the Colossians, writing to gentile Christians between 80 and 100 C.E., possibly in Asia Minor. The occasion, he argues, was a spiritual crisis in the Ephesian church in which gentile Christians had to be reminded that Christianity included Jews equally.

3

THE INTERPRETATION OF SCRIPTURE

> Eat like a human being what is set
>   before you,
> and do not chew greedily, lest you be
>   hated.
> Be the first to stop eating, for the sake
>   of good manners,
> and do not be insatiable, lest you give
>   offence.
>   The Wisdom of Jesus the Son of
>   Sirach (31:16–17)

Christianity was originally just one among many sects of Judaism that flourished in the first century C.E. It differed most from those other sects in its universalism, which contrasted sharply with the separatist nationalism that dominated Jewish sectarianism after the Maccabean revolt. Even the Essenes, in many respects similar to early Christians, did not share their universalistic outlook. For them, the Servant suffered exclusively for the redemption of Israel.

Sectarians were united in their adherence to the law that was recorded in scripture during the decades following the restoration. They derived their differences from its interpretation. To understand the distinctiveness of early Christians, we must understand how they interpreted scripture.

Water and Wine

The problem for Jesus and his disciples, as for the people who wrote about them, was to find the forms with which to distinguish their "new man" from traditional conceptions of the observant Jew and yet communicate his nature powerfully to their contemporaries in terms they could understand. It was a problem because the language that was familiar to their contemporaries already had other connotations attached to it. As Nock points out, speaking of Paul:

> The importance of these points of contact [between Christianity and the pagan mystery religions] is that they remind us that the Christian missionary had to use the language of the time, that this language often had religious connotations which were more or less living, and that a stray hearer might well regard the new teaching as something not different in kind from the other religions of the time. [Nock 1964:31]

Grabar (1968) deals with the same problem in his analysis of the origins of the earliest Christian iconography in painting and sculpture. Christian authors of the first century and Christian artists of the second, third, and fourth centuries used the same approach. They expressed themselves in the language—verbal or visual—that was used around them because this was the only way they could make themselves understood.

The earliest Christian iconography in the visual arts has few terms of its own. Christian artists borrowed heavily from the imagery of the circus and the hippodrome, but they were particularly inspired by the art of the imperial cult, which represented the political, military, and judicial powers of the emperor and his agents and the activities of the Roman state. They expressed the novelty of their ideas primarily by taking over known formulas and giving them new meaning, often juxtaposing old and new in the same work, or by composing similar ones by analogy.

Jesus was made to symbolize the problem of innovation and comprehension when he transformed water into wine at the wedding party at Cana in Galilee and hailed the bridegroom who kept the best wine for last (John 2:1–11). It is also symbolized in the parables of the cloaks and patches, the new wine and old skins, images found in all three synoptic gospels and in the Gospel of Thomas immediately following passages concerning commensalism and fasting:

> "No one tears a piece from a new garment and puts it upon an old garment; if he does, he will tear the new, and the piece from the new will not match the old. And no one puts new wine into old wineskins; if he does, the new wine will burst the skins and it will be spilled, and the skins will be destroyed. But new wine must be put into fresh wineskins. And no one after drinking old wine desires new; for he says, 'the old is good'. " [Luke 5:36–39; see also Matthew 9:16–17; Mark 2:21–22; Gospel of Thomas 47b–d, which suggest that Luke added the last line recognizing the complexity of the problem.]

The Gospel of Thomas brings all of these sayings together with the admonition against serving two masters (47a), which is found in Matthew (6:24) immediately followed by Jesus' bidding to "put away anxious thoughts about food and drink" (6:25) and in Luke (6:13) by an attack on the hypocrisy of the Pharisees (16:14). In addition, Matthew has Jesus conclude the parables about wheat and weeds, priceless treasures, and good and bad fish by saying:

> "Have you understood all this?" They said to him, "Yes." And he said to them, "Therefore every scribe who has been trained for the kingdom of heaven is like a householder who brings out of his treasure what is new and what is old." [Matthew 13:51–52]

Wine means words. So Elihu speaks to Job:

> I also will give my answer.
> I also will declare my opinion.
> For I am full of words,
> > the spirit within me constrains me.
> Behold my heart is like wine that has no vent;
> > like new wineskins, it is ready to burst.
> I must speak, that I may find relief;
> I must open my lips and answer. [Job 32:17–20]

The author of the Second Book of the Maccabees, composed circa 100 B.C.E. (Rost 1976:82), uses the same imagery:

At this point I will bring my work to an end. If it is found well written and aptly composed, that is what I myself hoped for; if cheap and mediocre, I could only do my best. For, just as it is disagreeable to drink wine alone or water alone, whereas the mixing of the two gives a pleasant and delightful taste, so too variety of style in a literary work charms the ear of the reader. Let this then be my final word. [2 Maccabees 15:38–39, *NEB*]

Above all, wine means the inspired words of God, although it is not always easy to distinguish them from their common counterparts. The opening passages of Acts (2), composed by the author of Luke, depict the apostles so filled with the Holy Spirit that they speak in the native tongues of every one of the "multitude . . . of Jews and proselytes" from "every nation under heaven" who surround them (5–11). Ironically, those who mock them for being drunk are right. They are "filled up with new wine" (13), like the prophet Jeremiah, who said: "I am like a drunken man, like a man overcome by wine, because of the Lord and because of his holy words" (Jeremiah 23:9).

The cloak was a common symbol of the cosmos (Jeremias 1963:117–18, 189). The letter to the Hebrews praises God, using the words of scripture (Psalms 102:25–27):

Thou, Lord, didst found the earth in the beginning,
and the heavens are the work of thy hands;
they will perish, but thou remainest;
they will all grow old like a garment,
like a mantle thou wilt roll them up,
and they will be changed.
But thou art the same,
and thy years will never end. [Hebrews 1:10–12]

The father blesses his prodigal son by covering him with his best robe (Luke 15:22). Luke returns to the image in Acts (10:11–12, 11:5–6), in the sheet that contains Peter's unorthodox meal, symbolizing a radically different creation, transformed and declared clean by God. In writing about wine and cloaks, early Christians were writing about the God-given words with which they could construct and communicate a new vision of the world.

Given Hengel's (1974) demonstration of the complexity of social and cultural relations during the Greco-Roman period, it is no longer possible to agree wholly with Nock that "the key to Christian doctrine is given to us by Jewish conceptions alone" (1964:43). Early Christianity, like every other Jewish sect, must be seen as a complex mixture of ideas and practices derived from a variety of sources, including sources outside Judaism. Nevertheless, as I have emphasized, early Christians, like other Jewish sectarians, felt themselves to be expressing the only true Jewish faith (see, for example, Matthew 19:28; John 6:33, 15:1; Acts 3:1; Romans 11; Galatians 6:16; 2 Timothy 3:15–17; James 1:1; 1 Peter 1:1, 2:4–10, 5:13; Revelations 4:10, 7:4–9, 14:3). So Luke describes the apostles in Acts:

> And day by day, attending the temple together and breaking bread in their homes, they partook of food with glad and generous hearts, praising God and having favor with all the people. [Acts 2:46–47]

They regarded scripture as the basis of their doctrine (e.g., Matthew 5.17; 22.40, Luke 24.27, 32, 44–45).[1] Indeed, one of their strongest arguments was that the facts of Jesus' life, and especially his ignominious death, provided the essential clue to understanding scripture (Ellis 1957; Lindars 1961). As Paul says:

> For I delivered to you as of first importance what I also received, that Christ died for our sins in accordance with the scriptures, that he was buried, that he was raised on the third day in accordance with the scriptures, and that he appeared to Cephas, then to the twelve. [1 Corinthians 15:3–5]

Early Christian iconography, though it borrowed from a variety of Jewish and non-Jewish sources, preserved this technique. One of the commonest ways of conveying the import of a New Testament scene was to juxtapose it to a familiar Old Testament scene, represented or construed in terms of its prophetic significance (Grabar 1968:111), a method synonymous with the doctrine of prefiguration known as typology. Grabar (1968:141)

---

1. Scripture for most Jewish sectarians from at least the second century B.C.E. included the Law (the five books of Moses), the Prophets (most of the major and minor prophets now represented in the Old Testament), and the Writings (such as Psalms, Proverbs, Job). The Samaritans recognized only the first of these three categories. Sadducees and Pharisees were divided on the status of the Prophets. Still other disagreements focused on books now included among the Apocrypha or Pseudepigrapha (see von Campenhausen 1972).

derives this technique from the Stoics' method of establishing significant resemblances between events widely separated in time and space. He believes that Philo was the first to apply this method to the Bible, thereby opening the way to a typological exegesis of the Old Testament by comparison with the New. This may account for why Christians continued to use typology in symbolism, even after Christianity diverged from Judaism. Nevertheless, it is important to remember that the technique was thoroughly embedded in Jewish tradition as well.

"Turning water into wine" was the commonest activity of sectarian Judaism, deriving the *living* Torah from scripture, revealing its *true* meaning, as opposed to the adulterated meaning that false believers, "dead to the law," as Paul describes them, had attached to it. Those small groups revealed the living Torah by interpreting scripture in relation to their lives, a process known as *midrash* perhaps epitomized in the oral Torah of the Pharisees, but one that Vermès considers to be "the ultimate purpose of all Jewish exegesis" (1961:229). In the words of the rabbinic midrash on Numbers-Deuteronomy (probably composed before 200 C.E.): "When you study the Torah, let the commandments not seem old to you, but regard them as given this very day" (cited in Sandmel 1978:445, n. 24). Within Judaism, this kind of exegesis probably dates to the period of Persian domination, when scripture first started to become fixed in form (Bloch 1957:1267–69). It is found throughout the literature of the postexilic period, including the New Testament, where all the midrashic forms are represented (ibid.:1279–80; Gouldner 1974 and Drury 1977 are recent studies from this perspective).

Midrash means "to search for, to strive, to understand the meaning, the content, of a scriptural text; to explain, to set forth in public the meaning of scripture" (Bloch 1957:1265). Bloch's research on the Dead Sea Scrolls suggests something of the way midrash worked during the period between the second century B.C.E. and the first century C.E. (ibid.:1265–67):

1. It derives from scripture. It is a meditation on the sacred texts, an explanation or interpretation of scripture.
2. It is not an activity of savants confined to their studies, but a popular genre concerned above all with instruction,

which almost certainly derived from the homilies that followed the liturgical reading of the Torah in the synagogue.

3. The text is scrutinized, verse by verse or word by word, in order to decipher its meaning, usually in the context of other passages from scripture that have been selected not randomly but in relation to a theme.
4. The meaning of the scripture is adapted to contemporary needs.
5. If the text concerns laws, then the purpose of the midrash is to determine the basic principles behind them in order to solve problems not handled in scripture *(halakhah)*. If the text is narrative, then the purpose is to determine the true significance of the events that are described *(haggadah)*.

Nehemiah's (8:1–12) description of the first reading of "the book of the law of Moses" following the return from Babylon is a good example of the use of midrash in the temple, but midrash has also been preserved in scripture. Redaction criticism in biblical studies, defined by Perrin as the search for "the theological motivation of an author as this is revealed in the collection, arrangement, editing, and modification of traditional material, and in the composition of new material or the creation of new forms" (1969:1), essentially requires scholars to trace the midrashic process, without assuming, as midrash does, that theology is embedded in culture and social organization.

Although the purpose of midrash was to elucidate the true meaning of scripture, the result was neither imitative of the original source or sources nor uniform among different sects. This is perhaps why biblical scholars have begun to find it useful to combine redaction criticism with structuralism (in a variety of forms), which emphasizes the logic of a text taken as a whole rather than as a concatenation of parts (see Kelber 1976a:179; Kelber 1976b). Vermès concludes from an analysis of transformations in the story of Balaam (Numbers 22–24) that new tradition, whatever its original purpose, never simply supplements or replaces old. The new totally transforms the old. Balaam does not become increasingly composite. He becomes a different person with every new text (1961:126). The same is true of the effect of midrash on the Torah as a whole. The rabbis' purpose was to achieve harmony among the diverse traditions that constituted scripture by combining and interweaving parallel accounts, eliminating discrepancies, clarifying obscurities, and completing what they considered to be gaps in the narrative. But because they believed that the whole of scripture manifested the same word of God, they carried the process further, treating not only Torah, but the prophets, and later even the other writings in the Hebrew canon in the same synoptic manner. "The result was exegetical symbolism and a consequent doctrinal evolution and enrichment" (1961:228).

Kee (1977:46–47) makes the same point about the single gospel of Mark. He emphasizes that Mark was not "tradition-bound," as might appear from scholarship that has concentrated on the history of his sources (see also Kelber 1976a:156–58). He imitated neither the letter nor the spirit of his several sources. Some of his transformations were so radical that it is impossible to ascertain whether the quotation derived from a Hebrew or Greek original or "some deviant or corrupt text." This is characteristic of both the form and content of Mark's work from beginning to end, including some of the most critical points in the narrative. The significance he derived from his sources was not simply the sum of their parts, but a transformation of them all, something wholly different.

A good example from contemporary Judaism is the latest version of the haggadah, or commentary, intended to accompany the passover meal that derives from the scriptural injunction to "tell your son" (Exodus 13:8). The passover haggadah was recently rewritten by Rabbi Herbert Bronstein, in consultation with colleagues, for the Central Conference of American Rabbis, publishers of all liturgical works for the 1.1 million members of the Reform movement in North America. Rabbi Bronstein's haggadah replaced a 1923 version, which he considered appropriate to its time but now "dull and thin." The new haggadah "restores the joy and meaning of the festival while reflecting our generation's recovery of a whole realm of the sacred, spiritual, mystical and ethical concepts" (Bronstein, quoted in Blau 1974:B1).

"The Haggadah," according to Rabbi Bronstein, "is like the libretto for an opera. The opera is the seder itself [the passover service], and the head of the seder, like the producer of an opera, can alter the libretto." His new version expresses what he believes to have been the original intent of the passover: the reliving of a history that moves from slavery to freedom, from degradation to dignity. It incorporates a selection from *The Diary of Anne Frank* and a poem by Samuel Halkin describing his release from a Soviet prison camp in 1959, translated from Yiddish into English. Rabbi Bronstein said he had to "fight" for the omission of other contemporary documents and events. Although the selections concern Jews, the purpose of the haggadah is more universal: in the words of the text, "the deliverance from bondage of people everywhere" (Blau 1974:B1). Most of the haggadah is in English, but it is opened from right to left like a Hebrew prayer book. It is illustrated by Leonard Baskin, son of an Orthodox rabbi, who, although not observant himself, accepted the commission enthusiastically because he believed in its sociological importance (ibid.).

Gluttony

Paul speaks ironically of his teaching as turning wisdom into folly (1 Corinthians 1:18–2:16; 4:10; 2 Corinthians 11–12). Indeed, one of the most astonishing transformations in early Christian writing is the last supper, in which Christ's crucifixion and resurrection are turned into a meal of bread and wine.

The meal described by Paul and the evangelists derives directly from contemporary Jewish practice (Nock 1964:76–77, 133–34; Couratin 1969:151).[2] Jews did not eat or drink without blessing

2. Principal references to the last supper, in the order in which they were written, are: 1 Corinthians 11:17–34; Mark 14:22–26; Matthew 26:26–30; Luke 22:-14–20; John 6:51–58. Other references include: Luke 24:30; 35; Acts 1:13; 2:42, 46–47; 20:7, 11; 27:35; 1 Corinthians 5:7; 10:1–4, 16–22; 12:11–13; Hebrews 13:10; 1 Peter 2:5, 9; 2 Peter 2:13; 1 John 5:6, 8; Revelations 1:10, 19:7, 9. Couratin (1969:137) says Matthew is wholly dependent upon Mark for his account of the last supper. Biblical scholars disagree about the text of Luke (ibid.; Bowman 1965:91). John does not describe the "eucharist." He describes the events he believes happened during and after the supper: Jesus washes the feet of the disciples and feeds Judas, signifying that Judas is his betrayer. John discourses most explicitly on the significance of eating and drinking the body and blood of Jesus following the feeding miracle (John 6). The historical and sociocultural differences among these accounts will be discussed at greater length in chapter 5.

God's name, and special thanksgivings to God for his mighty acts of creation and redemption were attached to the bread broken and distributed by the host at the beginning of the meal and to the "cup of blessing" that all drank from at its close.

Nock (1938:54–55) thinks that the very name of the Christian sacrament, "thanksgiving" *(eucharistia),* echoed in the opening "We thank Thee, God . . ." of the central prayer in so many early Christian liturgies, in which reference to the last supper is always parenthetical, indicates that the Christian prayer originated in a Jewish benediction over shared food. He finds further evidence in Paul's phrase "the cup of blessing" (1 Corinthians 10:16), which includes the word for blessing, *eulogia,* that appears on a Jewish cup. Even Jesus' supposed command, "Do this in remembrance of me," would not have been out of character in a Jewish prayer (Couratin 1969:51).

Yet even if the last supper was quite ordinary in some ways, it was also profoundly peculiar. The apostles did not consume the usual sacrificial animal, but the body and blood of Jesus himself. The bizarreness of the meal, according to Nock, is precisely what guarantees the authenticity of the report:

> The 'words of institution', as they are commonly called, have a clear formal similarity to Exodus 16.15, 'This is the bread which the Lord hath given you to eat' and 24.8, 'Behold the blood of the covenant which the Lord hath made with you concerning all these words'. The strangeness of what remains, and in particular the paradoxical character for a Jew of any suggestion of the drinking of blood, guarantee the substantial authenticity of the record. It is much harder to imagine someone else inventing the words than Jesus uttering them. [1964:125; see also Knox 1944:66–67; Goodenough 1956, 6:136]

According to Mosaic law, blood must be strictly separated from food (Leviticus 3:17; 7:26–27; 17:3–7, 10–14; 19:26; Deuteronomy 12:15–16, 20–28; 15:19–23; 1 Samuel 14:32–35; Ezekiel 33:25). The prohibition against eating blood was one of the most important laws in scripture. Even foreigners were not exempt (Leviticus 12:10–12). It was so important that, together with the interdiction against shedding human blood, it was referred back to the restoration of order after the chaos of the deluge, when the

Lord made the covenant with Noah that applied to all mankind (Genesis 9:4–5). It was therefore older and more universal than even the Decalogue, which was dated to the wilderness period and applied only to Israelites. As Pedersen points out, "blood had become a thing apart, the law concerning it came before all other laws" (1926, 4:341).

"Treason" Saul called it when the Israelite army, faint with hunger from the fast he had enforced on them at the battle of Michmash, seized the sheep and cattle of the defeated Philistines and ate the meat with the blood in it. It was for this sin that Saul built his first altar to the Lord (1 Samuel 14:31–35). The consumption of blood was among those transgressions punished by death that included failure to keep the sabbath (Exodus 31:14; Numbers 15:32–36), to observe circumcision (Genesis 17:14), and to celebrate the passover (Numbers 9:13). The reason for the prohibition is always the same: "the blood is the life," not simply the mortal life, but in some sense the spiritual essence of the creature, man or beast (Genesis 4:10; Job 16:18; 2 Maccabees 8:3):

> If any man of the house of Israel or of the strangers that sojourn among them eats any blood, I will set my face against that person who eats blood, and will cut him off from among his people. For the life of the flesh is in the blood; and I have given it for you upon the altar to make atonement for your souls; for it is the blood that makes atonement by reason of the life. [Leviticus 17:10–11] When the Lord your God enlarges your territory, as he has promised you, and you say, "I will eat flesh," because you crave flesh, you may eat as much flesh as you desire. . . . Only be sure that you do not eat the blood; for the blood is the life, and you shall not eat the life with the flesh. [Deuteronomy 12:20, 23]

In the synoptic gospels, Jesus is made to reveal himself secretly, to his disciples alone. As in the Dead Sea Scrolls, the synoptics frequently argue that "the secret of the kingdom of God" has been given exclusively to the members of the covenant community. Outsiders will hear only parables (e.g., Matthew 13:10–15; Mark 4:11–12, 34). Secrecy and allegory, the presentation of revelations with political implications in veiled form, are common in apocalyptic and other writing from Daniel onward

(Jeremias 1963:13–19). Biblical scholars have varying explanations for the incomprehension of Jesus' own disciples. I think one possibility, which Matthew and Mark especially seem to suggest, is that Christ's symbolism is so radical that even his disciples cannot comprehend it (see also John 10:6). They doubt his teaching on lesser issues, but when it comes to the sacrificial meal on which his new covenant is founded, they deny, they fall asleep, finally they abandon him.

It is John who emphasizes what a horrifying meal it was, although why he does so is a difficult question. Remembering that Jewish sectarians constantly reinterpreted scripture according to their circumstances, we should look for the answer in the social and cultural context of the community or communities to which John belonged or for which he was writing. Unfortunately, John's gospel has been the most difficult of the four to situate.

According to John, Jesus reveals his true nature in public, at the place where his decisive confrontations with the religious leaders of Galilee occur in all the gospels—the synagogue at Capernaum, built with money donated by a gentile (Luke 7:5). It is Jesus' last public appearance in Galilee. He has just finished the feeding miracle on the shores of the Sea of Galilee, comparable to the second feeding miracle of the four thousand described by Matthew (15:32–39) and Mark (8:1–9), representing the inclusion of the gentiles.

"The Jews" have already begun to "murmur at him" because he says, "I am the bread which came down from heaven." They respond, "Is not this Jesus, the son of Joseph, whose mother and father we know? How does he now say, 'I have come down from heaven?'" (John 6:42–43). But Jesus continues:

> "Truly, truly, I say to you, unless you eat the flesh of the Son of man and drink his blood, you have no life in you; he who eats my flesh and drinks my blood has eternal life, and I will raise him up at the last day. For my flesh is food indeed, and my blood is drink indeed. He who eats my flesh and drinks my blood abides in me, and I in him. As the living Father sent me, and I live because of the Father, so he who eats me will live because of me. This is the bread which came down from heaven, not such as the fathers ate and died; he who eats this bread will live for ever." [John 6:53–58]

John (6:59) stresses again that "this he said in the synagogue, as he taught at Capernaum."

"The Jews" dispute among themselves: "How can this man give us his flesh to eat?" (John 6:52). That they should also drink his blood was simply unthinkable. Even many of his disciples agree, "This is a hard saying; who can listen to it?" (John 6:60). Jesus asks, "Do you take offense at this?" Indeed, "after this many of his disciples drew back and no longer went about with him" (John 6:61, 6:66). Jesus has to ask the twelve whether they too want to leave him, knowing that one of them will betray him. He avoids Judea afterwards, "because the Jews sought to kill him" (John 6:67–7:1).

The last supper is horrifying by itself. But in context it is merely the last in a long series of culinary disasters, each of which is minutely described by early Christian authors. Here they are agreed. To the world, Jesus is a drunkard like his disciples and a glutton. He eats anything with anyone:

> John came neither eating nor drinking, and they say, 'He has a demon'; the Son of man came eating and drinking, and they say, 'Behold, a glutton and a drunkard, a friend of tax collectors and sinners!' [Matthew 11:18–19]

Matthew follows this passage with Jesus' prediction that the notoriously licentious gentile cities of Tyre, Sidon, and Sodom will be better off on the day of judgment than the law-abiding Bethsaida and Chorazin (Matthew 11:20–34). Luke, who repeats the passage, follows it with the story of the sinner at the Pharisee's feast. One of the Pharisees asks Jesus to eat with him. As soon as a sinner learns that Jesus is "at table in the Pharisee's house," she arrives to anoint his feet with her tears and dry them with her hair. The Pharisee is surprised that the alleged prophet does not recognize "what sort of woman this is." Jesus' response is to tell the parable of the money-lender and forgive the woman her sins (Luke 7:33–50).

On other occasions, Jesus' disciples "eat and drink" while John's disciples and the Pharisees fast, and yet Jesus justifies the action of his disciples: "Can the wedding guests fast while the bridegroom is with them?" he asks, alluding to the popular image of messianic salvation as a wedding banquet (Mark 2: 18–22; see also Matthew 9:14–17; Luke 5:33–39; 18:12).

Jesus and his disciples break the sabbath, token of the Lord's covenant with Israel and one of the fundamental observances distinguishing Jews from gentiles, because they pick corn to eat (Matthew 12:1–8; Mark 2:23–27; Luke 6:1–5). Breaking the sabbath is punishable by severance from kin and death (Exodus 31:14–15). Only Matthew tries to excuse them by saying that they were hungry.

Jesus' disciples break "the tradition of the elders," Mosaic law as interpreted by the scribes and Pharisees, because they do not wash their hands before they eat and therefore eat with "defiled hands" (Matthew 15:1–20; Mark 7:1–23). Jesus himself eats with Pharisees without washing his hands (Luke 11:37–41). In response to their objections, he cites scripture, a passage from Isaiah (29:13; see Matthew 15:5–7; Mark 7:6–7), which runs in its entirety:

> Then the Lord said:
> Because this people approach me with their mouths
> and honour me with their lips
> while their hearts are far from me,
> and their religion is but a precept of men, learnt by rote,
> therefore I will yet again shock this people,
> adding shock to shock:
> the wisdom of their wise men shall vanish
> and the discernment of the discerning shall be lost.
> [Isaiah 29:13–14, *NEB*]

Then he calls the crowd closer and says: "Hear and understand: not what goes into the mouth defiles a man, but what comes out of the mouth, this defiles a man" (Matthew 15:10–11; Mark 7:14–15). Matthew (15:12) notes that the statement offends the Pharisees.

It is at this point in the accounts of both Matthew and Mark that the Syrophoenician woman begs Jesus for crumbs. Matthew describes her as a Canaanite woman from the region of Tyre and Sidon. In either case, she is a gentile. She wants Jesus to drive an unclean spirit out of her daughter. Jesus is reluctant. According to Matthew, his own disciples want him to send her away. He says, "Let the children first be fed, for it is not right to take the children's bread and throw it to the dogs" (Mark 7:27; Matthew 15:24 is more explicit: "I was sent only to the lost sheep of the house of Israel"). But when the woman answers, "Yes, Lord; yet even the dogs under the table eat the children's crumbs," recognizing the Bread of Life for who he is, Jesus is so overwhelmed by her faith that he restores her daughter on the spot (Mark 7:27–30; Matthew 15:27–28). The multiplications of the loaves and fishes follow almost immediately in both gospels.

Jesus asks for water from the hands of a Samaritan woman in John (4:4–42), although, as John notes carefully, "Jews have no dealings with Samaritans" (John 4:9). The woman herself is horrified: "How is it that you, a Jew, ask a drink of me, a woman of Samaria?" (John 4:9). The incident is said to have taken place at Jacob's well: *"our* father Jacob, who gave us the well and drank from it himself," as the Samaritan woman describes him (John 4:12). Jesus asks the woman to give him water ostensibly because his disciples, whom he would normally ask, "had gone away into the city to buy food" (John 4:8). In accepting it, he makes the Samaritan woman one of his own disciples. She recognizes him as a prophet; he admits to being the messiah (John 4:19, 26). When his disciples return, he refuses the food they have brought him, having already eaten:

> Meanwhile the disciples besought him, saying, "Rabbi, eat." But he said to them, "I have food to eat of which you do not know." So the disciples said to one another, "Has any one brought him food?" Jesus said to them, "My food is to do the will of him who sent me, and to accomplish his work." [John 4:31–34]

Jesus consistently eats and drinks with "many tax-collectors and sinners" (Matthew 9:10–13; Mark 2:15–17). The taxgatherer Levi holds "a great feast in his house" for Jesus, to which he has invited "a large company of tax collectors and others" (Luke 5:27–32). Jesus actually asks to be a guest at the house of Zacchaeus, "a chief tax collector, and rich," who "received him joyfully" (Luke 19:1–10). Worse yet, he receives them all at his own table (Matthew 9:10–13; Mark 2:15–17). According to Matthew, he receives taxgatherers even into his own circle of disciples (9:9, 10:3).

The spectacle of Jesus "receiving sinners and eating with them" (Luke 15:1) causes murmuring among the Pharisees and scribes. Jesus frequently explains the purpose of his commensalism: "to seek and to save the lost" (Luke 19:10; see also Matthew

9:12–13; Mark 2:16–17; Luke 5:31–32, 15:1–10, and others). But Luke expresses it graphically in the parable of the prodigal son, which immediately follows one of these murmuring episodes (Luke 15:11–32).

The good son who stayed home and worked for his father represents the Jews, while the prodigal son, wild and uncouth, represents a diaspora Jew or possibly a gentile. Jeremias (1963: 132), who interprets the younger son as a Jew of the diaspora, points out that the eldest sons of Jewish families at this time received twice the inheritance of younger sons and that a younger son would therefore have found the thriving cities of the diaspora very attractive.

Ironically, it is the "far country," not Judea, that is hit by a "great famine." The younger son attaches himself to "one of the citizens of that country," who sends him to feed swine. He gets so hungry that "he would gladly have fed on the pods that the swine ate; and no one gave him anything" (Luke 15:16). "Perishing with hunger," he returns home, where even his father's hired servants have more bread than they can eat.

The prodigal son disavows his kinship out of shame: "Father, I have sinned against heaven and before you; I am no longer worthy to be called your son; treat me as one of your hired servants" (Luke 15:18–19). His angry elder brother would also prefer to deny his kinship. He refuses to join the feast on the fatted calf. But the father will reunite his two sons into one family:

> [The elder son says], "Lo, these many years I have served you, and I never disobeyed your command; yet you never gave me a kid, that I might make merry with my friends. But when this son of yours came, who has devoured your living with harlots, you killed for him the fatted calf!" And he said to him, "Son, you are always with me, and all that is mine is yours. It was fitting to make merry and be glad, for this your brother was dead, and is alive; he was lost, and is found." [Luke 15:29–32]

4

FOOD SYMBOLISM IN THE JUDAIC TRADITION

> I am the Lord your God,
> who brought you up out of the land of Egypt.
> Open your mouth wide, and I will fill it.
>
> Psalms 81:10

In the last chapter, I argued that early Christian writers, concerned with distinguishing their "new man" from traditional conceptions of the observant Jew, interpreted him in the eyes of the world as "a glutton and a drunkard." The phrase is almost certainly an allusion to the insubordinate son and his fate according to scripture:

> If a man has a stubborn and rebellious son, who will not obey the voice of his father or the voice of his mother, and, though they chastise him, will not give heed to them, then his father and his mother shall take hold of him and bring him out to the elders of his city at the gate of the place where he lives, and they shall say to the elders of his city, "This our son is stubborn and rebellious, he will not obey our voice; he is a glutton and a drunkard." Then all the men of the city shall stone him to death with stones; so you shall purge the evil from your midst and all Israel shall hear and fear. [Deuteronomy 21:18–21][1]

1. This passage is immediately followed by the description of the procedure appropriate to hanging a criminal on a tree after his execution to which early Christians referred in writing of Jesus' crucifixion (Deuteronomy 21:22–23; see John 19:31; Acts 5:30; 10:39; 13:29; Galatians 3:13; 1 Peter 2:24).

In early Christian writing, the father welcomed his rebellious son back into his household. Yet the question remains: why should food have been so controversial? Why should it have been such a powerful means of exalting Jesus as well as condemning him? If "no one would crucify a teacher who told pleasant stories to enforce prudential morality" (C.W.F. Smith 1948:17), why should the teacher be crucified for "gluttony"? Presumably because gluttony, like the parables in which he also expressed his rebellious doctrine, was related to bitterly disputed theological and social issues.

In this chapter, I will argue that food, articulated in terms of who eats what with whom under which circumstances, had long been one of the most important languages in which Jews conceived and conducted social relations among human beings and between human beings and God. Food was a way of talking about the law and lawlessness that dated at least to the Babylonian Exile in the mid-sixth century B.C.E., when the Pentateuch and Deuteronomic books are estimated to have taken nearly final form. In these books and in the books of the prophets and other writings composed during the early postexilic period that Jews regarded as scripture:

1. The power of the Lord is manifested in his ability to control food: to feed is to bless, to confer life; to feed bad food or to starve is to judge or punish, to confer death.
2. Acceptance of the power and authority of the Lord is symbolized by acceptance of his food.
3. Rejection of the power and authority of the Lord is symbolized by seeking after food he has forbidden.
4. People "limit" or "tempt" the Lord—that is, question the extent of his power or authority—by questioning his ability to feed them.
5. The Lord's word is equated with food.
6. Eating joins people with the Lord or separates them.

Blessing

The power and authority of the Lord is manifested in his ability to control food: to feed is to bless. In the Pentateuch, God's commandments signify his personal activity, by virtue of which all things exist in the universe. Yahweh, as the creator and sustainer of the entire world, is conceived as operating through his word, his *fiat,* at once the expression of his will and its execution. His command is the underlying principle of all creation, all orderliness in the course of nature. History is providential because God may give or withhold as he alone chooses.

God's first command on creating living beings and putting them in their places defines the food through which they will persist or perish. Thus the Psalmist praises God:

> O Lord, how manifold are thy works!
> In wisdom hast thou made them all;
> the earth is full of thy creatures. . . .

> These all look to thee,
> to give them their food in due season.
> When thou givest to them,
>   they gather it up;
> when thou openest thy hand,
>   they are filled with good things.
> When thou hidest thy face,
>   they are dismayed;
> when thou takest away their breath,
>   they die and return to their dust.
> When thou sendest forth thy Spirit, they are created;
> and thou renewest the face of the ground.
>   [Psalms 104:24, 27–30]

God's creation proceeds through a series of re-creations, distinguished by the foods his new creatures may and may not eat. Thus Adam and Eve in Eden may eat everything in the garden except the fruit of the tree of knowledge of good and evil (Genesis 2:16–17). But when they eat the forbidden fruit and are cast out, they must eat "the plants of the field," bread in the sweat of their faces, for "cursed is the ground because of you; in toil you shall eat of it all the days of your life" (3:17–18).

Noah and his seed, the remnant saved from the flood, may eat all things except meat with blood in it: "Every moving thing that lives shall be food for you; and as I gave you the green plants, I give you everything. Only you shall not eat flesh with its life, that is, its blood" (9:3–5). The children of Israel, passed over in the smiting of Egypt, are instructed to eat the passover meal, which represents in its food and in the manner of its consumption their salvation at the hand of the Lord. The passover is forbidden to the foreigner (Exodus 12).

The children of Israel are delivered in the wilderness by God's gifts of water from a wandering rock (Exodus 17) and manna which they are told to store in a vessel on the altar as a sign of his divine power: "I fed you in the wilderness when I brought you out of the land of Egypt" (Exodus 16:32). Canaan is the land he has promised them, a "land flowing with milk and honey [where] they will eat and be satisfied" (Jubilees 1:7–8). When they arrive, they are instructed first of all in the dietary rules: "This is the law pertaining to beast and bird and every living creature that moves through the waters and every creature that swarms upon the earth, to make a distinction between the unclean and the clean and between the living creature that may be eaten and the living creature that may not be eaten" (Leviticus 11:46–47; see also Deuteronomy 14:3–29).

The Lord stands by his children in adversity: "Thou preparest a table before me in the presence of my enemies" (Psalms 23:5; see also Psalms 81:7–16; Ruth 1:6). The Jerusalem that the Lord has restored to the Jews following the Babylonian Exile will nourish them like a mother with the wealth of the nations:

> That you may suck and be satisfied
> with her consoling breasts;
> that you may drink deeply with delight
> from the abundance of her glory . . .
>
> Behold, I will extend prosperity
>   to her like a river,
> and the wealth of the nations
>   like an overflowing stream;
> and you shall suck, you shall
>   be carried upon her hip,
> and dandled upon her knees.
> As one whom his mother comforts,
>   so I will comfort you;
> you shall be comforted in Jerusalem.
>   [Isaiah 66:11–13]

Nourishment is an important feature of worldly relations among the nations also. The same metaphor is used of human political leaders and prophets to symbolize their power and authority over the people: Elisha (2 Kings 4:42–44), Saul (2 Samuel 5:2; 2 Chronicles 11:2), and David (Psalms 78; Ezekiel 34:23–24).

Early Christian writers relied on this imagery to represent the divine power and authority of Jesus. The multiplication of the loaves and fishes is recounted six times: twice by Matthew and Mark, once each by Luke and John; "clearly the church cherished the memory of it" (Harvey 1970:140). Jesus' feeding miracles parallel the scriptural stories of the Passover and God's miraculous gift of manna in the wilderness (John 6:4).

Jesus gives the same command to his disciples that the Lord gave to Saul and David: "Feed my sheep."

> When they had finished breakfast, Jesus said to Simon Peter, "Simon, son of John, do you love me more than these?" He said to him, "Yes, Lord; you know that I love you." He said to him, "Feed my lambs." A second time, he said to him, "Simon, son of John, do you love me?" He said to him, "Yes, Lord; you know that I love you." He said to him, "Tend my sheep." He said to him the third time, "Simon, son of John, do you love me?" Peter was grieved because he said to him the third time, "Do you love me?" And he said to him, "Lord, you know everything; you know that I love you." Jesus said to him, "Feed my sheep." [John 21:15–17]

Paul feeds his companions on what he predicted would be a disastrous ship voyage, and they escape their captors and reach land safely (Acts 27:33–38). He feeds his flock of Corinthians as "babes in Christ . . . with milk, not solid food," to acquaint them gradually with the Lord's wisdom (1 Corinthians 3:1–2).

The Lord often has to seek out the sheep whom his faithless shepherds did not feed, but fed on, abused, lost, or left to be devoured by wild beasts:

> I myself will search for my sheep, and will seek them out. As a shepherd seeks out his flock when some of his sheep have been scattered abroad, so will I seek out my sheep, and I will rescue them from all places where they have been scattered on a day of clouds and thick darkness. And I will bring them out from the peoples, and gather them from the countries, and will bring them into their own land; and I will feed them on the mountains of Israel. . . . I will seek the lost, and I will bring back the strayed, and I will bind up the crippled, and

75

> I will strengthen the weak, and the fat and the strong I will watch over; I will feed them in justice. [Ezekiel 34:11–13, 16; see also Proverbs 30:11–14; Isaiah 9:20, 40:11, 56:8–11; Joel 2:26; Micah 3:3; Zechariah 11:16]

Thus Jesus feeds and eats with bad characters to seek out and save what was scattered and lost. Indeed, it is precisely the hungry, the poor and persecuted, who Jesus, like the prophets before him, predicts will inherit the earth (e.g., Isaiah 57:15, 61: 1–11, 66:2; Jeremiah 24; Micah 4:6–8; Matthew 5:3–12, Luke 6:20–26).

Judgment

To feed bad food or starve is to judge or punish. It is inconceivable that the Lord should not feed a faithful flock, but the faithless deserve different treatment. The Lord's destructive power is also conveyed through the medium of food. His treatment of Adam and Eve provides the paradigm for all that follows:

> Come now, let us reason together, says the Lord . . .
> If you are willing and obedient,
> you shall eat the good of the land;
> But if you refuse and rebel,
> you shall be devoured by the sword;
> for the mouth of the Lord has spoken.
> [Isaiah 1:18–20; see also Isaiah 58:13–14; Hosea 4:16]

Destruction may come as feast or famine. The people of Israel complain to Moses and Aaron in the desert:

> Would that we had died by the hand of the Lord in the land of Egypt, when we sat by the fleshpots and ate bread to the full; for you have brought us out into this wilderness to kill this whole assembly with hunger. [Exodus 16:3]

The Israelites envisage their salvation as a heavenly wedding banquet. The Lord's judgment, on the other hand, is a funeral feast in which the victim is Judah and the guests are wild beasts and birds of prey (Isaiah 34:6; Jeremiah 46:10; Ezekiel 39:17–24; Zephaniah 1:7), an image that is taken up in Revelations

(19:17–18) to symbolize the destruction of the enemies of Christ. The Lord also takes food away:

> "I gave you cleanness of teeth in all your cities,
> and lack of bread in all your places,
> yet you did not return to me," says the Lord.

> "And I also withheld the rain from you
> when there were yet three months to the harvest;
> I would send rain upon one city,
> and send no rain upon another city;
> one field would be rained upon,
> and the field on which it did not rain withered;
> so two or three cities wandered to one city
> to drink water, and were not satisfied;
> yet you did not return to me," says the Lord.
> [Amos 4:6–8; see also 4:9–11;
> Deuteronomy 28:64–66; Ezekiel 14:12–13]

He feeds the faithless with bad or poisonous food, or he permits them to die of their own greed (Exodus 16; Numbers 11:32–34; Job 20:10–23; Psalms 8:4–5; 106:14; Jeremiah 8:14, 9:15, 23: 15). He instructs Jeremiah to destroy all the nations, including Israel, with the "wine of wrath" (Jeremiah 25:15), a deliberate inversion of the messianic "cup of salvation" described in the Psalms (116:13):

> "Then you shall say to them, 'Thus says the Lord of hosts, the God of Israel: Drink, be drunk and vomit, fall and rise no more, because of the sword which I am sending among you.'
> "And if they refuse to accept the cup from your hand to drink, then you shall say to them, 'Thus says the Lord of hosts: You must drink!' " [Jeremiah 25:27–28; see Jeremiah 13:13–14; Psalms 75:7–8; Isaiah 51:17–23; Ezekiel 23:31–34; Revelations 14:10; 16; 17:6]

The cup reappears in early Christian writing, where it is turned against Christ himself. When he finally accepts the Roman soldiers' "sour wine," he dies, evoking, according to John (19:28),one of the deadliest curses in scripture:

> They gave me poison for food,
> and for my thirst they gave me vinegar to drink.

77

Let their own table before them become a snare;
let their sacrificial feasts be a trap.
     [Psalms 69:21–22; see also
Matthew 27:48;
     Mark 15:36; Luke 23:37]

Paul cites the curse again in his letter to the Romans: "Let their table become a snare and a trap, a pitfall and a retribution for them" (Romans 11:9).

The same imagery is used in speaking of worldly relations among kingdoms and nations. [2] The Israelites are a field of late summer corn devoured by locusts (Amos 7:1–3; see also Joel 2:25), a basket of ripe summer fruit: "The end has come upon my people Israel; I will never again pass by them" (Amos 8:2). Jerusalem is a stewpot filled with "choice bones" (Ezekiel 24:4). The Lord has put it on the fire to cook. The king of Babylon will eat it:

Nebuchadrezzar the king of Babylon has devoured me,
he has crushed me;
he has made me an empty vessel,
he has swallowed me like a monster;
he has filled his belly with my delicacies,
he has rinsed me out. . . .

[The Lord promises vengeance.]
While they are inflamed I will prepare them a feast
and make them drunk, till they swoon away
and sleep a perpetual sleep
and not wake, says the Lord.
     [Jeremiah 51:34; 39; see also Psalms 80:12–13;
     Ezekiel 11:3–7; Hosea 7:8–9; Zechariah 11:4]

The imagery is reversed in another of Jeremiah's visions. He sees two baskets of figs set out in front of the temple, one of first-ripe figs that are very good, the other of figs that are very bad, "so bad they are not fit to eat" (Jeremiah 24:1–3). God inter-

2. It is in this spirit, perhaps, that in March 1970 four hundred members of the Jewish War Veterans held a "foodless banquet" in the Jade Room of the Waldorf Astoria to protest against President Nixon's dinner in honor of President Pompidou in the Grand Ballroom next door. France had just sold 110 Mirage jets to Libya, while refusing 50 to Israel (New York Times 1970:29).

prets the figs that are good to eat as the exiles of Judah who surrender to the king of Babylon and keep his peace; they will be restored to their land. The rotten figs are the ones who remain in Judah or flee to Egypt against his will. These he will scatter among foreigners, where no one will associate with them:

> Like the bad figs which are so bad they cannot be eaten, so will I treat Zedekiah the king of Judah, his princes, the remnant of Jerusalem who remain in this land, and those who dwell in the land of Egypt. I will make them a horror to all the kingdoms of the earth, to be a reproach, a byword, a taunt, and a curse in all the places where I shall drive them. And I will send sword, famine, and pestilence upon them, until they shall be utterly destroyed from the land which I gave to them and their fathers. [Jeremiah 24:8–10; see also 29:17–18]

Jesus returns to Jeremiah's imagery, when he curses the fig tree that fails to satisfy his hunger:

> On the following day, when they came from Bethany, he was hungry. And seeing in the distance a fig tree in leaf, he went to see if he could find anything on it. When he came to it, he found nothing but leaves, for it was not the season for figs. And he said to it, "May no one ever eat fruit from you again." And his disciples heard it. [Mark 11:12–14]

In Mark's text the fig tree stands immediately before the temple. Jesus follows his curse by cleansing the temple and the fig tree is found "withered away to its roots" the next day (Mark 11:15–21).

Acceptance and Rejection

Acceptance or rejection of the power and authority of the Lord is symbolized by acceptance or rejection of his food. The Psalmist praises the Lord: "The Lord is my chosen portion and my cup . . . yea, I have a goodly heritage" (Psalms 16:5–6). Habakkuk too will rejoice in the "God of my salvation" even in times of want, when the trees yield no fruit, the fields yield no food, and the herds dwindle (Habakkuk 3:12–18). Yet this is not the inevitable response of God's children. The Lord gives Ezekiel a vision of the siege of Jerusalem and the subsequent exile in the form of an unclean meal. He orders Ezekiel to prepare bread from mixed grains, including even the inferior millet and spelt, to bake the bread over human dung, rendering it unclean (Deuteronomy 23:12–14), and to eat it in small rations for 390 days. He is to do all this where everyone can see him because the unclean food is a sign: "Thus shall the people of Israel eat their bread unclean, among the nations whither I will drive them" (Ezekiel 4:13). When Ezekiel desperately protests: "Ah Lord God! Behold, I have never defiled myself; from my youth up till now I have never eaten what died of itself or was torn by beasts, nor has foul flesh come into my mouth" (Ezekiel 4:14), the Lord relents and allows him to use cow's dung instead of human dung as fuel.

Jesus Christ is no less reluctant to drink the bitter cup. Three times in the garden of Gethsemane he prays to God to take it away: "Abba, Father, all things are possible to thee; remove this cup from me; yet not what I will, but what thou wilt" (Mark 14:36; see also Matthew 26:39–42; Luke 22:41–42; John 18:11). This time the Lord does not relent. Jesus Christ asks his disciples, "Are you able to drink the cup that I drink?" They answer, "We are able," though in the end, they are not (Mark 10:38; see also Matthew 20:22–23). Paul uses the same imagery to condemn idolatry:

> I do not want you to be partners with demons. You cannot drink the cup of the Lord and the cup of demons. You cannot partake of the table of the Lord and the table of demons. Shall we provoke the Lord to jealousy? Are we stronger than he? [1 Corinthians 10:20–22]

But only a few prophets would obey the Lord by eating even the really difficult meals he has prepared for them. Mostly the Israelites lust after forbidden fruit. Esau sells his birthright to his twin brother, Jacob, in exchange for a dish of red lentil broth. Thus he acquires the name Edom, "Red," whence the ambiguous Edomites, kin to the Israelites but, because of their patriarch's thoughtless hunger, symbolic of those whom God did not choose (see, for example, Malachi 1:2–3; Romans 9:10–13; Hebrews 12:16).

The Israelites demand worldly food from God after he has given them the divine manna, "supernatural food," as Paul describes it to the Corinthians (1 Corinthians 10:3). He sends them wild birds, so that they cannot say afterward that he was ever powerless. Then he destroys them for their insatiable greed (Exodus 16; Numbers 11:32–34; Psalms 106:14):

> he rained flesh upon them like dust,
> winged birds like the sand of the seas;
> he let them fall in the midst of their camp,
> all around their habitations.
> And they ate and were well filled,
> for he gave them what they craved.
> But before they had sated their craving,
> while the food was still in their mouths,
> the anger of God rose against them
> and he slew the strongest of them,
> and laid low the picked men of Israel.
> In spite of all this they still sinned;
> despite his wonders they did not believe.
> [Psalms 78:27–32]

Even in Canaan, idolatrous Israelites do not "sow righteousness" or "reap the fruit of steadfast love" (Hosea 10:12–13; see also Jeremiah 2:7). Hosea's marriage to Gomer will bear witness to their faithlessness and to the Lord's redemptive love:

> And the Lord said to me, "Go again, love a woman who is beloved of a paramour and is an adultress; even as the Lord loves the people of Israel, though they turn to other gods and love cakes of raisins." [Hosea 3:1]

Paul summarizes up the story of the golden calf by quoting scripture: "The people sat down to feast and rose up to revel" (1 Corinthians 10:7 *NEB*; see Exodus 32:6).

Doubt

People question the Lord's power and authority by questioning his ability to feed them. It is expressly forbidden in scripture to "challenge" or "test" God, to "limit" him by questioning the extent of his power or authority (Deuteronomy 6:16; quoted by Jesus in Matthew 4:7 and Luke 4:12). Yet it happens continually, usually represented in terms of faithlessness over food. The Israelites tempt God in the wilderness when they murmur against

Moses, Aaron, and the Lord himself, for bread, meat, and drink successively (Exodus 16; 17):

> Yet they sinned still more against him,
> rebelling against the Most High in the desert.
> They tested God in their heart
> by demanding the food they craved.
> They spoke against God, saying,
> "Can God spread a table in the wilderness?
> He smote the rock so that water gushed out
> and streams overflowed.
> Can he also give bread, or provide meat for his people?"
>
> Therefore, when the Lord heard, he was full of wrath;
> a fire was kindled against Jacob,
> his anger mounted against Israel;
> because they had no faith in God,
> and did not trust his saving power. [Psalms 78:17–22]

Satan tempts Jesus fasting in the wilderness by challenging him to turn stones into bread (Matthew 4:1–11; Mark 1:13; Luke 4:1–13). Jesus himself has to counsel his anxious disciples to trust in the Lord:

> O men of little faith . . . do not seek what you are to eat and what you are to drink, nor be of anxious mind. For all the nations of the world seek these things; and your Father knows that you need them. [Luke 12:28–30; see also Matthew 6:25–32]

God's Food Is His Word

Two assumptions are implicit in all the examples of divine and human behavior discussed so far. The first is that the food God provides is his word; the food embodies his wisdom. The second is that eating God's wisdom should establish a binding agreement, a covenant, among the eaters to abide by his word.

The first of these assumptions is stated explicitly in a variety of ways. The unleavened bread of the passover, for example, is intended by the Lord "as a sign on your hand and as a memorial between your eyes, that the law of the Lord may be in your mouth; for with a strong hand the Lord has brought you out of

Egypt" (Exodus 13:9). God's saving food in the wilderness is like-wise to be commemorated. Manna must be preserved in a vessel on the altar in the temple to "make you know that man does not live by bread alone, but that man lives by everything that pro-ceeds out of the mouth of the Lord" (Deuteronomy 8:3; see also Exodus 16:32–35). Both the manna and the rock were called "God's Wisdom" (Psalms 42:23). The association of wisdom with food underlies many other passages in scripture (for example, Psalms 36:9, 42:1–3; Proverbs 10:11, 13:14, 14:27, 16:22, 24:13–14; Isaiah 12:3; Jeremiah 17:13):

> Wisdom has built her house,
> she has set up her seven pillars.
> She has slaughtered her beasts,
> she has mixed her wine,
> she has also set her table.
> She has sent out her maids to call
> from the highest places in the town,
> "Whoever is simple, let him turn in here!"
> To him who is without sense she says,
> "Come, eat of my bread and drink
>   of the wine I have mixed.
> Leave simpleness, and live, and walk
>   in the way of insight."
>   [Proverbs 9:1–6]

At least two of the prophets eat the book thereby acquiring the gift of prophecy. The Lord commands Ezekiel:

> "But you, son of man, hear what I say to you; be not rebellious like that rebellious house; open your mouth, and eat what I give you." And when I looked, behold, a hand was stretched out to me, and, lo, a written scroll was in it; and he spread it before me; and it had writing on the front and on the back, and there were written on it words of lamentation and mourning and woe. And he said to me, "Son of man, eat what is offered to you; eat this scroll, and go, speak to the house of Israel." So I opened my mouth, and he gave me the scroll to eat. And he said to me, "Son of man, eat this scroll that I give you and fill your stomach with it." Then I ate it and it was in my mouth as sweet as honey. [Ezekiel 2:8–3:3; see also Jeremiah 15:16; Revelation 10:8–11]

The association of wisdom with bread or manna, milk, honey, "living water," and especially wine, pervades the literature of the postexilic period (see, for example, Ecclesiasticus 9:9, 24:19–23, the Odes of Solomon 6:8–18; 11:7; 30, Jubilees 24:19, 25, 1 Enoch 17:4, 2 Esdras 8:4, and the Dead Sea Scrolls [Dupont-Sommer 1961:101, 211, 235, 241]). It also occurs frequently in the work of Philo, Jesus' contemporary. A passage describing the repellant behavior of the gourmand, enslaved to "strong drink and fish and dainty cakes," suggests that *what* was eaten was really more important than *how* it was eaten: "It was this which led those who had taken no mere sip of philosophy but had feasted abundantly on its sound doctrines to the theory [of the tripartite nature of the soul]" (*The Special Laws*, 4:92).[3]

Jesus preaches the same message: "Blessed are those who hunger and thirst for righteousness, for they shall be satisfied" (Matthew 5:6; see also 1 Corinthians 3:1–3; Hebrews 6:4–5, 1 Peter 2:1–3; 2 Peter 1:8). He quotes Deuteronomy (8:3, cited above) in response to the devil who tempts him while he is fasting in the wilderness. He tells his disciples to beware of the leaven of the Pharisees, although they become confused and think he is speaking about bread and not ideas. They have just come from the multiplication of the loaves and fishes and forgotten to take any of the leftovers with them. He has already cautioned them against false prophecy, which he compares to thorns masquerading as grapes (Matthew 7:15–20, 12:33, 13:22–23; Luke 6: 43–45). Nevertheless, he has to explain again:

> "How is it that you fail to perceive that I did not speak about bread? Beware of the leaven of the Pharisees and Sadducees." Then they understood that he did not tell them to beware of the leaven of bread, but of the teaching of the Pharisees and Sadducees. [Matthew 16:11–12; see also Luke 12:1]

3. The same association is found throughout the Talmud and Midrashim, the rabbinic commentaries on scripture (Goodenough 1956, 6:182–216). Joseph Caro's (1488–1575) great summary of Jewish law, printed in 1565, is called "the Prepared Table" *(Shulḥan Arukh)*. With Moses Isserles's glosses incorporating divergent Ashkenazi practices, known as "the Tablecloth" *(Mappah)*, it was the standard manual of Jewish law for centuries, "the revered and reviled symbol of orthodox rabbinism . . . the *Summa* of rabbinic orthodoxy" (Werblowsky 1962:1, 7; see also *Encyclopaedia Judaica*, 3:586, 14:1475).

Food Symbolism in the Judaic Tradition

Pharisees may have regarded themselves, or certain of their outstanding teachers, as living embodiments of the law, but for Christians, Jesus Christ is the only true prophet. For Paul he is "the wisdom of God" (1 Corinthians 1:24), "in whom are hid all the treasures of wisdom and knowledge" (Colossians 2:3), as for John he is the one in whom "the Word became flesh and dwelt among us, full of grace and truth" (John 1:14). He is "the supernatural Rock" (1 Corinthians 10:4), "the true vine" (John 15:1), "the bread of life" (John 6:48). He said it himself, according to John:

> "I am the living bread which came down from heaven; if any one eats of this bread, he will live for ever; and the bread which I shall give for the life of the world is my flesh." [John 6:51]

Commensalism and Covenant

The consequence of eating God's words is the covenant, "the creator of all rights and duties" in Judaism (Pedersen 1926, 2: 309), with which he binds people together in his name:

> Come, all who are thirsty, come, fetch water;
> come, you who have no food, buy corn and eat;
> come and buy, not for money,
>   not for a price, wine and milk.
> Why spend money and get what is not bread,
> why give the price of your labour
>   and go unsatisfied?
> Only listen to me and you will have
>   good food to eat,
> and you will enjoy the fat of the land.
> Come to me and listen to my words,
> hear me, and you shall have life:
> I will make a covenant with you,
>   this time for ever,
> to love you faithfully as I loved David.
>   [Isaiah 55:1–3, *NEB*]

Pedersen (1926, 2:306, n. 1) even argues for a connection between the word for "covenant" *(berith)* and the verb "to eat" *(bārā)*. Food is the commonest form of gift in scripture, given to relatives (Genesis 32:3–21), acquaintances (Genesis 43:1–11), kings (1 Chronicles 12:38–40; 2 Samuel 16:1; 17:27–29), and prophets (1 Samuel 9:6–7; 1 Kings 14:1–3; Amos 7:12; Micah 3:5). Table fellowship is synonymous with fellowship in all aspects of life (see, for example, Genesis 14:18–20; 26:26–31; 29:22, 27–28; 31:44–46, 51–54; Joshua 9:3–15; Judges 9:26–28; 2 Samuel 3:20; 9:7, 10–11; Proverbs 15:17; 17:1). A person who shares table fellowship with another "enjoys his salt" (Ezekiel 4:14). A particularly intimate covenant is therefore called a "covenant of salt" (Numbers 18:19; 2 Chronicles 13:5; Ezra 4:14; but compare Leviticus 2:13; Job 21:11). Thus Jesus says to his disciples: "Have salt in yourselves, and be at peace with one another" (Mark 9:50; see also Matthew 5:13; Luke 14:34–35; Colossians 4:6).

Refusal to eat together severs the relationship (1 Samuel 20:34). Those who do not eat or drink together are without any obligation to one another, if not actually enemies. The worst kind of traitor is the traitor with whom one has shared food (Psalms 41:9; Obadiah 1:7; Matthew 26:21; Mark 14:17; Luke 22:21; John 13:18, 24–27).

Commensalism, according to Robertson Smith, was thought of "as confirming or even as constituting kinship in a very real sense" (1889:257). Thus Isaac requested a meal of his favorite food from Esau, the elder of his twin sons, in order to recognize him formally as his first-born in the presence of the Lord and bestow his paternal blessing upon him before he died (Genesis 27). Esau, a skilled hunter, was to feed his father with a "savory food . . . such as he loved," made of game Esau had hunted and prepared himself. Indeed, Isaac preferred Esau because he kept him supplied with game (25:28). Jacob, favored by their mother Rebecca, "was a quiet man, dwelling in tents" (25:27).

Jacob tricked Esau out of his paternal blessing and established himself as first-born by disguising his tame flesh and food to appear wild. Using goatskins on his hands and neck to deceive his aged father into thinking he was the red and hairy Esau, he fed Isaac with kids from his own flock that Rebecca had cooked to taste like game. The blessing could not be revoked, because the meal was eaten. When Esau came in with his food shortly afterwards, Isaac "trembled violently," but said: "Who was it then that hunted game and brought it to me, and I ate it all before you came, and I have blessed him?—yes, and he shall be blessed" (27:33).

It should be noted that Esau, having sold Jacob his birthright for a dish of pottage, had married a gentile to the great grief of his parents, who now pleaded with Jacob to marry one of his mother's brother's daughters so that he might receive the blessing God had bestowed on Isaac and Isaac's father Abraham (27:46–28:4).

Eating and drinking together is also symbolic of sexual love and marriage, as in the Song of Solomon and in Jesus ben Sirach's blunt warning:

> Never dine with another man's wife,
> nor revel with her at wine;
> lest your heart turn aside to her,
> and in blood you be plunged into destruction.
> [Sirach 9:9]

So it expresses the relationship of Israel to God's wisdom, the perfect marriage:

> he who holds to the law will obtain wisdom.
> She will come to meet him like a mother,
> and like the wife of his youth
>   she will welcome him.
> She will feed him with the bread
>   of understanding,
> and give him the water of wisdom to drink.
> [Sirach 15:1–3]

Faithless Israelites "set a table for Fortune and fill cups of mixed wine for Destiny" (Isaiah 65:11), but the faithful feed Yahweh in a variety of celebratory meals held throughout the year, the counterpart of God's meals, the means by which both parties identify and maintain their common obligation in the covenant. Such ceremonies are described as "eating before God" (Exodus 18:12; Deuteronomy 12:7, 18). As Paul says, preaching against partnership with the demons of idolatry, "Consider the people of Israel; are not those who eat the sacrifices partners in the altar?" (1 Corinthians 10:18). God's portion is the fat and blood of each sacrificial animal, the first fruits, and a tithe of all produce.

The occasion in the wilderness when the Israelites first pledged to honor and obey the Lord's covenant was marked by a meal in which the elders of Israel, led by Moses, saw God and ate before him:

> Then Moses and Aaron, Nadab, and Abihu, and seventy of the elders of Israel went up, and they saw the God of Israel.... And he did not lay his hand on the chief men of the people of Israel; they beheld God, and ate and drank.
>
> The Lord said to Moses, "Come up to me on the mountain, and wait there; and I will give you the tables of stone, with the law and the commandment, which I have written for their instruction." [Exodus 24:9–12]

God's place among the Israelites for all eternity is to be represented by bread on the altar: "You shall set the bread of the Presence on the table before me always" (Exodus 25:30). Israel's place at the table is represented by the division of the bread into twelve loaves arranged in two rows of six each: "Every sabbath day Aaron shall set it in order before the Lord continually on behalf of the people of Israel as a covenant for ever" (Leviticus 24:8).

The covenant is commemorated annually in the passover eaten in the first month of the new year by "all the congregation of Israel" exclusively (Exodus 12:47). God's portion is every first-born male animal: in essence, Israel (Exodus 13:11–16). Like the bread of the Presence, the passover meal celebrated not only the past deliverance of Israel, but also the future salvation that God had promised his people. The expectation of the prophet predicted in Deuteronomy (18:15, 18), who would come at Passover to deliver Israel from the bondage of Rome, just as Moses had delivered Israel from Egypt, was "one of the liveliest popular beliefs in pre-Christian Judaism" (Black 1961:158).

Salvation was frequently envisaged as a heavenly banquet that would confer everlasting life. The prophet Isaiah had described it:

> On this mountain the Lord of hosts will make for all peoples a feast of fat things, a feast of wine on the lees, of fat things full of marrow, of wine on the lees well refined. And he will

destroy on this mountain the covering that is cast over all peoples, the veil that is spread over all nations. He will swallow up death for ever, and the Lord God will wipe away tears from all faces, and the reproach of his people he will take away from all the earth. [Isaiah 25:6–8]

Idolaters were explicitly excluded, to go hungry and thirsty, to cry while God's faithful servants rejoiced (Isaiah 65:13–14). As noted above, the heavenly banquet was frequently represented as a marriage feast, celebrating the perfect marriage of Israel to the Lord, a most expressive image of the purity so passionately desired by Jews in both religious and socio-political matters.

Some Jews expected to eat fish at the heavenly wedding banquet (Goodenough 1956, 5:35–41). Leviathan (Job 41) was to be slain on that day and the flesh distributed to the surviving remnant (Isaiah 27:1; 2 Baruch 29:4; 4 Ezra 6:52; Ginzburg 1909–39, 5:43–46). The rabbis assured the faithful that, having scales and fins, Leviathan's flesh was kosher. To those who had fulfilled the law would be given the special prerogative of eating the head (Goodenough 1956, 5:37, 38). Another tradition anticipated a duel between Leviathan and Behemoth, after which the flesh of both terrible monsters would be distributed to the faithful Israelites at the heavenly feast, the ultimate reward of the most righteous (2 Baruch 29:4; 4 Ezra 6:51–52).

Fasting was part of this commensal system. Fasting was interpreted as witholding food, thus punishing the self as God punished the Israelites for their gravest transgressions. It was also interpreted as eating the self, as "offering one's own blood and fat on the altar of the temple," as the Rabbi Shesheth expresses it in the Talmud (Berakoth 17a; see also 32b). There was no greater sacrifice, no stronger appeal to the Lord to exercise his part in the agreement.

Jews offered themselves on occasions that called for the most critical intervention of the Lord: the death of kings (1 Samuel 31:13, 2 Samuel 1:12), war (1 Samuel 7:6, 14:24), famine (Joel 1:14; 2:12, 15). Thus the Talmud includes fasting among the forms of self-affliction required on Yom Kippur, the Day of Atonement, when Israelites should collectively confess their sins and pray for forgiveness (Leviticus 23:27–32).

Josephus tried to date the captures of Jerusalem in 63 B.C.E.

(by Pompey) and 37 B.C.E. (by Soius and Herod) to the Day of Atonement (Smallwood 1976:appendix D). Other fast days were deliberately intended to commemorate national rather than personal disasters for which the collective sins of the people were held responsible. The Ninth of Ab, a national day of mourning and fast day second only to Yom Kippur, commemorates no fewer than five of these: Nebuchadnezzar's destruction of Solomon's temple, dated to 587 B.C.E.; the fall of the second temple in 70 C.E.; the capture of Bethar, which signaled the defeat of the Bar Cochba revolt in 135 C.E.; and the plowing up of Jerusalem and of the temple by the Romans following the revolt in the same year.

The Priestly Code identified the table of the Lord with the altar of the Jerusalem temple. But other views also prevailed, as I have mentioned, and it seems that on critical occasions sacred meals might be created out of any repast. These impromptu transformations provide some of the clearest examples of the use of commensalism to identify the parties to an agreement and confirm their common obligation.

Gideon, who had reason to wonder about the Lord's commitment to the Israelites, doubted the reality of his angel emissary: "Pray sir, if the Lord is with us, why then has all this befallen us? And where are all his wonderful deeds which our fathers recounted to us?" (Judges 6:13). The angel agreed to wait while Gideon got him a "present," so Gideon prepared him a meal. When the angel consumed it by fire, vanishing in the process, Gideon "perceived that he was the angel of the Lord" and that he would indeed win against the Midianites with the Lord's help (Judges 6:11–24).

Jesus provided his own test meals to prove the reality of his resurrection to his doubting disciples by transforming breakfasts and suppers into sacrificial offerings (Luke 24:29–32; John 21:6–14). When he broke the bread and gave it to them, "their eyes were opened, and they recognized him; and he vanished out of their sight" (Luke 24:31). Recounting their experience later, they told "how he was known to them in the breaking of the bread" and he appeared again. This time to prove he was not a "spirit," he urged them to touch him and said: " 'Have you anything here to eat?' They gave him a piece of broiled fish, and he took it and ate before them." [Luke 24:35–43].

Fasting was particularly liable to personal interpretation. King David fasted to appeal to the Lord not to let his son die, but when the child died, he refused to fast as he should have (2 Samuel 12:16–23). Ezra would have fasted to achieve understanding, fasting being the accustomed means of receiving visions and other individual manifestations of the Lord's interest, if the angel had not instructed him to "go into a field of flowers where no house has been built, and eat only of the flowers of the field, and taste no meat and drink no wine, but eat only flowers, and pray to the Most High continually—then I will come and talk with you" (2 Esdras 9:24–25). Although Ezra had to speak first, he was granted visions of the last days of Zion.

The Jewish community of Persia agreed to fast with Esther for God's support in persuading King Ahasuerus not to exterminate them (Esther 4:16–17). When their appeal was granted, Esther, as queen of Persia, inaugurated a national holy day, Purim, to commemorate both the fasting and the feasting that followed (9:26–32).

Commensalism and Sectarianism

It is this persistent individualistic or personal strain, exemplified in the prophets, heroes, and heroines of scripture, often associated in some way with weakness, poverty, orphan, or outcast status, but intermittently translated into national policy, that helps to explain why, as Black says, "every meal in Judaism was in a sense a religious meal" (1961:115). God's covenant was binding not just on the nation but on all the individual Israelites who made up the nation. Individuals, interpreting God's word differently, were bound to embody it in different forms, and, as we have seen, food was one of the most important of these forms.

It was logical, therefore, that Jewish sectarians would choose to express and maintain their doctrinal differences through food. Although the details of their disputes with one another are sometimes obscure (Isenberg 1975:36; Lightstone 1975; see also Simon 1967), it is clear that they ate very different meals. The Sadducees seem to have been associated with the Jerusalem temple and its sacrificial observances, organized by the priests around the altar. But throughout Israelite history the prophets had railed at the priests for "despising the table of the Lord" with their improper offerings (Malachi 1:6–14).

One alternative was the fasting traditionally associated with prophets. John the Baptist's followers seem to have observed fasting as a distinctive practice, although he is otherwise characterized in early Christian writing as one "whose food is locusts and wild honey" (Mark 1:6; Matthew 3:4). The Essenes also removed the table of the Lord to its place of origin in the desert. They broke with the Hasmoneans, probably around 150 B.C.E., on the appointment as high priest of the Maccabean Jonathan, whom they considered illegitimate because he did not belong to the line of Zaddok, the traditional occupants of the hereditary office according to scripture (Hengel 1974, 1:251). In organizing their own priestly community, they reinterpreted the central act of sacrifice associated with the temple to establish a "new covenant." Although their meal seems to have had eschatological significance, like the meals of the temple priests and the Baptists (Black 1961:109), it was organized very differently. The altar of the community was their own dinner table. The sacrifice was their own food, consumed daily under circumstances designed to ensure perfect purity. According to Josephus, after bathing in cold water and putting on special clothing, "they assemble in a private apartment which none of the uninitiated is permitted to enter; pure now themselves, they repair to the refectory, as to some sacred shrine". The meal is conducted by a "priest" and surrounded by prayers. Afterwards, "laying aside their raiment, as holy vestments, they again betake themselves to their labours until the evening. On their return they sup in like manner. . . ." Participation was restricted to the elect. A candidate might be enrolled in the order after a probationary period of three years: "but, before he may touch the common food, he is made to swear tremendous oaths" (*The Jewish War* 2:129–32, 139–42; see also Vermès 1975:27; Dupont-Sommer 1961:86–90 *passim*). Those unfortunate enough to be turned out of the community faced dismal prospects:

> the ejected individual often comes to a most miserable end. For, being bound by their oaths and usages, he is not at

liberty to partake of other men's food, and so falls to eating grass and wastes away and dies of starvation. This has led them in compassion to receive many back in the last stage of exhaustion, deeming that torments which have brought them to the verge of death are a sufficient penalty for their misdoings. [*The Jewish War* 2:143–44]

The Pharisees broke with the Hasmoneans about fifty years later, in the reign of John Hyrcanus (134–104 B.C.E.), apparently because of disagreements about the law and the status of oral tradition (Hengel 1974, 1:305–6). What we know of their beliefs and practices is primarily what the rabbis of Yavneh and Usha, their successors, thought proper and important and therefore preserved. This turns out to be "almost entirely the internal record of the life of the party and its law, the party being no more than the two factions that dominated after 70, the laws being mainly rules of how and what people might eat with one another" (Neusner 1971, 3:319). Nevertheless, it accords with what we know from the polemical accounts of the Pharisees in early Christian documents (ibid.:304).

Although the dietary rules were enjoined on all Israelites, the Pharisees seem to have been primarily associated with their elaboration. Neusner (1971, 3:304) estimates that 67 percent of their legal pericopae deal with dietary laws. A similar emphasis is apparent in the Talmud, which incorporated their oral torah. The *Encyclopaedia Judaica* (6:40) stresses the fact that talmudic dietary law is "exceedingly complex." A great deal of the Talmud is devoted to the subject, including one entire tractate *(Ḥullin)*. One of the four sections of the *Shulḥan Arukh* deals exclusively with dietary laws (the *Yoreh Deʾah*). According to the Talmud, "As long as the temple stood, the altar atoned for Israel. But now a man's table atones for him" (Berakoth 55a, cited by Neusner 1977:671; Dresner 1966:40 echoes these sentiments exactly).

Neusner (1971, 1973c) interprets the Pharisees initially responsible for developing this law as Jews who arrogated to themselves and to all Jews the status of temple priests and who therefore kept the purity rules enjoined on temple priests. They took literally the commandment "You shall be to me a kingdom of priests and a holy nation" (Exodus 19:6). In other words, they were very similar to other sectarians. Where they seem to have differed most was in the inclusiveness of their community. Every Jew, every Jewish home, every Jewish table, possessed the sanctity of the priest, the temple, and the great altar, provided Levitical laws of cleanliness were observed. This seems to have been why they elevated teaching and learning to sacred acts: all the people should be holy, not just a chosen few.

In practice, the Pharisees still seem to have distinguished themselves not only from the temple priesthood and isolationists like the Essenes and the Baptists, but also from the *am ha-arez* who, because of their indisposition to learning were virtually gentiles. Even at their most inclusive, the dietary rules distinguished Jews from gentiles. This is clearly expressed in the dietary rules of Leviticus (11) and Deuteronomy (14:2–21), God's first commandment to the Israelites concerning their patrimony filled with strangers.

Douglas interprets these rules as "merely developing the metaphor of holiness on the same lines" as other negative rules and positive commandments in the Old Testament. She concludes from an analysis of the characteristics of holiness in the Old Testament that holiness is exemplified by completeness and conformance to the proper categories: "holiness requires that different classes of things shall not be confused" (1966a: 53):

> If the proposed interpretation of the forbidden animals is correct, the dietary laws would have been like signs which at every turn inspired meditation on the oneness, purity and completeness of God. By rules of avoidance, holiness was given a physical expression at every encounter with the animal kingdom and at every meal. Observance of the dietary rules would thus have been a meaningful part of the great liturgical act of recognition and worship which culminated in the sacrifice in the Temple. [Ibid.:57]

It is surely true that the dietary rules represent holiness, the separation unto God of the children of Israel. But Douglas neglects to observe that God is purifying unto himself a chosen people by means of his commandments. Social relations are an integral part of holiness:

> the Lord has declared this day concerning you that you are a people for his own possession, as he has promised you, and

that you are to keep all his commandments, that he will set you high above all nations that he has made, in praise and in fame and in honor, and that you shall be a people holy to the Lord your God, as he has spoken. [Deuteronomy 26:18–19]

One social group is distinguished from all others in the practice of the dietary rules; Jews are distinguished from non-Jews. The rules make a political as well as a religious statement. The distinction of Jews from gentiles is represented in the separation of clean animals from abominable things. The political and social significance of the dietary rules enjoined by Mosaic law is stated unequivocally in the passages that immediately precede two of the three major statements of the rules in Leviticus and Deuteronomy:

You shall therefore keep all my statutes and all my ordinances, and do them; that the land where I am bringing you to dwell may not vomit you out. And you shall not walk in the customs of the nation which I am casting out before you; for they did all these things, and therefore I abhorred them. But I have said to you, 'You shall inherit their land, and I will give it to you to possess, a land flowing with milk and honey.' I am the Lord your God, who have separated you from the peoples. You shall therefore make a distinction between the clean beast and the unclean, and between the unclean bird and the clean; you shall not make yourselves abominable by beast or by bird or by anything with which the ground teems, which I have set apart for you to hold unclean. You shall be holy to me; for I the Lord am holy, and have separated you from the peoples, that you should be mine. [Leviticus 20: 22–26]

You are the sons of the Lord your God . . . you are a people holy to the Lord your God and the Lord has chosen you to be a people for his own possession, out of all the peoples that are on the face of the earth.
You shall not eat any abominable thing. These are the animals you may eat . . . [Deuteronomy 14:1–4]

The second text is repeated twice in Deuteronomy, at 7:6 and again at 14:2–4. Whereas the earlier text instructs the Jews not to make marriages or other covenants with the foreigners, but to defeat them in war (Deuteronomy 7:1–5), the second text instructs them not to eat any abominable thing (Deuteronomy

14:3–21). In other words, to eat abominations is to marry foreigners and make treaties with them. Not to eat the beasts is not to marry them, not to make treaties with them, but to destroy them.

Commensalism and Apostasy

It seems fairly clear that these meals had as much to do with history as with eschatology. They were the means and end of distinguishing the chosen many or few from those who were not, in life as in perpetuity. The hair-splitting rules concerning food were a way of talking about the endless proliferation of groups that resulted from the search for true believers.

Yet even at the furthest reaches of purity, as exemplified in the Essenes' monastic table, shut away from the world, surrounded at mealtime by the most elaborate precautionary ritual, the traitor slipped through. The food and drink of the Teacher of Righteousness was transformed by the betrayal of table fellowship that defined the "Community of the New Covenant":

> All who ate my bread lifted the heel against me. . . . I ate the bread of groaning and my drink was in tears without end. . . . My bread was changed into quarreling and my drink into an enemy that entered my bones, causing the spirit to stagger and consuming strength. They changed the work of God by their transgression according to the mysteries of sin. [Dupont-Sommer 1961:216–18]

So Jesus suffered the company of Judas at the last supper (Matthew 26:23; Mark 14:20; Luke 22:21; John 13:18, 24–27). The traitor was there; he was required by scripture (Psalms 41:9), a necessary embodiment of that accursed mixture that had haunted the Israelites, breeding conflict, from the earliest days of their existence. The terrible irony of Judas was not his presence at the table; it was the fact that this Judas was an apostate to the Jews. The apocryphal and pseudepigraphic literature of the inter-Testamental period reflects the history of this struggle, expressed metaphorically in food. As God's word came to be concentrated in the law, so food law came to represent the whole law.

Food Symbolism in the Judaic Tradition

Pious Jews refused to eat gentile food as they refused to eat with gentiles, for both were taken as the sign and means of assimilation to the gentile way of life. Nevertheless the Book of Tobit, allegedly written during the Assyrian exile, but probably written under Hellenistic rule in Egypt or western Syria around 200 B.C.E. (Rost 1976:63), suggests that they were not always in the majority:

> Now when I was carried away captive to Nineveh, all my brethren and my relatives ate the food of the Gentiles; but I kept myself from eating it, because I remembered God with all my heart. [Tobit 1:10–12]

So does the nationalist Jesus ben Sirach, writing in Jerusalem around 190 B.C.E. (ibid.:68), who warns on the eve of the Maccabean revolt: "Receive a stranger into your home and he will upset you with commotion, and will estrange you from your family." (11:34). Hengel interprets this warning "an allusion to the frequent contacts of the Jewish Hellenists with non-Jewish friends, by which the confines of Jewish morality and religion which separated Israel from the non-Jewish world were shattered" (1974, 1:152).

Self-rule, which was the consequence of the Maccabean revolt, did not restore purity. The Hasmoneans were soon quarreling among themselves, using the traditional symbolism, over the nature of Judaism and the relationship of Jews to gentiles. The Talmud records a rabbinic legend about one of their civil wars, in which a pig is used to represent the idea that "nobody should teach his son Greek wisdom":

> When the kings of the Hasmonean house fought one another, Hyrcanus was outside and Aristobulus within [the walls of Jerusalem]. Each day they used to let down [money] in a basket, and haul up [animals] for the continual offerings. An old man there, who was learned in Greek wisdom, spoke with them [Hyrcanus's group] in Greek, saying, 'As long as they carry on the Temple-service, they will never surrender to you'. On the morrow they let down [money] in a basket and hauled up a pig. When it reached half way up the wall, it stuck its claws [into the wall] and the land of Israel was shaken over a distance of four hundred parasangs. At that time they declared, 'Cursed be a man who rears pigs and

97

cursed be a man who teaches his son Greek wisdom.' [Sotah 39b][4]

Some writers argued for mutual tolerance: the author of the story of Esther, for example. The Book of Esther was probably written in the early Hellenistic period some time after 300 B.C.E. (Rost 1976:199), possibly in Alexandria. The story concerns a Jewish orphan, the adopted daughter of a paternal relative exiled in Babylon with the rest of the Judean king's entourage. The first chapter sets the tone of Persian court life under King Ahasuerus by describing customary commensal behavior:

> Drinks were served in golden goblets, goblets of different kinds, and the royal wine was lavished according to the bounty of the king. And drinking was according to the law, no one was compelled; for the king had given orders to all the officials of his palace to do as every man desired. [Esther 1:7–8][5]

The queen refuses to come to the king's table when summoned. To teach her and all the wives in the kingdom to obey their husbands, the king calls all the virgins together to select a more tractable replacement. Esther is among them. She accepts her allowance of food, and when first summoned to the king's presence, takes nothing with her except what the king's eunuch advises (Esther 2:9, 15). The king chooses Esther to be his queen.

Esther keeps her "race and family" secret, at the request of Mordecai, her foster-father. Meanwhile, Haman, the king's chief officer, warns him against the Jews:

> There is a certain people scattered abroad and dispersed among the peoples in all the provinces of your kingdom; their laws are different from those of every other people, and they do not keep the king's laws, so that it is not for the king's profit to tolerate them. [Esther 3:8]

---

4. According to Josephus, who also recounts this story, Passover was the occasion on which the animal was required. In his version, Hyrcanus's men took the money but sent no animal, and so Aristobulus's men prayed to God "to exact satisfaction on their behalf from their countrymen," and God sent a windstorm "to destroy the crops of the entire country." [*The Jewish Antiquities*, 14:25–28]

5. See also 1:22 and 3:12, which emphasize the same politico-religious ideal, using the equivalent of food: language.

Food Symbolism in the Judaic Tradition

With the king's permission, Haman conspires to exterminate the Jews. Persuaded by Mordecai to identify herself with the Jews rather than the gentiles to whom she is now related by marriage, Esther invites Haman and the king to two banquets. During the second meal, she reveals that she is a Jew and pleads for the right of her people to defend themselves against those who wish to kill them and plunder their possessions. Because Esther has fasted to enlist God's aid, her plea is granted and the Jews are permitted to organize and defend themselves. Haman is killed, Esther receives his house and Mordecai his office, second only to that of the Persian king, where he works for the good of his people and promotes the welfare of all their descendants.

The Letter of Aristeas, written about 130 B.C.E., suggests that Jews and gentiles worship the same god, although by different names (Letter of Aristeas 15–16). After explaining some of the distinctive features of Judaism, the author concludes with a description of the sort of benign monarchy that would permit the peaceful coexistence of different kinds of people. The description is conveyed in a series of table conversations between King Ptolemy II Philadelphus and the seventy-two Jewish scholars he has called together to translate the Torah into Greek.

The meals exemplify the political ideal. The Jewish scholars have accepted the Egyptian king's invitation to dine, by which the king intended "to extend the right-hand of friendship." King Ptolemy not only lodged his Jewish guests in "the best quarters," but he commanded "the special officer appointed to look after the Jews . . . a very conscientious man . . . to make the necessary preparations for each one . . . in accordance with their own customs, in order that there may be no discomfort to disturb the enjoyment of their visit [and] in order that he might not withhold from them the highest possible honor" (179–83). He says to them: "Everything that you may have occasion to use . . . shall be prepared [for you] in a befitting manner and for me also with you" (181).

King Ptolemy's practice, according to the author, is still maintained, "for as many cities [as] have [special] customs in the matter of drinking, eating, and reclining have special officers appointed to look after their requirements" (182).

Josephus reports in *The Jewish Antiquities* two cases—apparently historically valid (Smallwood 1976:127–28)—in which the Romans in 49 and 43 B.C.E. exempted Jews in the province of Asia from military service so that they would not be compelled to desecrate the sabbath or eat forbidden food. Nevertheless, the very existence of the Letter of Aristeas, described as "a piece of Jewish propaganda" (Rost 1976:103), like much of Josephus's own writing, suggests that comprehension and tolerance were probably the exception rather than the rule.

Scholars are divided on the nature and extent of anti-Semiticism in the ancient world. According to Daniel, who cites much of the voluminous literature on the subject, "anti-Semiticism was more deeply ingrained and more widespread than many modern scholars allow" (1979:64 see also Baron 1952, I:188–95). The vast majority of comments in the Hellenistic-Roman literature are negative, evidence of "an impassable chasm between the Jews and their neighbours" (ibid.:46). He acknowledges Rome's tolerance of foreign religions, including Judaism, but argues that popular feeling remained anti-Jewish even if legal reprisals were rare. Despite the growing evidence of Hellenization or Romanization among Jews during the inter-Testamental period, even in Palestine, "Jews remained Jews, sufficiently different to attract attention, most of which was unpleasant" (ibid.: 48–49). Their differences, according to contemporary sources, included their insistence on their god as the only god, their law as the only law, and themselves as the only holy people; their social exclusiveness; their alleged hatred of humanity; their poverty; and their strange practices, including circumcision and abstention from pork (ibid.:49–64; Smallwood 1976:123–24).

Daniel's assessment of the situation as overwhelmingly negative must be considered extreme, since it does not explain the paradox he rightly recognizes as an important problem of the period: how a group of people, allegedly so disliked, could have been such successful proselytizers. Nevertheless, the existence of sharp conflict focused on stereotyped views of customary behavior is indisputable. Which side seized on the prohibition of pork as exemplary of Jewish wisdom is unclear. Daniel (1979:56, n. 64) points out that swine were often honored in the Greek world—for example, at Eleusis—and so the Greeks were understandably confused by the Jewish belief that the animal was unclean. Jews so abhorred the pig that it was referred to as *davar aher* ("another thing," that is, something unmentionable by name) in the Talmud, and in Aramaic as "that species" (*Encyclopaedia Judaica,* 13:506). Whatever the reasons, pork, together with food offered to idols, is a recurrent theme in the dispute.

Gentiles restricted themselves to satirizing the Jews in literature ; thus Juvenal mocks "a long-standing clemency [that] allows pigs to attain old age" (Daniels 1979:56 Smallwood 1973:123). Gentile practices, however, seem to have been more barbaric, particularly during and after the Maccabean revolt. This is the conclusion one draws from the Jewish literature that survives from the period, which abounds in stories of gentile rulers who tried to force their food on Jews (as God would have forced it on Ezekiel, warning him of just such an eventuality), and Jews who died rather than eat it. As the dietary laws became identified with the whole law, so the denial of the dietary laws became equivalent to apostasy.

The Book of Daniel, written about 170 B.C.E. to rally support for the Maccabean revolt (Rost 1976:199; Sandmel 1978:28), establishes the piety of its main character in the very first chapter by having Daniel and his three companions, in contrast to the majority of Jewish exiles at the Persian court, refuse their daily allowance of food and wine from the royal table. Subsisting on vegetables and water, they were "better in appearance and fatter in flesh than all the youths who ate the king's rich food" (Daniel 1:15). Belshazzar, however, dies as a result of the feast in which he uses the vessels of gold and silver his father Nebuchadnezzar had stolen from the sanctuary at Jerusalem (5:1–30).

As Hengel notes (1974, 1:269–70), court histories like those of Daniel and Tobit contrast dramatically with Josephus's history of the Tobiads at the Egyptian court, who became the leaders of the Hellenist party (*The Jewish Antiquities,* 12:160–224). Josephus gives equal attention to the riches of the royal table, but says nothing of the dietary rules that are so important to Daniel and Tobit. The Tobiad Josephus is a different kind of hero, "a noble and generous man who led the Jewish people from poverty and miserable circumstances to a brighter way of life" (*The Jewish Antiquities,* 12:224; see also 12:160). Hengel characterizes this as the chief theme of the Jewish Hellenists, con-

sistent with their program as summarized in the first book of the
Maccabees (1:11).

Later additions to Daniel, such as Bel and the Dragon—possibly written during the second half of the first century B.C.E. but
before 70 C.E. (Rost 1976:94)—elaborate on the same themes.
Daniel proves that Bel is merely an idol of clay and bronze by
showing that it cannot eat; the priests and their families have
consumed its food (Bel and the Dragon 1–22). He destroys another
idol, a snake, by feeding it cakes of pitch, fat, and hairs (23–27).
As a consequence, the Babylonians accuse King Astyages of having "become a Jew" (28) and force him to feed Daniel to the lions.
An angel of the Lord transports a prophet and his meal to the
lion pit. The prophet shouts: "Daniel, Daniel take the dinner
which God has sent you!" and Daniel replies: "Thou hast remembered me, O God, and has not forsaken those who love thee."
Daniel eats and is not eaten. His enemies are thrown into the pit
and devoured instantly (28–42).

Food is associated with sex in Judith as it was in Esther. The
Book of Judith was probably written during the Hasmonean period in the latter part of the second century B.C.E. (Metzger 1977:
76). The beautiful, pious, and chaste Jewish widow Judith brings
her own food and cooking vessels when she visits the Assyrian
commander-in-chief Holophernes in his camp, explaining that
she cannot eat his, "lest it be an offense" (Judith 12:2). But what
happens if your supply runs out, he asks, "for none of your people is here with us" (12:3). Judith's reply identifies her food with
her moral and political obligation: "As your soul lives, my lord,
your servant will not use up the things I have with me before the
Lord carries out by my hand what he has determined to do"
(12:4). When Holophernes extends his invitation again, this time
to seduce her, she fulfills that obligation. She chops his head off
and delivers it back to the Israelites, carrying it in her food bag
as if she were leaving the camp for her early morning prayers
(12:10–13:10).

The apocryphal Additions to the Book of Esther were written
by a Jew probably living in Jerusalem as part of a colony of
diaspora Jews from Egypt and are variously dated to 130, 114, 77,
or the end of the first century B.C.E. (Rost 1976:87). The Additions
show many interesting differences from the earlier version that
are more in keeping with the sentiments expressed in the Book

of Judith. Esther does not accept the bed and board of the gentile king so easily (2:9–15). In addition to keeping her identity secret, Mordecai instructs her to "fear God and keep his commandments just as she had done when she was with [the Jews]." So Esther makes no change in her way of life (2:20). The king's decision to exterminate the Jews is followed by a copy of his edict in which the Jews are more strongly characterized as "stand[ing] constantly in opposition to all men, perversely following a strange manner of life and laws, and . . . ill-disposed to our government, doing all the harm they can so that our kingdom may not attain stability" (13:5). Esther's decision to reveal her identity and plead for her people is followed by a prayer to God that concludes:

> save us by thy hand, and help me, who am alone and have no helper but thee, O Lord. Thou hast knowledge of all things; and thou knowest that I hate the splendor of the wicked and abhor the bed of the uncircumcised and of any alien. Thou knowest my necessity—that I abhor the sign of my proud position, which is upon my head on the days when I appear in public. I abhor it like a menstruous rag, and I do not wear it on the days when I am at leisure. And thy servant has not eaten at Haman's table, and I have not honored the king's feast or drunk the wine of the libations. Thy servant has had no joy since the day that I was brought here until now, except in thee, O Lord God of Abraham. O God, whose might is over all, hear the voice of the despairing, and save us from the hands of evildoers. And save me from my fear! [14:14–19]

The first book of the Maccabees, probably written between 103 and 63 B.C.E. (Rost 1976:79), describes the decree of Antiochus Epiphanes IV that "all should be one people and that each should give up his customs" or die (1 Maccabees 1:41). "Many even from Israel" did comply (1:43), those who subscribed to the argument of the "lawless men": "Let us go and make a covenant with the Gentiles round about us, for since we separated from them, many evils have come upon us" (1:11). But there were also many for whom eating unclean food meant apostasy. They "stood firm and were resolved in their hearts not to eat unclean food. They chose to die rather than to be defiled by food or to profane the holy covenant; and they did die. And very great wrath came upon Israel" (1:62–64).

The second book of the Maccabees, probably written around 100 B.C.E. (Rost 1976:82, 83), describes the same event, but includes the stories of the elder Eleazar, one of the leading teachers of the law, and Hannah and her seven sons, who died terrible deaths by torture for refusing to eat pork and thereby transgress ancestral law (2 Maccabees 6:7–7:42).

The author of 4 Maccabees, possibly written during Christ's lifetime, in the first half of the first century C.E., was a Jew, probably from Alexandria, thoroughly conversant in Greek language and philosophy, who used his Hellenistic education to defend the law (Rost 1976:110). He too concentrates on the efforts of Antiochus Epiphanes IV to force Jews "to eat unclean meats and thus abjure the Jewish religion" (4 Maccabees 4:26), but he devotes thirteen chapters of detailed description to the grisly martyrdoms of Eleazar and the mother and her seven sons (5–18).

In an eloquent farewell address, Eleazar identifies the dietary laws with the whole law to prove that the law is the epitome of reason (4 Maccabees 5:16–38). The author's praise of Eleazar's heroism is based on precisely the same equations:

> O priest, worthy of the priesthood, you neither defiled your sacred teeth nor profaned your stomach, which had room only for reverence and purity, by eating defiling foods. O man in harmony with the law and philosopher of divine life! [7:6–7]

The third book of Maccabees is actually an account of the efforts of the Egyptian king Ptolemy IV Philopater to force the Egyptian Jews to apostasize some fifty years prior to the Maccabean period. It was written in Greek by an Alexandrian Jew during the last third of the first century B.C.E. (Rost 1976:107). The author emphasizes that the Jews maintained unswerving loyalty and good will to the dynasty. Nevertheless, they encounter intolerance, expressed in the familiar identification of food with religion and politics:

> because they worshipped God and conducted themselves by his law, they kept their separateness with respect to foods. For this reason they appeared hateful to some; but since they

adorned their style of life with the good deeds of upright people, they were established in good repute among all men. Nevertheless those of other races paid no heed to their good service to their nation, which was common talk among all; instead they gossiped about the differences in worship and foods, alleging that these people were loyal neither to the king nor to his authorities, but were hostile and greatly opposed to his government. So they attached no ordinary reproach to them. [3 Maccabees 3:4–7]

In this case, however, the king is persuaded by an aged priest, Eleazar, to repent and become the patron of the Jews, who make the counter-argument that "those who for the belly's sake had transgressed the divine commandments would never be favorably disposed toward the king's government" (3 Maccabees 7:11). The king agrees and gives them license to destroy the ones who had transgressed the law of God. So they put to "a public and shameful death" more than three hundred of their countrymen who had become defiled, and "kept the day as a joyful festival since they had destroyed the profaners" (7:14–15). Although the exact historical circumstances of the book are unknown, it is clear that 3 Maccabees was written to console and instruct Egyptian Jews, who were threatened several times during the first century B.C.E. by Roman efforts to change their civic status (Metzger 1977:294).

Philo reports that Jewish women were offered "swine's flesh" and tortured if they refused to eat it during anti-Jewish riots in Alexandria ca. 38 C.E. (*Flaccus,* 95–6); see also Smallwood 1976:237–42). Alexandrian Jews met with the emperor Gaius in Rome in 40 C.E. to discuss their civil rights and religious liberty. In *The Embassy to Gaius,* Philo describes the meeting as a brutal farce, constantly interrupted by Gaius's commands to workmen constructing festival pavilions around them. After one of these interruptions, he turned to the Jews and asked them "this grave and momentous question, 'Why do you refuse to eat pork?'."[6] While his courtiers burst into peals of laughter, the Jews answered: "Different people have different customs and

---

6. Box (1939:92), who argues that Philo was strongly influenced by contemporary conventions of the mime in this account, believes that the question itself comes from a mime.

the use of some things is forbidden to us as others are to our opponents . . . just as many don't eat lamb, which is so easily obtainable." Whereupon Gaius also laughed and said: "Quite right too, for it's not nice." Finally, he returned mockingly to the subject of their visit: "We want to hear what claims you make about your citizenship" (*The Embassy to Gaius,* 361–63).

According to Josephus, the Romans tortured the Essenes during the first Jewish revolt (66–74 C.E.) for refusing to renounce the dietary rules:

> They were racked and twisted, burnt and broken, and made to pass through every instrument of torture in order to induce them to blaspheme their lawgiver and to eat some forbidden thing; yet they refused to yield to either demand, nor even once did they cringe to their persecutors or shed a tear. Smiling in their agonies, mildly deriding their tormentors, they cheerfully resigned their souls, confident that they would receive them back again. [*The Jewish War,* 2:152–53]

In 70 C.E., after the destruction of the temple and the fall of Jerusalem, the Romans sent a complete legion, supported by auxiliaries, to replace the lesser military units that had guarded the city. "Was it malicious humor or pure chance?" asks Smallwood (1976:333), that the chosen legion was X Fretensis, whose emblem was the boar.

X Fretensis remained garrisoned in Jerusalem in 135 C.E., after the defeat of the Bar Cochba revolt. Its emblem appeared on the coinage issued by the city under its new name of Aelia Capitolina, though Rome had previously been careful to avoid using even representations of the emperor on troop ensigns and coins circulated in Judea (Smallwood 1976:148, 165–67). The same motif was carved over the west gate, which stood near the camp (ibid.: 457). It signified to all: *Romanae potestati subiacere Iudaeos.*

5

THE LAST SUPPER

Christ, our paschal lamb has been
sacrificed. Let us, therefore, celebrate
the festival, not with the old leaven,
the leaven of malice and evil, but
with the unleavened bread of sincerity and truth.

1 Corinthians 5:7–8

In the last chapter, I argued that food was the embodiment of
God's word, his wisdom, for a people who would have no graven
images. The food God provided was his word. The food he prohibited was idolatry. The constant struggle over food that resulted in one creation after another was the constant struggle
over doctrine that resulted in the repeated redefinition of Israel
and the Israelite. God's word, as represented in scripture, was
not a dead formula. The word was realized in creative, life-
giving, death-dealing speech, which transformed wisdom into
practice, as food is transformed into flesh.

During the postexilic period, as God's word came to be increasingly concentrated in the law, so food law came to represent the whole law. At the time of Jesus Christ, food was the
word, and food law was the law, not only to Jews but to gentiles
who dealt with Jews, using their knowledge of the language to
their own political and religious advantage.

It is not surprising in this context that gluttony should epito-
mize all dangerously unlawful behavior, and indeed this is precisely the philosophy of Philo, Jesus' contemporary. Trying to
explain why the dietary rules should have been the first of the

Lord's commandments to the Israelites in the Promised Land, he develops a three-part theory of the soul, in which reason is centered in the head, high spirit in the chest, and desire, often called hunger and thirst, in the space around the navel and diaphragm, "almost at the outermost boundary." As an "animal insatiable and incontinent it should be pastured in the region where food-taking and copulation dwell" (*The Special Laws*, 4:93–94).

Moses knew this and legislated against passion. But rather than enumerate the passions individually, he chose "that one whose field of activity is the belly" to stand for all of them. He admonished and disciplined gluttony first,

> holding that the other forms will cease to run riot as before and will be restrained by having learnt that their senior and as it were the leader of their company is obedient to the laws of temperance. What then is the lesson which he takes as his first step? Two things stand out in importance, food and drink; to neither of these did he give full liberty but bridled them with ordinances most conducive to self-restraint and humanity and what is chief of all, piety. [*The Special Laws*, 4:96–97]

Moses censured some of his own contemporaries as "gluttons . . . who let their belly go uncontrolled and rebelled against holiness" (*The Special Laws*, 4:126–27). So Jews eventually came to interpret what they considered the gluttony of early Christians as apostasy. But it is not at all clear that apostasy is what early Christians intended by their behavior. It is more likely, judging from the New Testament accounts, that Jesus Christ and his followers felt themselves to be acting completely within the law, even while they advocated a radically different interpretation. Early Christians used the law to establish a new covenant, and because they believed they were faithful to the true meaning of Judaism, they stated their interpretation of the law in the language of the law, that is, food. Their interpretation of the new covenant in food is the subject of this chapter.

The Heavenly Wedding Banquet

The heavenly marriage feast as an image of salvation was as popular among Christians as it was among other Jews. Paul explains the relationship of Jesus and his church in terms of conjugal love (e.g., 2 Corinthians 11:2; see Isaiah 54:5–8; Hosea 2:16, 19–20). The author of the letter to the Ephesians also elaborates on this theme (5:22–33). Jesus is the bridegroom (Matthew 9:14–17, 25:1–13; Mark 2:18–20; Luke 5:33–39; John 2:1–11, 3:29), whereas the New Jerusalem, like Israel, but now including "men . . . from every tribe and tongue and people and nation" (Revelation 5:9), is "the Bride, the wife of the Lamb" (Revelation 22:9; see also 19:7–8, 21:1–3, 22:17).[1]

"Blessed are those who are invited to the marriage supper of the Lamb. . . . These are the true words of God" (Revelation 19:9). Babylon, "the great harlot," "mother of harlots and of earth's abominations . . . drunk with the blood of saints and the blood of the martyrs of Jesus" (Revelation 17:1, 6) will be destroyed. The wedding supper of the Lamb that is described in the final passages of Revelation will take place in "a new heaven and a new earth" as predicted in scripture (Revelation 21:1; see also Isaiah 65:17, 66:22). The book closes with the wedding invitation:

> The Spirit and the Bride say, "Come." And let him who hears say, "Come." And let him who is thirsty come, let him who desires take the water of life without price. . . .
> He who testifies to these things says, "Surely I am coming soon." Amen. Come, Lord Jesus! [Revelation 22:17, 20]

The invitation is extended to everyone, for the wedding supper of the Lamb will be very different from the heavenly wedding feast anticipated by the Pharisee (Luke 14:15), and more like that anticipated by the fearful servant, who recognizes that the Lord reaps where he has not sown (Matthew 25:24, 26; John 4:37). Not only is the bride radically transformed to represent gentiles as well as Jews, but so are the rest of those present at the feast.

All the social relationships traditionally expressed in the heavenly marriage feast will be reversed in order. The places of honor will become the places of dishonor: "everyone who exalts himself will be humbled, and he who humbles himself will be exalted" (Luke 14:11; see also Matthew 23:12; Luke 1:51–53, 16:14–15,

---

1. The Revelation of John was probably written by a Jewish-Christian prophet living in Asia Minor toward the end of the reign of Domitian, ca. 90–95 C.E., a time when Christians were severely persecuted for not observing the imperial cult (Kümmel 1975:466–72).

18:9–14; James 4:6; 1 Peter 5:5–6). Tax-gatherers and prostitutes are entering the Kingdom of God ahead of Pharisees and Sadducees (Matthew 21:31; Luke 7:29, 50, 18:9–14). The poor, the crippled, the lame, and the blind are the guests at the wedding supper, replacing friends, brothers, other kin, and rich neighbors (Luke 14:7–14).

The invited guests refuse to come to the marriage feasts described by Matthew (22:1–10), Luke (14:15–24), and Thomas (64). The angry master of the house sends his servant to bring in the poor, crippled, blind, and lame (Luke 14:21–22). And when there is still room at the table, he sends him out again beyond the city walls, which had been built in Nehemiah's time (ca. 444 B.C.E.) to protect the reconstructed temple and keep out unwanted Samaritans and other foreigners (Bowman 1965:54). He is to invite everyone he can find, "both good and bad" in Matthew's version (22:10). So the banquet table is packed with diners.

As the bridegroom at the wedding in Cana in Galilee distinguished himself by serving the poor wine first and the good wine last (John 2:1–11), so shall the first be last and the last first at the banquet in the Kingdom of Heaven (Matthew 19:30, 20:16, 21: 28–32; Mark 10:31; Luke 13:30). Isaiah's vision (65:13–14) has been completely reversed:

> I tell you, many will come from east and west and sit at table with Abraham, Isaac, and Jacob in the kingdom of heaven, while the sons of the kingdom will be thrown into the outer darkness; there men will weep and gnash their teeth. [Matthew 8:11–12, immediately following the curing of the Roman centurion's servant]

According to Jeremias (1963:178–80), the parable attributed to Jesus is a transformation of a popular story of the time, which recurs in Aramaic in the Palestinian Talmud. Originally, it was an Egyptian folktale about reversals of fortune in the afterlife, which Jeremias dates to before 331 B.C.E. (ibid.:183). Alexandrian Jews had brought it to Palestine, transforming it in the process to a story about a rich tax-gatherer and a poor scholar. When the tax-gatherer died, the whole city stopped work to attend his burial, yet when the scholar was buried, no one noticed. God was not unjust. The tax-gatherer, although a sinner by definition, had done one good deed in spite of himself, and because he had died and no subsequent evil could annul it, he had to be rewarded. Using his new and ill-gotten wealth, the tax-gatherer attempted to join the company of the city councillors by inviting them to eat with him. When they unanimously refused, he invited the city's beggars to eat the food so it would not be wasted, showing the councillors that he would have nothing more to do with them. As Jeremias says (ibid.:179–80), it must have come as quite a shock to his followers to find Jesus in the role of tax-gatherer and to hear him say: "For I tell you, none of those men who were invited shall taste my banquet" (Luke 14:24).

The story recurs in the parable of the rich man and poor Lazarus, also recounted by Luke (16:19–31). Here the conclusion of the story is transformed (Jeremias 1963:182–86). The scholar's colleague had a dream that revealed the ultimate fate of the two men: the poor scholar wandered in well-watered gardens of heavenly beauty; the rich publican stood on the bank of a stream and strained to drink but could not. The rich man in Luke's second parable "feasted sumptuously every day," arrayed in the finest clothes (Luke 16:19). Lazarus begged in a heap at his gate while the dogs licked his sores. He would gladly have eaten what fell from the rich man's table, if only it had been offered to him (Luke 16:20–21). Lazarus's miserable condition would have suggested a sinner to Jewish listeners (Jeremias 1963:18). But when both men die, Lazarus joins the righteous at the heavenly banquet, occupying the most honored place at the right hand of Abraham. The rich man thirsts in hell. Even kinship with Abraham will not save him or anyone who ignores Moses and the prophets (Luke 16:29–31).

The Last Supper

All the feeding miracles in early Christian writing may be summarized as narratives that, in purporting to describe Jesus' life (as perhaps they do), essentially explain it. The last supper, a description of what happened on the last night of his life, is an answer to the final crucial question: why he died, or rather, why he was killed like a common criminal, as scripture required.

Like the heavenly wedding banquet of the early Christians, their last supper is also a transformation of familiar material. But what material? Are Paul, the synoptics, and John, for example, even referring to the same kind of meal? How has it been transformed? What does the meal actually include? The evidence is ambiguous enough to accommodate a variety of interpretations.

Paul's account is the earliest (1 Corinthians 11:23–26). His Jesus speaks of the bread that is his body and the cup that is "the new covenant in [his] blood," which should be eaten and drunk in memory of him and of his sacrifice: "For as often as you eat this bread and drink the cup, you proclaim the Lord's death until he comes" (11:26).

Mark (14:12–26) uses slightly different words to refer to the bread and the cup, and he emphasizes the cup more than Paul does. Furthermore, he does not include the instruction to do this "in remembrance of me." Matthew (26:17–30) seems to have copied Mark fairly closely (or vice versa). Luke's version (22: 7–39), though similar to the accounts of Mark and Matthew, reverses the order of the bread and cup, and according to some manuscripts, adds a second cup at the end of the meal. Some manuscripts also include instructions of remembrance, which nevertheless differ from those of Paul.

John's last supper (John 13:1–30) does not mention the bread and cup at all. He concentrates on the episode, unique to his gospel, in which Jesus washes his disciples' feet and then feeds his betrayer, Judas. Jesus' statements identifying his body and blood with the bread and wine occur in John's version of the miraculous feeding of the five thousand (John 6:1–30), where they are more strongly and elaborately worded than in any other account, evoking a violent response.

All of the evangelists agree that the crucifixion occurred on a Friday, the day before the sabbath, and that the last supper took place the night before. According to the synoptics, that Friday was the fifteenth of Nisan, the first day of Passover, marked by the first full moon after the vernal equinox. The last supper was therefore a passover seder. According to John, the Passover coincided with the sabbath that year. Jesus' last supper and crucifixion took place on the fourteenth of Nisan, the "preparation day" before Passover (John 18:28; 19:14, 31). The crucifixion coincided with the slaughter of the paschal lambs. It is unlikely that the Passover fell on a Friday in any year between 27 and 34 C.E., the period in which Jesus' death probably occurred. The possible occurrence of the eve of Passover on a Friday in 30 or 33 C.E. is why these years are sometimes suggested for his death (Smallwood 1976:168, n. 82).

None of these authors describes a last supper that can be identified with any one traditional Jewish meal. In fact, their descriptions seem to combine elements of many kinds of meals, which is not surprising, given the common association of ceremonies in Judaism.

By declaring his blood to be the blood of the covenant: "This cup is the new covenant in my blood" (1 Corinthians 11:25; see also Matthew 26:28; Mark 14:24; Luke 22:20), Jesus related the last supper to the occasion on which the old covenant was made. The earlier covenant was also established through a sacrifice: having read the Israelites "all the words of the Lord and all the ordinances," Moses took the blood of the sacrifice and threw half of it against the altar and the other half on the people, and said: "Behold the blood of the covenant which the Lord has made with you in accordance with all these words" (Exodus 24:8). By virtue of the blood of the covenant, Moses and the other leaders of Israel ascended to God and ate and drank in his presence. Jesus anticipates the same experience when he says: "Truly, I say to you, I shall not drink again of the fruit of the vine until that day when I drink it new in the kingdom of God" (Mark 14:25; see also Matthew 26:29; Luke 22:18). According to Luke, he says this of the whole meal: "I have earnestly desired to eat this passover with you before I suffer; for I tell you I shall not eat it until it is fulfilled in the kingdom of God" (22:16).

Both Paul (2 Corinthians 3:6–18) and the author of the letter to the Hebrews (8:1–13, 9:18–28, 10:16–17) elaborate on the parallel between the Mosaic and Christian covenants, arguing that Jesus established the new covenant predicted by Jeremiah:

> Behold, the days are coming, says the Lord, when I will make a new covenant with the house of Israel and the house of Judah, not like the covenant which I made with their fathers

when I took them by the hand to bring them out of the land of Egypt, my covenant which they broke, though I was their husband, says the Lord. But this is the covenant which I will make with the house of Israel after those days, says the Lord: I will put my law within them, and I will write it upon their hearts; and I will be their God, and they shall be my people. And no longer shall each man teach his neighbor and each his brother, saying, 'Know the Lord,' for they shall all know me, from the least of them to the greatest, says the Lord; for I will forgive their iniquity, and I will remember their sin no more. [Jeremiah 31:31–34]

The author of Hebrews cites this passage in full, adding that "in speaking of a new covenant he treats the first as obsolete. And what is become obsolete and growing old is ready to vanish away" (Hebrews 8:13).

Many Jews believed that the messiah would repeat the miracle of the manna when he came (Nock 1964: 128). Paul gives Jesus the name for manna, "God's Wisdom" (1 Corinthians 1:24). Both Paul (1 Corinthians 10:1–4) and John (6:14, 30–59) directly connect the miracle of the manna with the feeding miracles and the last supper. In Revelation (2:17), Jesus promises the "hidden manna." According to a tradition recorded in 2 Maccabees (2:1–8), the prophet Jeremiah hid the manna that had been preserved before the ark containing the tablets of the law (Exodus 16:32–35), saying that it would not be revealed "until God gathers his people together again and shows his mercy" (2 Maccabees 2:7). The hidden manna would be the food at the heavenly banquet (Harvey 1970:795–96).

In commanding his disciples to commemorate the last supper (Luke 22:19; 1 Corinthians 11:23–26), Jesus echoes the Lord's exhortations to the Israelites concerning the manna and the passover, to perpetually commemorate their salvation from bondage in Egypt (Exodus 12:14). The letter to the Hebrews (2:14–15) compares the bondage in Egypt to the bondage imposed by the fear of death.

The author of Hebrews is also careful to demonstrate (e.g., at 10:1–18) that Jesus is a far more perfect offering for sin than the traditional blood of goats and bulls (Leviticus 4, 5, 6, 9, 16). Other passages in early Christian writing compare interpret Jesus' sacrifice as a first fruits offering (e.g., Romans 8:23; 1 Corinthians 15:20; Colossians 1:15–20; compare Exodus 23:19; Leviticus 23:10–11; Numbers 15:17–21; Deuteronomy 18:4); or as a creative act that gave rise to the "first fruits" represented by his disciples (James 1:18; Revelation 14:4) even as the Israelites once represented "the first fruits of [the Lord's] harvest" (Jeremiah 2:3; see Hosea 9:10; Romans 11:16).

The last supper is also a prefiguration of the heavenly wedding feast (Matthew 26:29; Mark 14:25; Luke 22:16, 18). Luke (22:27) depicts the disciples at the last supper quarreling jealously over who should rank highest among them, just like the participants at the wedding feasts he describes. As before, Jesus puts the highest in the place of the lowest, the servant in the place of the leader. In John (13:13–17), he washes his disciples' feet (see also Mark 10:35–45; Matthew 20:24). The disciples will be judges of Israel when next they eat together with Jesus at the fulfillment of this passover meal in the kingdom of heaven:

> You are those who have continued with me in my trials; and I assign to you, as my Father assigned to me, a kingdom, that you may eat and drink at my table in my kingdom, and sit on thrones judging the twelve tribes of Israel. [Luke 22:28–30; see also Matthew 19:28–30]

The last supper also resembles the *kiddush* that inaugurated every sabbath as well as the annual feast days. The kiddush, pronounced over a cup of wine, was a special prayer of thanks to God for choosing Israel and hallowing her above all nations, giving her as a heritage the particular holy day in question. The prayer was sometimes followed by the blessing and distribution of bread. Goodenough (1956, 6:134–41), among others, has argued that the last supper was a kiddush ceremony.

Last Supper and Passover

The Latin church, which has chosen to adopt the synoptic chronology, celebrates the last supper as a passover meal, using unleavened bread. The Greek church interprets John's chronology to mean that the last supper was not a passover meal, and therefore uses leavened bread (Buttrick 1962, 2:74). Scholars are similarly divided concerning the timing and the content of the meal and its relationship to the passover.

There is no way of resolving the argument without additional evidence; in fact, the argument is probably unresolvable. It is most likely that the last supper was deliberately ambiguous in traditional terms. Early Christian writers seem to have chosen this opportunity to reinterpret several of the major feasts by which Jews expressed their relationship to other human beings and to God, stressing one or another according to their different circumstances and intentions. Later interpretations must likewise reflect the particular historical circumstances in which they were developed. Nevertheless, I would like to contribute to the continuing debate by suggesting that although the last supper was intended to refer ambiguously to a variety of sacrifices, the passover sacrifice was the focus.

I would interpret each of these stories of Jesus as a kind of midrash on the life of Moses as depicted in the books of Exodus, Leviticus, Numbers, and Deuteronomy, beginning, in some instances, with Jesus' birth, and ending with his death. The midrash focuses on the covenant and the law that is its most important part, the sacrifice that ratifies the covenant, and the temple and priesthood established to carry out the sacrifice.

The last suppers described by early Christian writers are, in this context, "new passover haggadahs" exactly analogous to Rabbi Bronstein's more recent version. This, at least, seems to be the most explicitly stated view of the participants.

Paul, author of the earliest reports, calls Jesus "our paschal lamb" in his first letter to the Corinthians (1 Corinthians 5:7). Christians too are part of the meal:

> Your boasting is not good. Do you not know that a little leaven leavens the whole lump? Cleanse out the old leaven that you may be a new lump, as you really are unleavened. For Christ, our paschal lamb, has been sacrificed. Let us, therefore, celebrate the festival, not with the old leaven, the leaven of malice and evil, but with the unleavened bread of sincerity and truth. [5:6–8]

A later passage in the same letter states that Christ's body is the bread. Christians are "one loaf, one body" in eating the bread together (10:17, *NEB*). Paul must exhort the Corinthians to stop becoming so divided that "it is not the Lord's supper that you eat. For in eating, each one goes ahead with his own meal, and one is hungry and another is drunk" (11: 20–21). The last supper is the sacrifice that seals the "new covenant": "any one who eats and drinks without discerning the body eats and drinks judgment upon himself" (11:29).

The authors of the synoptic gospels also represent the last supper, the meal that will be fulfilled in heaven, as a passover seder (Matthew 26:2, 17–19; Mark 14:1, 12–16; Luke 22:1, 7–13, 15). Jesus says to his disciples: "You know that after two days the Passover is coming, and the Son of man will be delivered up to be crucified" (Matthew 26:1–2; see also Mark 14:1–2; Luke 22:1–2). His disciples ask him: "Where will you have us go and prepare for you to eat the passover?" (Mark 14:12; see also Matthew 26:17; Luke 22:7–8). In the versions of Matthew (26:30) and Mark (14:26), Jesus and his disciples conclude the meal with "a hymn," probably the Hallel (Psalms 113–118) associated with the passover service (Harvey 1970:201; May and Metzger 1979:1208).

John refers to an earlier occasion when Jesus went to Jerusalem for Passover (John 2:3): it was "when he was in Jerusalem at the Passover feast, [that] many believed in his name when they saw the signs which he did" (2:23). The feeding of the five thousand, where Jesus uses the eucharistic language characteristic of Paul and the synoptic gospels, is also made to take place when "the Passover, the feast of the Jews, was at hand" (6:4). The "Passover of the Jews" was again at hand when many people who had come up to Jerusalem from the country for the occasion stood in the temple looking out for Jesus and asking one another: "What do you think? That he will not come to the feast?" For "the chief priests and the Pharisees had given orders that if anyone knew where he was, he should let them know, so that they might arrest him" (11:55–57). It is six days before Passover when Jesus eats supper with Lazarus, whom he has raised from the dead. There Mary annoints his feet with costly perfume, which he associates with his imminent death and burial (12:1–8).

Nevertheless, it was "before the feast of the Passover [that] Jesus knew that his hour had come to depart out of this world to the Father" (John 13:1). Some biblical scholars have argued that

John altered the date to meet contemporary Jewish objections that none of these events—Jesus' arrest, trial, and crucifixion—could have taken place on a holy day. But this seems unlikely in view of his contentious attitude toward "the Jews" elsewhere in the gospel. Jeremias (1966:88), a proponent of the passover theory, emphasizes that John's last supper would still be surrounded by the atmosphere of the Passover even if it occurred the evening before the feast. But it could also be argued that John placed the crucifixion a day earlier so that it, rather than the preparations for the meal, would coincide with the slaughter of the passover lambs (John 19:31; see also 18:28, 19:14). Like Paul, he may have intended to make the identification of Jesus' death with the passover sacrifice even more explicit than it is in the synoptic gospels.

John has already had John the Baptist announce Jesus at the very beginning of the gospel as "the Lamb of God, who takes away the sin of the world" (John 1:29, 36; see also 1 Peter 1:19). Furthermore, only John emphasizes that Jesus' bones were not broken in the crucifixion. The Jews had requested Pilate to have the legs of the condemned men broken to hasten their deaths so that the bodies could be taken down before the sabbath, but Jesus is already dead. Nevertheless, one of the soldiers does stab his side with a lance, immediately releasing blood and water (John 19:31–39). John makes his point stronger by adding:

> He who saw it has borne witness—his testimony is true, and he knows that he tells the truth—that you also may believe. For these things took place that the scripture might be fulfilled, "Not a bone of him shall be broken." And again another scripture says, "They shall look on him whom they have pierced." [John 19:35–37]

The first quotation comes from the passover haggadah in Exodus (12:46; see also Numbers 9:12; Psalms 34.20), which prohibits breaking the bones of the paschal lamb. The prohibition is repeated in Jubilees (49:13–14), a passover haggadah dated to about 109–105 B.C.E., which may have been written by an Essene at Qumran (Rost 1976:132–33) and which John might therefore have known (Charlesworth 1972). The phrase from Jubilees—"of the children of Israelites no bone shall be crushed . . . they shall not break a bone thereof"—derives from the identification of the Israelites with the paschal lambs, which seems to be what John too wants to convey. The second citation, from Zechariah (12:10; see also Psalms 22:16–17; Revelation 1:7), reminds the reader and listener that Jesus was a first-born son. This Passover did not spare him.

Harvey (1970:361) finds it difficult to imagine that Jesus would deliberately hold his own celebration of the Passover one day earlier than everyone else. Black (1961), however, bases his explanation of the inconsistencies in the chronologies of the gospels precisely on the fact that the use of different calendars was one of the hallmarks of Jewish sectarianism.

The calendar had long been a source of disagreement between the Samaritans and the Jews, who both insisted that their calendar alone conformed to God's time. (Black 1961:57, 60, 65, 199–201; Bowman 1965:112). In contrast to the solar calendar of the Samaritans, the festal calendar associated with the Jerusalem temple was organized according to a lunisolar year. Feasts fell on different days in different years, sometimes on the sabbath, giving rise to conflicting religious obligations that Sadducees and Pharisees were not unanimous in resolving. The Essenes separated from the temple in part because they chose to adopt a solar calendar more like that of the Samaritans, in which sabbaths and feast days were fixed (Hengel 1974, 1:234–35; Bowman 1976:115–16). Thus their Passover did not fall on the same day as that of the Jerusalem temple, which they regarded as violating divine order.

Nock (1938:58–59) points out that the "Lord's day" mentioned in Acts (20:7), Paul's first letter to the Corinthians (16:2), and Revelation (1:10), the day on which Jesus was believed to have been resurrected and the day on which the Lord's supper was celebrated each week, was the day after the sabbath. Furthermore, early Christians observed Wednesday and Friday as fast days, in preference to the traditional Jewish fast days, Monday and Thursday. The choice of Friday as a fast day actually involved a breach of Jewish custom (see Judith 8:6), although this custom was not legally binding or universally observed. This selection of new holy days, "like Mohammed's choice of Friday, shows a consciousness of novelty which characterized the movement in spite of its fidelity to Jewish tradition" (ibid.:58).

If Jesus had chosen to characterize his mission as a new exodus by following the older Mosaic festival calendar, which was still in use outside Jerusalem, then his passover may actually have been an illegal meal (Black 1961:201). Black notes Mark's emphasis (14:12–16) on the secrecy of the meal, and suggests that it was the illegality of the last supper that gave Judas his final opportunity to betray Christ: "In carrying off the sop, he took evidence with him to the priests and the Pharisees that an illegal feast had been celebrated. In that case, Jesus was challenging Pharisaic law in its stronghold, Jerusalem itself" (ibid.).

It is significant that both the Passover and Jesus' sacrifice signified the beginning of a new time and a new people, a new nation. With the institution of the Passover, the Lord founded the nation of Israel and initiated a new time; the month of Passover was made the first month of the new year (Exodus 12:1–2). With the sacrifice of Jesus, "a new humanity" was born into a "new heaven and new earth" (Ephesians 2:15; Revelation 21:1; see also Romans 8:19–23; Ephesians 4:24; Colossians 3:9–11; James 1:18; 2 Peter 3:13). Jesus is "the bright star of dawn" (Revelation 22:16).

The Passover Seder

The other major problem in interpreting the relationship of Jesus' last supper to the passover has to do with the constituents of the two meals, the order (*seder*) in which they were eaten, and the narrative (*haggadah*) with which they were associated, a problem exacerbated by the fact that there is no detailed evidence for the organization of the passover in Jesus' time.[2] A passage in the passover haggadah of Jubilees describes "all Israel . . . eating the flesh of the paschal lamb and drinking the wine and . . . lauding and blessing, and giving thanks to the Lord God of their fathers" for deliverance from evil bondage in Egypt (49:6).

Philo refers to the passover throughout his writing, but particularly in *The Special Laws* (2:144–75). He describes it there as

2. Ashkenazic Jews continue to refer to the passover meal on the first night as a seder, after the order of the meal; Sephardic Jews call it a haggadah, after the story involved.

a domestic festival celebrated by the whole people and based on a meal that includes not only the sacrificial victim and the wine, but also "food . . . of a different and unfamiliar kind, namely, unleavened bread." The purpose of the meal is "not as in other festive gatherings, to indulge the belly with wine and viands, but to fulfill with prayers and hymns the custom handed down by their fathers" concerning the exodus from Egypt. *Quaestiones et Solutiones in Genesin et in Exodum*, a document attributed to Philo, but possibly written a little later, also describes the passover as a domestic meal that required small male animals to be cooked and eaten together with unleavened bread and bitter herbs in accordance with the prescriptions outlined in the book of Exodus (see Segal 1963:30–32).

The earliest complete account of the meal is found in the tractate on the passover included in the Mishnah, compiled 175–200 C.E. According to the Mishnah (Pesahim 5:3, 6:2), the sacrifice of the paschal lambs occurred "between the evenings in its appointed time" as required by scripture (Exodus 12:6; Numbers 9:3). Samaritans and Sadducees interpreted the phrase as meaning the hour between dusk and dark. Pharisees interpreted it as meaning late afternoon, from the time when the sun inclined toward its setting to its disappearance (Charles 1913, 2:80). The lambs were slaughtered in the temple court by the people themselves. Priests stood by with bowls to catch the blood which was dashed against the base of the altar. The Levites, assistants to the priests, intoned the Hallel, repeating it if necessary, until the sacrifices were finished (Mishnah Pesahim 5:5–7). No food was to be eaten until nightfall. Even the poor must not eat until they reclined, a practice normally restricted to the rich, and even the poor must not drink fewer than four cups of wine during the meal (Mishnah Pesahim 10:1). The order of the service was as follows:

1. The first cup of wine was mixed with water and spices. The head of the seder recited the kiddush, or benediction, over the day and then over the wine. The Mishnah (Pesahim 10:2) notes that the houses of Shammai and Hillel, Pharisaic schools that existed in Palestine circa 10 B.C.E.–70 C.E. (Neusner 1975:82), disagreed about whether the prayer over the day or the prayer over the wine came first.
2. Unleavened bread, lettuce, *haroseth*, and in the days of

the Jerusalem temple the whole roasted carcass of the passover lamb were brought to the table. The Mishnah notes disagreement among the rabbis about whether the haroseth, finely ground fruit, nuts, and spices mixed with wine or vinegar, was a "commandment," that is, a religious obligation (Pesahim 10:3). Several varieties of grains might be used to make the unleavened bread (2:5). Several different varieties of vegetables, herbs, or greens might be used to fulfill the obligation to eat bitter herbs, including lettuce, chicory, pepperwort, snakeroot, and dandelion or horseradish (2.6). Participants should follow the customs of the community in which they live concerning whether they may work until midday on the day before Passover (4.1) or whether they may eat flesh roast on the night of Passover (4:4).

3. While the food was on the table, a second cup of wine was mixed, and the son asked his father (or his father instructed him how to ask) the following questions:

> Why is this night different from other nights? For on other nights we eat seasoned food once, but this night twice; on other nights we eat leavened or unleavened bread, but this night all is unleavened; [some texts add: on other nights we eat all other manner of vegetables, but this night bitter herbs]; on this night we eat flesh roasted, stewed, or cooked, but this night all is roast [some texts add: on other nights we dip but once, but this night twice]. (Mishnah Pesahim 10:4)

The Talmud (Pesahim 115b, 116b) indicates that these questions were to serve as models. They could be and were replaced or augmented by others.

4. The father instructed the son according to his understanding by reciting the passover haggadah. The core of the haggadah was a midrashic commentary on Deuteronomy 26:5–10, preceded by an introductory statement that "begins with the disgrace and ends with the glory" (Mishnah Pesahim 10:4). Deuteronomy 26:5–10 was very familiar because it was part of a confessional that pilgrims recited every year when they brought their first fruits to the temple at Shavuot, the Feast of Weeks (Glatzer 1979:30). The midrash would have varied according to the midrashist and his company. The Talmud (Pesahim 116a) indicates that there were different tradi-

tions concerning the introduction. It cites two, one beginning with the verse "We were Pharaoh's slaves," the other with "In the beginning our fathers were idolators."

5. The Hallel was recited to the end of Psalm 113 (house of Shammai) or to the end of Psalm 114 (house of Hillel). Rabbis differed over whether the psalms should be followed by a benediction, and if so, what benediction (Mishnah Pesahim 10:6).

6. The Mishnah says nothing of grace before meals, a prayer over the bread, but it was probably included (Jeremias 1966:86).

7. The meal was eaten. This phase in the sequence, which the Mishnah does not describe, was later called the *shulḥan arukh* or "prepared table" (*Encyclopaedia Judaica,* 13:168), whence the title of Joseph Caro's great synthesis of Jewish law.

8. The third cup of wine was mixed and the grace after meals was recited (Mishnah Pesahim 10:7).

9. A fourth cup of wine was mixed for the completion of the Hallel, Psalms 114–118 (house of Shammai) or Psalms 115–118 (house of Hillel). Participants could drink more wine between the second and third cups (i.e., during the meal), but they could drink no more wine between the third and fourth cups (Mishnah Pesahim 10:7), lest insobriety interfere with the completion of the Hallel (Blackman 1951–56, 2:221).

10. The participants could not depart for revelry *(afikoman)* after the meal (Mishnah Pesahim 10:8). The after-dinner revelry that commonly followed banquets was prohibited so that attention would not be diverted from the passover (Danby 1933:151, n. 9). The Talmud (Pesahim 119b–120a), which translated the word as "the practice of going from one company to another," "dinner music," or "dessert," interpreted the phrase to mean that the participants should not finish the meal with a sweetmeat or dessert to ensure that the taste of the passover offering remained in the mouth (Blackman 1951–56, 2:221). Since there was no passover sacrifice after the destruction of the temple, the Talmud (Pesahim 109a, b) reinterpreted the afikoman as a piece of the unleavened bread that was hidden at the beginning of the meal for the children to find at the end. Everyone then ate some. The afikoman was thus a way of

keeping the children awake and aware during the long ceremony, and also served as a symbolic reminder of the paschal lamb that had been eaten at the end so its taste would remain in the mouth (Pesahim 109a, 119b–120a). Glatzer cites a formula customarily pronounced before eating the afikoman in Sephardic and Oriental rites: "In memory of the Passover sacrifice, eaten after one is sated" (1979:57).

The passover meal was a symbolic re-enactment, rendered in food, of the miraculous deliverance of the Jews from bondage in Egypt. Each kind of food that was eaten stood for some aspect of the way in which God had saved his chosen people before and would save them again in the future. The host was bound to explain the significance of the meal to the next generation every time it was eaten, and special efforts were made to ensure that they got the message.

The Mishnah cites in this context Rabban Gamaliel's requirement, based on Exodus (12:8), that three foods must be explained or the father has not fulfilled his obligation. The three foods are the passover, the unleavened bread, and the bitter herbs:

> 'Passover'—because God passed over the houses of our fathers in Egypt [Exodus 12:27]; 'unleavened bread'—because our fathers were redeemed from Egypt [Exodus 12:39]; 'bitter herbs'—because the Egyptians embittered the lives of our fathers in Egypt [Exodus 1:4]. In every generation a man must so regard himself as if he came forth himself out of Egypt, for it is written, *"And thou shalt tell thy son in that day saying, It is because of that which the Lord did for me when I came forth out of Egypt"* [Exodus 13:8. [This whole sentence is omitted by older sources (Danby 1933:151, n. 1).] Therefore we are bound to give thanks, to praise, to glorify, to honour, to exalt, to extol, and to bless him who wrought all these wonders for our fathers and for us. He brought us out from bondage to freedom, from sorrow to gladness, and from mourning to a Festival-day, and from darkness to great light, and from servitude to redemption; so let us say before him the *Hallelujah*. [Mishnah Pesahim 10:5]

The rabbis interpreted every other element in the meal in the same way. Two cups of wine, associated with the kiddush and the grace after meals, were customary on sabbath and holiday meals. The additional cups, associated with the passover haggadah and the completion of the Hallel, were added to mark the joy of the occasion (*Encyclopaedia Judaica,* 3:292). The "four cups" *(arba kosot)* stood for the four terms of redemption in Exodus 6:4 (Exodus Rabbah 6:4). They are also explained in the Palestinian Talmud as corresponding to the four cups of Pharaoh mentioned in Genesis (40) or the four ancient kingdoms that oppressed Israel and for which God requited Israel with four cups of consolation (TJ Pesahim 10:1, 37b–c). The Talmud (Pesahim 118a) notes that some rabbis later required a fifth cup to stand for the fifth term of redemption mentioned in the same passage of Exodus. The fifth cup was sometimes called "Elijah's cup," Elijah being the traditional forerunner of the messiah of future salvation. The haroseth represented the mortar mixed by the Jews as slaves (Blackman 1951–56, 2:217; Danby 1933:150, n. 7). According to scripture (Exodus 12:11), the whole meal was to be eaten "in haste," the participants dressed to travel, "your loins girded, your sandals on your feet, and your staff in your hand," but the Mishnah (Pesahim 9:5) notes that "the Passover of the generations" differs in lasting seven days.

Several meanings seem to have been attributed to the bread. In Exodus (12:33–34, 39), the bread commemorates the hasty departure of the Jews from Egypt, so hasty that they had not time to prepare ordinary bread. For the same reason, Deuteronomy (16:3) interprets it as "the bread of affliction," signifying the suffering of the Jews in Egypt. Philo cites the first interpretation, but also considers other possibilities, including one that is startlingly familiar in form. Pointing out that in springtime, when the feast is held, the crops are not yet ripe for harvest, he suggests that the "imperfection of this fruit which belonged to the future" is paralleled by the unleavened food, which is also imperfect but promises future abundance (*The Special Laws,* 2: 158). Noting "another suggestion made by the interpreters of the holy scriptures ... that food, when unleavened, is a gift of nature, when leavened is a work of art," he argues that the springtime feast is therefore a reminder of the creation of the world and its earliest inhabitants, who used nature's gifts in their pure state before pleasure, mediated through art, had got the upper hand (ibid.:159–60). He finds this interpretation confirmed by the fact that the bread of the Presence is also unleavened:

> These statements are especially guaranteed by the exposure of the twelve loaves corresponding in number to the tribes, on the holy table. They are all unleavened, the clearest possible example of a food free from admixture, in the preparation of which art for the sake of pleasure has no place, but only nature, providing nothing save what is indispensable for its use. [*The Special Laws,* 2:161]

Still another interpretation of the unleavened bread is included in Paul's characterization of Jesus as the paschal lamb, cited at the beginning of this chapter. Leaven is equated with "malice and evil"; unleavened bread means "sincerity and truth" (1 Corinthians 5:7–8).

Harvey (1970:199) argues that the unleavened bread did not have a specific meaning like the lamb or the bitter herbs because it originally belonged to the Feast of Unleavened Bread, not the Passover. This is why Jesus could freely pronounce the bread his "body." But it seems clear from the Mishnah and other sources that there were opportunities for diverse interpretations at virtually every point in the service. Different groups of Jews probably differentiated themselves in the way they organized the meal to fit their particular ideological and practical requirements, exactly as they do today.

Bowman (1965:262–66) attempts to fill out Mark's version of the last supper by accounting for the full complement of dishes and recitations probably customary in the time of Jesus. Jeremias (1966) tries to do the same for all four gospels. Opponents of the passover theory, besides noting the inconsistencies in the chronologies of early Christian writers, argue that the important distinction between "a general reference to an event and a narrative account of that event" should not be masked with hypothetical reconstructions (Robbins 1976:25, n. 13).

In fact, the most critical ingredients of the passover service are conspicuously absent from the last supper. No account, except perhaps Luke's, mentions more than one cup of wine. Only Mark (14:26) and Matthew (26:30) conclude the meal with a "hymn," which may be the Hallel. There are no references to bitter herbs or haroseth. The very narrative concerning the

Passover is missing, and the most important part of the meal, the paschal lamb, is not even mentioned (Bultman 1972:265, n. 5). On the other hand, perhaps early Christians were dealing with some more comprehensive set of comparisons in attempting to relate the original redemption of the Jews from Egypt to their present circumstances. To evaluate this possibility, it is necessary to examine more closely the issue of style in midrash.

Style in Midrash

If the story of Jesus in its various forms can be viewed as a midrash on the story of Moses, then our approach to some of the problems posed by the last supper might focus on the range of possibilities that midrash provided for interpretation. The purpose of midrash, to reveal the true word of God by explaining scripture, was usually achieved by analyzing one passage of scripture in relation to others. Although the passages were usually selected according to a theme, they were not literal parallels. Bloch emphasizes that midrash goes beyond simple literal explanation, later distinguished as *peshat*. It "tries to penetrate into the spirit of scripture, to scrutinize the text more profoundly and to draw from it interpretations that are not always obvious" (1957:1264–65). This is one reason midrash has become synonymous among scholars with the creation of fables, a misconception that Bloch's article is intended to dispel.

Bloch cites the Talmud (Yebamot 24a) to prove that the rabbis clearly distinguished midrash from peshat (ibid.:1265). We know less of the relationship between the two forms of explanation during the inter-Testamental period, however. The evidence discussed above in this chapter and in chapter 3 suggests that styles of explanation during the inter-Testamental period varied widely, from the more literal, as exemplified in the transformations in the story of Abraham (Vermès 1961:67–126), to the more "interpretive," as exemplified in the transformations in the story of Balaam (ibid.:127–77). Styles of interpretation were probably selected according to the audience in view. Clearly, however, given the varieties of Jewish "tradition" that flourished under Hellenistic and Roman influence during this critical period, it cannot be assumed that interpretations were literal or "traditional" according to whether their author or his audience was Jewish or gentile. Such conspicuously hybrid creatures as the early Christian writers and their readers and listeners cannot be consigned to simplistic categories of gentile Christians ignorant of, or uninterested in, Jewish custom, or vice versa. We must assume communication that involved not just bilingualism, but "biculturalism," although this word is hardly adequate to describe what seems to have been a very heterogeneous cultural and social environment.

Daube (1971) has shown that Paul made recondite allusions to Jewish law by analogy and without explanation when writing to the Corinthians on the very technical subject of the marital status of converts to Christianity, and the Corinthian Christians were a particularly diverse group. Derrett (1973:101) interprets Daube's discovery as meaning that "Paul made no conscious concession to the intellectual foreignness of the Gentile proselyte element amongst his correspondents." But intellectual foreignness may not have been an important consideration. Perhaps Paul could assume that gentiles in the church understood him well enough or would understand him through instruction. Early Christian documents sometimes include explanations of Jewish custom (e.g., Mark 7:3–4; John 2:6, 4:9), but this does not imply that details left unexplained in the texts that survive from the period were not understood.

Derrett (1970, 1971, 1973, 1977, 1979) has written extensively on the complex points of Jewish law and custom that early Christian writers appear to take for granted. Paul's reference to Jesus as "our paschal lamb" should be included here; as Jeremias rightly notes (1966:223, n. 1), it "presupposed as self-evident the familiarity of the Corinthian community with this comparison, a comparison widespread in early Christian literature" (John 1:29, 36; 19:36; 1 Peter 1:19; Revelations 5:6, 9, 12; 12:11).

Recent analyses of Mark emphasize his creativity and originality (Kee 1977; Kelber 1976a). John (6:1–71) deliberately stages a confrontation between the literalists and "those who are accustomed to turn literal facts into allegory," as Philo once put it (*The Special Laws*, 2:147). He does so precisely in speaking of Jesus' last supper, suggesting not only that he was well aware of the alternatives, but that he advocated a more interpretive approach to the meal, as compared, for example, to the very conservative approach of the Jubilees (49) haggadah. Paul does the same in his first letter to the Corinthians (1 Corinthians 11:17–34).

In fact both radical and conservative explanations apply to the last supper. Only as long as the meal is taken in isolation it is fair to say that "there is evident desire [in Mark] to link up the last supper with the Passover, even though the details of the Passover are imperfectly grasped" (Kee 1977:31), that "the Evangelists have little interest in such a thoroughly Jewish activity," or that Mark introduces the Passover only as "a general framework for emphasizing the importance of the death of Jesus" (Robbins 1976:26, 25, 29). Once the crucifixion and resurrection are included, this cannot be said at all. The sequence of events in the last supper, the crucifixion, and the resurrection must be interpreted as a radical transformation of the passover seder precisely because there is such a close point-by-point correspondence between the two.

The inclusion of the crucifixion and the resurrection in the meal is again the logic of the participants. It is they who emphasize that Jesus' sacrifice is the whole point of the meal. His death and resurrection *is* the meal. His words concerning the bread and wine make no sense except in the context of these transformations in his flesh and blood, as he himself is constantly made to emphasize before, during, and after the last supper. This is particularly true of the accounts of Paul and Mark, which subordinate even the resurrection to the crucifixion. Paul is very explicit in this regard: "For as long as you eat this bread and drink the cup, you proclaim the Lord's death until he comes" (1 Corinthians 11:26). But all the gospels are filled with enough allusions to Jesus' death that they have been described as passion narratives with extended introductions (see Donahue 1976:1).

Although uncertainties remain concerning the celebration of the Passover in the first century C.E., I would like to suggest an interpretation relating the passover to the last suppers described by early Christian writers in which the last supper is simply the preliminary, including the benediction over the wine (the kiddush) and the benediction over the bread, the grace before meals. The crucifixion is the main part of the meal, the *shulḥan arukh* or "prepared table." The cross is the table of the Lord where the bitter herbs and the paschal lamb are consumed.

The first cup of wine accompanies the kiddush. The second

cup is offered in the garden of Gethsemane, the third immediately before the crucifixion, and the fourth, the one that the host finally takes, is offered at the end. The resurrection, a tradition that became very important to the church, but nevertheless seems almost tacked on the earliest accounts, is the afikoman. It is another transformation of the hidden manna, which is probably also the basis for the passover tradition of the mazzah (or unleavened bread) that is hidden by the host at the beginning of the meal and found by the children at the end. The passion narrative is the passover haggadah. Jesus himself intones the Hallel.

The eucharist, commemorating the last supper in which Jesus prefigured his crucifixion and resurrection, is a symbolic representation of salvation in food patterned exactly after the passover. The difference is that in this case, as in Jesus' interpretation of the heavenly marriage feast and other traditional statements about politico-religious and social relations, the significance of the meal—the food, the host, the guests, the circumstances—is absolutely reversed. Temple and sacrifice, family, priesthood, and nation are radically redefined. This point is best demonstrated by examining each of the significant features of the meal in turn.

Time

Scripture is emphatic that the passover must be held at its appointed time (Exodus 12:6, 18, 23:15). The passover haggadah in Jubilees warns that "there may be no passing over from day to day, and month to month, but on the day of its festival let it be observed" (Jubilees 49:14; see also 49:1, 7–10, 12, 15). The Passover occurred at midnight:

> At midnight the Lord smote all the first-born in the land of Egypt, from the first-born of Pharaoh who sat on his throne to the first-born of the captive who was in the dungeon, and all the first-born of the cattle. And Pharaoh rose up in the night, he, and all his servants, and all the Egyptians; and there was a great cry in Egypt, for there was not a house where one was not dead. [Exodus 12:29–30]

The passover meal was consequently celebrated after night-fall.

Early Christian writers are equally emphatic that Jesus' death occurred at "an appointed time" (Matthew 26:1–2, 18, 45; Mark, 14:1; Luke 22:53; John 12:23; 13:1, 16:31–32). But the day of the Lord is unpredictable. Jesus is constantly exhorting his followers to be ready, to stay awake and aware, for he will come like a thief in the night at an unexpected hour (Matthew 24:43–44; Mark 13:35; Luke 12:39–40; 1 Thessalonians 5:2; 2 Peter 3:10; Revelation 3:3, 16:15). They must be prepared to leave in haste, just as the Israelites had to leave in haste from Egypt (Exodus 12:11; Mark 13:14–20, 33–37; Matthew 24:15–22, 42–44; Luke 21:34–36). The last supper may actually have been held at an illegal hour by temple standards. When the passover finally comes, it comes not at midnight but at midday. But this midday, a darkness suddenly covers the land, and it is Jesus who echoes the cry of the Egyptians:

> And when the sixth hour had come, there was darkness over the whole land until the ninth hour. And at the ninth hour Jesus cried with a loud voice, "E′lo-i, E′lo-i, la′ma sabach-tha′ni?" which means, "My God, my God, why hast thou forsaken me?" [Mark 15:33; see also Matthew 27:45–50; Luke 23:44–46; John 19:14, 28–30]

The time of the crucifixion undoubtedly had many different meanings for early Christians. Darkness in scripture was symbolic of ignorance and evil (e.g., Job 12:24–5, 24:13–17, 34:22; Micah 3:6; John 9:4–5; Romans 13:12), as Jesus himself suggests when he is arrested in Luke (22:53): "When I was with you day after day in the temple, you did not lay hands on me. But this is your hour, and the power of darkness."

A dark cloudy day also implied a day of judgment (Job 15:23; Ezekiel 30:3, 34:12; Joel 2:2, 31; Acts 2:20), including, ironically, Jesus' own. Paul, in his first letter to the Thessalonians, develops this theme in a midrash on Jesus' parable of the householder and the thief:

> For you yourselves know well that the day of the Lord will come like a thief in the night. When people say, "There is peace and security," then sudden destruction will come

upon them as travail comes upon a woman with child, and there will be no escape". But you are not in darkness, brethren, for that day to surprise you like a thief. For you are all sons of light and sons of the day.[1 Thessalonians 5:2–5]

Paul suggests that the darkness may also have signified a return to the dark primordial chaos out of which a new creation would emerge (Genesis 1:2), as, in Jewish time reckoning, new days were born out of night. This new day would banish night forever, as scripture predicted (Zechariah 14:7; Revelation 21:23–25, 22:5).

By replicating and yet inverting the critical hour, early Christian writers identified the crucifixion with the passover at the same time they distinguished it as unique. Evil and degradation would give way to glory in this history too, but the nation born of Jesus' sacrifice would be absolutely different from the nation born out of Egypt.

Place

The passover must be sacrificed at the temple in Jerusalem: "You may not offer the passover sacrifice within any of your towns which the Lord your God gives you; but at the place which the Lord your God will choose, to make his name dwell in it, there you shall offer the passover sacrifice" (Deuteronomy 16: 5–6; see also 16:2, 11). Again, the Jubilees haggadah is especially emphatic on this point (Jubilees 49:16–22).

Jesus' sacrifice occurs outside the temple at a place that is absolutely taboo according to temple law. Although the temple must not be contaminated by anything having to do with death (Leviticus 21:1–3), Jesus is sacrificed at "Golgotha (which means the place of a skull)" (Mark 15:23; see also Matthew 27:33, John 19:17), or as Luke puts it, "the place which is called The Skull" (Luke 23:33).

When he dies, the temple curtain that hung before the Holy of Holies, the inner sanctuary representing God's presence among the Israelites, was "torn in two, from top to bottom" (Matthew 27:51; Mark 15:28; Luke 23:45; see also Exodus 26:31–35; 2 Kings 19:14–15; 2 Chronicles 6:1–2, 18–21; Hebrews 9.3, 8; 10:19–20). John (19:23–24) expresses the same idea in contrasting terms. It is Jesus' robe, his cosmos, that is "without seam, woven from top to bottom." Because they cannot tear it, the soldiers cast lots for it, fulfilling scripture into the bargain (Psalms 22:18).

Golgotha is the supreme repudiation of the Jerusalem temple. But the theme recurs throughout early Christian writing, notably in the cleansing of the temple recounted in all four gospels. The synoptics place the event within the passion narrative where it provokes the hostility that leads to Jesus' arrest and crucifixion (Matthew 21:12–13; Mark 11:15–19; Luke 19:45–48). Mark (14:58) and Matthew (27:61) cite the false witnesses at his trial, who accuse Jesus of saying: "I will destroy this temple that is made with hands, and in three days I will build another, not made with hands."

John's version coincides with Passover (John 2:13–22). Jesus himself speaks the words attributed to false witnesses in Mark and Matthew, and John takes care to state Jesus' meaning explicitly, opposing the literalists and the allegorists in yet another context:

> The Jews then said, "It has taken forty-six years to build this temple, and will you raise it up in three days?" But he spoke of the temple of his body. When therefore he was raised from the dead, his disciples remembered that he had said this; and they believed the scripture and the word which Jesus had spoken. [John 2:20–22]

The orientation of the Christian mission is outward, in contrast to the inward orientation of the first Passover. Scripture exhorts that "none of you shall go out of the door of his house until the morning. For the Lord will pass through to slay the Egyptians; and when he sees the blood on the lintel and on the two doorposts, the Lord will pass over the door, and will not allow the destroyer to enter your houses to slay you" (Exodus 12:22–23, 46). This orientation may explain the Mishnaic prohibition on "going from one company to another" that the rabbis attributed to the distraction of revelry.

But Jesus and his disciples leave the last supper in every version. They go out into the garden of Gethsemane, where, as if in fulfillment of the threat implied in the Exodus narrative, Jesus is not passed over. He is seized by his enemies, by his God, taken to Golgotha, and crucified.

All four gospels emphasize that Jesus is buried by a pious

Christian, Joseph, in his or a "known tomb" (Matthew 27:57–61; Mark 15:42–47; Luke 23:49–54; John 19:38–42), although it is more likely that Jesus was buried by those who had crucified him and that "those who knew the site did not care and those who cared did not know the site" (Crossan 1976:152). But he vanishes from that place to reappear "where two or three are gathered in my name" (Matthew 18:20), in every person according to his promise. So Mark's Jesus appears to his disciples for the last time while they are eating and instructs them to "go into all the world and preach the gospel to the whole creation." And they go forth and preach everywhere, while the Lord goes with them and confirms their messages with his signs (Mark 16:14–20).

Matthew develops the idea further. The closing passages of his gospel correspond to the closing passages of Deuteronomy: Moses stands on the top of Mount Nebo so that before he dies the Lord can show him the land of Canaan to which he has brought the Israelites. Canaan is consecrated to the Jews alone; it is their patrimony (Deuteronomy 34:1–4). Jesus instructs his disciples to meet him for the last time on a mountain in Galilee. There they survey the world, and he instructs them "to make disciples of all nations" (Matthew 28:18–19).

Luke goes further still. At the end of his gospel, Jesus instructs the disciples to "stay in the city, until you are clothed with power from on high." So they return joyfully to Jerusalem, where they remain "continually in the temple blessing God" (Luke 24:49, 52–53). Luke devotes a second book, the Acts of the Apostles, to explaining how God's "chosen instruments" carried his "name before the Gentiles and kings and the sons of Israel" (Acts 9:15).

The Community

Like the time and place of the meal, the agents of the sacrifice are also dramatically transformed. The Lord instructs Moses concerning the passover:

> Tell all the congregation of Israel that on the tenth day of this month they shall take every man a lamb according to their fathers' houses, a lamb for a household; and if the household is too small for a lamb, then a man and his neigh-

bor next to his house shall take according to the number of persons. . . . and you shall keep it until the fourteenth day of this month, when the whole assembly of the congregation of Israel shall kill their lambs in the evening. [Exodus 12:3–4, 6]

This is precisely the procedure reported in the Mishnah (Pesahim 5:5–7). The lamb is killed by and for the family: "The ordinance of the passover [is] no foreigner shall eat of it" (Exodus 12:43). Slave, sojourners, hired servants, and strangers may partake of the passover only if they are circumcised and thus made native-born (Exodus 12:44–49). Any Jew who is capable of keeping the passover, and yet does not, shall be cut off (Numbers 9:13; Jubilees 49:9).

The family is also the focus of everything that follows. The blood of the lamb is applied with hyssop to the two doorposts and the lintel of the house in which it is eaten, to distinguish the houses of the Israelites that will be passed over (Exodus 12:7, 13, 22–23). Later it is thrown against the altar of the temple, the corporate house of Israel, to commemorate the event that gave birth to the nation. Each family eats its lamb inside its own house, and no part of the flesh may be taken outside the house (Exodus 12:46). In fact, it is forbidden to leave the family house at all during the course of the night (Exodus 12:22). The precepts concerning the unleavened bread imply that people normally spent the Passover week with their families in their houses (Exodus 12:15–20). As Philo interpreted it, the Passover, "as commanded by the law," was a time when "the whole people, old and young alike, (were) raised for that particular day to the dignity of the priesthood" and every house was "invested with the outward semblance and dignity of a temple" (*The Special Laws* 2:145, 148; see also *Moses* 2:224).

In celebrating the deliverance of Jewish families from the Egyptians as the chosen people of God, the Passover celebrated the birth of the nation of Israel. The Passover constituted so great a part of the Jews' conception of their God and their relationship to him that they swore by it: "As the Lord lives who brought up the people of Israel out of the land of Egypt" (Jeremiah 23:7). Texts describing the Passover (Exodus 13:1–16) and the subsequent entry into the Promised Land (Deuteronomy 6:4–9, 11:13–21) were written on parchment made from the skins of clean animals and kept in boxes attached not only to the house but to the person. Scripture required it:

> as a sign on your hand and as a memorial between your eyes that the law of the Lord may be in your mouth; for with a strong hand the Lord has brought you out of Egypt. . . . And you shall write them on the doorposts of your house and on your gates. [Exodus 13:9; Deuteronomy 6:9; see also Exodus 13:16; Deuteronomy 11:20]

The *mezuzah* ("doorpost"), a case usually in the form of a Torah scroll, was put on the right hand doorpost facing in, perhaps to commemorate the blood of the lamb. The *tefillin* (literally "prayers," but translated in Matthew's Greek [23:5] as "phylacteries") were also made from the skins and veins of clean animals and worn by Jewish men from the age of thirteen years and a day on the left arm and forehead during morning prayers. Samaritans did not wear them (*Encyclopaedia Judaica*, 15:898). Tefillin are first mentioned in the Letter of Aristeas (159). A mezuzah parchment and fragments of tefillin have also been found in caves at Qumran near the Dead Sea, probably dating to the first half of the first century C.E. (ibid., 11:1475–76; 15:903–4). Josephus ascribes both the tefillin and the mezuzah to the time of Moses, as befits established custom (*The Jewish Antiquities*, 4:213).

Given the significance of the Passover, it is not surprising that it was emphasized particularly in times of nationalist reform in the history of Israel. Different historians used different descriptions of participation in the event to reflect different visions of the nation they wished to see established. According to 2 Kings (23:21–23), probably written during the Babylonian exile (May and Metzger 1979:413), the Passover was ignored for centuries during the period in which the judges and kings ruled Israel until the reform instituted by Josiah in 621 B.C.E. The Passover he organized to celebrate the fulfillment of the newly rediscovered law marked the climax of his effort to rid the nation of foreign "abominations." The Book of Ezra, written during the postexilic period, attributes Ezra's re-establishment of the Passover in Judah following the exile to similar reasons. It was celebrated only for the exiles and for "every one [among the unexiled] who had joined them and separated himself from the pollutions of the peoples of the land" (Ezra 7:21).

The Chronicler expresses a different vision of the nation in the postexilic period—a return to the boundaries of Solomon that included both kingdoms—by rewriting pre-exilic history. His history emphasizes that King Hezekiah "sent to all Israel and Judah" to come to his Passover (2 Chronicles 30:1) and that "all Judah and Israel . . . were present" at the Passover of Josiah (2 Chronicles 35:18). Ezra's Passover is described again in 2 Esdras (7:10–15), probably written toward the end of the first century B.C.E. to denounce the wickedness of Rome, disguised as "Babylon" (Metzger 1977:1). In fact, the revolts against Rome "repeatedly took place at the Passover" (Jeremias 1966:207; see also Smallwood 1976:106, 146, 157, 263–66).[3]

Scripture is unequivocal concerning the agents appointed to slaughter and consume the passover. Although the ritual was subject to different interpretations in different times, the key figures were always Jews. The identity of those responsible for Jesus' sacrifice is less clear-cut. Indeed, the question of who killed Jesus has provoked more controversy than almost any other issue in early Christian writing. The evangelists interpret the involvement of Jews and Romans quite differently, for reasons that are probably best understood in relation to their own later circumstances. Matthew blames the Romans more than Mark or John, who blame primarily the Jews. Luke's Jesus is condemned by the mob, absolving both authorities, though Luke blames the Sanhedrin in Acts (5:30). All of them make it clear in a variety of ways that Jesus' death was voluntary, a self-sacrifice.

Scholars have tried to defend one version against another by arguing that the Sanhedrin could not have met on a holy day; that their actions do not reflect the Mishnaic code concerning proper trial procedure (admittedly of a later date); that a crucifixion could not have been held on a holy day; that Jews executed criminals by stoning, not crucifixion; that the Jews or,

---

3. Explaining the recent custom of including readings in memory of the Holocaust in the passover seder, the publishers of the Shocken edition of the passover haggadah note that the uprising in the Warsaw Ghetto occurred at Passover 1943 (Glatzer 1979:v).

conversely, the Romans had no legal jurisdiction in this case (see Winter 1974). Yet the most striking feature of the evangelists' diverse accounts is that despite every possible objection to the participation of either Jews or gentiles, they succeed in involving both in a very complicated and ambiguous alliance. Jews and gentiles sacrificed Jesus together. He was their common sacrifice, and by his own consent.

As Jews and gentiles are implicated in the crucifixion, so the loyal and the treacherous, the loving and the hateful, the doubting, ignorant, and cowardly are present at the last supper. The meaning of these motley crowds is not merely that everyone is potentially a traitor (Robbins 1976), that individual communities of early Christians were plagued with factionalism (e.g., Kelber 1976a; Weeden 1976), or that there was and always will be, as scripture requires, a deadly reminder of the accursed mixture, although these are all probably valid interpretations. The "traitor" is there now and forever because he is a participant in the new covenant. He slaughters the sacrifice. He eats it; indeed, he is especially fed. He is and always will be one of the chosen people, an essential member of the new Christian community. As Jesus says, "Did I not choose you, the twelve, and one of you is a devil?" (John 6:70).

Jesus' passover transforms this collection into a community of priests just like every other passover before and after. Their corporate body is the temple "not made by hands" that is raised in three days by his resurrection from the dead (Romans 12:3-8; 1 Corinthians 12:4-31). That Paul, the former Pharisee, should be one of the most eloquent proponents of this vision is not surprising, since it is essentially Pharisaic doctrine with one critical difference. Christians, like Pharisees, would arrogate to every individual the status of temple priest, but they would not restrict themselves to one nation. They would interpret the royal house to include members "from every tribe and tongue and people and nation" (Revelations 5:10). God's promise to Israel has been extended to the world:

> you are a chosen race, a royal priesthood, a holy nation, God's own people, that you may declare the wonderful deeds of him who called you out of darkness into his marvelous light. Once you were no people but now you are God's people;

once you had not received mercy but now you have received mercy. [1 Peter 2:9–10]

The Sacrifice

The sacrifice appropriate to this world-wide community of priests is not the domestic meal, riddled with dietary rules, that severs Jews from gentiles at every bite. It is voluntary self-sacrifice, the only possible means of confounding the distinctions between eater and eaten, edible and inedible, that persist in dividing them (Romans 12:1). In contrast to the animal of the passover sacrifice, a year-old male sheep or goat, "without blemish" (Exodus 12:3–6), as stipulated in the Holiness Code (Leviticus 22:22–25), Jesus' sacrifice is a human being, "born of woman, born under the law" (Galatians 4:4), who is reviled, beaten, and spat on before he is finally crucified together with criminals. The blood of his sacrifice is his own blood, not the blood of goats and calves (Hebrews 9:12). Jesus' humanity is emphasized in all accounts by his agony in the garden of Gethsemane and his suffering on the cross.

Prophets had railed for centuries against the sacrificial practices of the temple (e.g., Psalms 50:7–15; Isaiah 1:10–17; Jeremiah 6:20, 7:21–22; Hosea 6:6; Micah 6:6–8; Amos 5:21–24), contrasting righteousness, obedience to God's commandments, with empty ritual: "I desire steadfast love and not sacrifice, the knowledge of God, rather than burnt offerings" (Hosea 6:6; see also Matthew 9:13, 12:7). The issue of animal versus human sacrifice was part of that argument. To early Christians, Jesus' sacrifice was a more genuine expression of the relationship of humanity to God. Human sacrifice is superior to animal sacrifice as Jesus-manna is superior to Moses-manna (John 6:48–51), as "the fleshly tables of the heart" are superior to "tables of stone" (2 Corinthians 3:3), as Abel's gift was superior to Cain's (Hebrews 12:25).

The superior merit of human sacrifice is implied in the importance given to fasting, but it is addressed directly in Abraham's near sacrifice of Isaac, recounted in Genesis (22:1–18). God instructs Abraham to sacrifice Isaac, his only son, the son of his old age, as a burnt offering on a hill in the land of Moriah. Abraham takes Isaac to the place. He carries the fire and the knife. Isaac carries the wood. When Isaac asks after the sacrificial animal, Abraham answers: "God will provide himself the lamb for a burnt offering, my son" (Genesis 22:8).

They arrive. Abraham builds the altar, arranges the wood, and binds Isaac. Just as he takes up the knife, an angel of the Lord intervenes and tells him not to touch his son. He is to sacrifice a ram in Isaac's place. God now knows that Abraham is so obedient to God's will that he would sacrifice his only son and heir. God blesses him for his obedience, promising to multiply his descendants "as the stars of heaven and as the sand which is on the seashore" (Genesis 22:17), whence the Israelites.

Vermès (1961:193–227), who has traced the transformations in the story, notes a striking contrast between the biblical and medieval accounts, which focus on Abraham, and the targumic accounts from the inter-Testamental period, in which a pious Isaac actively seeks to participate in his own sacrifice. The Targums, translations of scripture from Hebrew into Aramaic made during this period, frequently reflect ideological changes in their choices of equivalents and occasional midrashic embellishments. Vermès relates the transformation in Isaac's role during this period to the theological problem of martyrdom that arose as a result of religious persecution, beginning in 167 B.C.E. in the reign of Antiochus Epiphanes. The martyrdom of Hannah and her seven sons, recorded in 2 Maccabees (7) may have been the critical event (ibid.: 203–4). It is frequently compared to the binding of Isaac in midrashic literature. In other words, Jews had already made a connection between Isaac and the suffering servant of Deutero-Isaiah (Isaiah 42:1–4, 49:1–6, 50:4–11, 52:13–53:12) before the theme was taken up in early Christian writing.

Vermès agrees with Jeremias (1966) that the last supper was a passover meal, but he finds it more difficult to equate John's "Lamb of God" with the paschal lamb. He believes that the story of Abraham and Isaac inspired a theology during the inter-Testamental period in which all lamb sacrifice, especially the passover lamb, was a memorial to Isaac's willing obedience "with its effects of deliverance, forgiveness of sin and messianic salvation" (Vermès 1961:225). Thus Christ is the lamb that God promised to provide in Genesis (22:8). This time he is sacrificed.

The Last Supper

The Death of Isaac and the Destruction of Kinship

In the story of Abraham and Isaac, God stays the hand of Abraham, and blesses him for his willing obedience by granting him the numberless descendants, who, through the Passover, come to constitute the nation of Israel. In the story of Jesus, God himself sacrifices his only begotten son, a son who was born of a virgin, who never married, and who never had one child of his own.

In the true spirit of midrash, the evangelists used Jesus' passion to harmonize two different, and at points conflicting, scriptural stories of the birth of Israel. An older story about Abraham and Isaac, in which the Israelites were not distinguished as chosen under the law, was incorporated into the more recent story of the Passover, in which they were. In bringing them together, they transformed them both. Isaac died in Jesus' passover. His sacrifice celebrated not only the death of the nation, but an end to the kinship on which the nation was based by law. The union of Jews and gentiles could be achieved only by destroying the relationship between fathers and sons.

It is difficult to imagine a stronger or more horrifying statement of the destruction of kinship than God's sacrifice of Isaac, which is perhaps why the evangelists are so careful to prepare their readers to accept it. The domestic life of the prophet is a sign of the judgement and redemption he preaches, exactly as in scripture (Isaiah 8:1-4; Jeremiah 16:1-13; Ezekiel 24:15-27; Hosea 1:2-9). Jesus' mother is the virgin Mary. His father is the Holy Spirit. He has neither home nor family in any conventional sense. He says so in both Matthew (8:20) and Luke (9:58): "Foxes have holes and birds of the air have nests; but the Son of man has nowhere to lay his head." His answer to those who inform him while he is preaching at Capernaum in Galilee that his mother and brothers have arrived, "to seize him, for people were saying, 'He is beside himself' " (Mark 3:21, 31), echoes the lawyer's question, "And who is my neighbor?":

> "Who are my mother and my brothers?" And looking around on those who sat about him, he said, "Here are my mother and my brothers! Whoever does the will of God is my brother, and sister, and mother." [Mark 3:33-35; repeated in Matthew 12:46-50 and Luke 8:19-21]

His disciples must do likewise and give up "house or brothers or sisters or mother or father or children or lands" for the sake of Jesus and for the gospel (Mark 10:29; repeated in Matthew 19:29 and Luke 18:29–30). Jesus means to bring about the destruction of conventional kinship relations that Micah predicted would herald the last judgment:

> Do you think that I have come to give peace on earth? No, I tell you, but rather division; for henceforth in one house there will be five divided, three against two and two against three; they will be divided, father against son and son against father, mother against daughter and daughter against her mother, mother-in-law against her daughter-in-law and daughter-in-law against her mother-in-law. [Luke 12:51–53; Matthew (10:36) concludes: and a man's foes will be those of his own household.]

If Jesus had addressed his remarks only to gentile disciples, they would have surprised no one. Converts to Judaism terminated all family ties, acquiring Jewish names that were unrelated to the names of their fathers. They were considered "newly born children" and referred to as "children of Abraham (our father)" (*Encyclopaedia Judaica*, 13:1184). But Jesus does not. He treats Jews like gentiles. All three of the synoptic gospels record the event in which one of the disciples asks leave to bury his father before following Jesus. It is a sacred and legally binding duty expressive of the solidarity of kin in life and death (Pedersen 1926, 2:460, 495–96). But Jesus replies: "Follow me, and leave the dead to bury their own dead" (Matthew 8:22; see also Mark 1:20; Luke 9:59–62), alluding to a passage in scripture (1 Kings 19:20–21) that emphasizes his point. In scripture, Elijah did permit Elisha to return to his father and mother to kiss them goodbye before he followed the prophet to become his disciple. In Jesus' view, cited by Luke (9:62): "No one who puts his hand to the plough and looks back is fit for the kingdom of God."

John stages a more direct confrontation with "the Jews," playing, as usual, on the ambiguous relationship between the literal and metaphorical meanings of his words. Jesus tells Jews who neither believe him nor love him, but seek to kill him, that they are not the children of God and Abraham as they insist: they are children of the devil (John 8:30–41):

If you were Abraham's children, you would do what Abraham did, but now you seek to kill me. . . . If God were your Father, you would love me, for I proceeded and came forth from God. . . . Why do you not understand what I say? It is because you cannot bear to hear my word. You are of your father the devil, and your will is to do your father's desires. He was a murderer from the beginning and has nothing to do with the truth. . . . He who is of God hears the words of God; the reason why you do not hear them is that you are not of God. [John 8:39–47]

"The Jews" respond literally by accusing Jesus of being a Samaritan and saying that he is possessed by a demon. (Note that the Samaritans have already identified Jesus as a Jew in John 4:9.) Jesus responds by moving from the literal back to the spiritual. He is not possessed; he is honoring his Father (John 8:48–49). This is what he says "to the crowds and to his disciples" in Matthew (23:1, 9): "Call no man your father on earth, for you have one Father, who is in heaven." The theme is developed further in later Christian writing. Every family in heaven and earth takes its name from the Father (Ephesians 3:15; see also Galatians 6:10; Hebrews 3:4–6).

The destruction of kinship will accompany the destruction of the temple and of the nation at the end of the age, when

brother will deliver up brother to death, and the father his child, and children will rise against parents and have them put to death; and you will be hated by all for my name's sake. But he who endures to the end will be saved. [Mark 13:12–13; repeated in Matthew 24:9–13; Luke 21:16–19]

All this devastation is "but the beginning of the birth-pangs" of the new age, when the gospel will be preached "to all nations" (Mark 13:8, 10; see also Matthew 24:8, 14). John symbolizes both the death and the new life when he completes his account of the crucifixion by confronting Jesus with his mother in the presence of the "disciple whom he loved":

When Jesus saw his mother, and the disciple whom he loved standing near, he said to his mother, "Woman, behold, your son!" Then he said to the disciple, "Behold, your mother!"

And from that hour the disciple took her to his own home. [John 19:26–27]

Jesus' Passover

This is the message conveyed in Jesus' command to commemorate his passion in the last supper, otherwise so similar to the Lord's command to commemorate the Passover in the passover seder. Jesus' use of bread and wine to interpret his death and resurrection is no different from the use of bitter herbs and haroseth to represent embitterment and mortar, enslavement and liberation. Both meals are composed of foods that must be translated as they are eaten. According to Paul and the evangelists, Jesus' words are incomprehensible to his listeners until they are spelled out in this way.

The difference is in the words of his command. It is not "tell your son" (Exodus 12:14, 24–27, 13:8), implying a community based on kinship, in which knowledge passes from father to son, and the purpose of ritual is frequently to reconcile one with the other (Malachi 4:6). It is "you," whoever you may be: man, woman, child, Jew, or gentile. You do this in remembrance of me, "for as often as you eat this bread and drink the cup, you proclaim the Lord's death until he comes" (1 Corinthians 11:24–26; see also Luke 22:19). Jesus' purpose in this meal is

> to reconcile the whole universe to himself, making peace through the shedding of his blood upon the cross—to reconcile all things, whether on earth or in heaven, through him alone. [Colossians 1:20]

Therefore, he does not celebrate Passover with his family as required by scripture. He celebrates it with his disciples. They represent the relationship of "family" or "kin" as he conceived it under the new law. God's children are no longer "brothers" in the traditional sense of being related by descent, however ideally construed. Brotherhood is no longer restricted to Israelites. "God's household" (Ephesians 2:19) has been completely transformed.

In contrast to the passover that brings the family together, Jesus' sacrifice breaks it apart to create new bonds. Self-sacrifice embodies the new law to love one another. The "word made flesh" is the food that has to be consumed. The passover that does not spare the first-born Israelite has identified the priest with his victim. So Jesus officiates at his own consumption, the crucifixion that will be his salvation, and so must every Christian after him. It is he who offers, then finally accepts the wine that seems to mark his fall from grace to degradation; he who says the Hallel that affirms his resurrection from degradation to glory.

The four cups of Jesus' passion reverse the traditional order of the passover. The wine of salvation seems to turn into the wine of wrath. Jesus himself presents the first cup, the kiddush cup with which he blesses the day (Matthew 26:27–29; Mark 14: 23–25; Luke 22:17–18). He resists the cup from his "Father" in the garden of Gethsemane, but he will drink it if it is his father's will (repeated three times in Matthew 26:39–44 and Mark 14:36–39; once in Luke 22:42–44 and John 18:11). He refuses the wine mixed with the sedative myrrh (Mark 15.23; Matthew 27:34 says it is mingled with gall, a bitter liquid), which the Roman soldiers offer him immediately before the crucifixion.

When he finally cries out in agony, "My God, my God, why hast thou forsaken me" (Matthew, Mark; according to John, he says "I thirst"), they offer him vinegar, taunting him with salvation in certainty of his death: "Let us see whether Elijah will come to save him" (Matthew 27:49; see also Mark 14:36); "If you are the king of the Jews, save yourself" (Luke 23:37). Even one of the criminals "rails at him": "Are you not the Christ? Save yourself and us!" (Luke 23:39). He drinks the fourth cup and dies the accursed death that rends the temple curtain in two and evokes the Roman centurion's statement of faith: "Truly this man was the Son of God" (Mark 15:36–39; see also Matthew 27: 48–54; Luke 23:36–47; John 19:29–30); Deuteronomy 21:23).

The wine does it. The blood of the lamb that saved the first-born Israelites when they painted it on the lintels and doorposts of their houses with hyssop is the wine of wrath that kills the first-born Israelite when it is handed up to him on hyssop (John 19:29). By drinking the wine that is the blood, the participant "cuts himself off from his kin" exactly as the law requires (Leviticus 7:27, 17:10–14). But by drinking "the life of the flesh" (Leviticus 17:11), he acquires that life. The separation from kin that is synonymous with death is only the prelude to eternal life in Jesus Christ.

> He who loves father or mother more than me is not worthy of me; and he who loves son or daughter more than me is not worthy of me; and he who does not take his cross and follow me is not worthy of me. He who finds his life will lose it, and he who loses his life for my sake will find it. [Matthew 10: 37–39]

Jesus' Hallel is transformed by the same ironic reversals. In contrast to the four cups, which seem to mark the fact that God has "set [his] face against that person who eats blood" (Leviticus 17:10), the text incarnate in his passion promises salvation to those with the faith to endure to the end. Psalms 113–118, attributed to Moses in a first-century C.E. tradition recorded in the Talmud (Berakoth 56a), praise God for his fidelity to the covenant. They encourage the Israelite to trust in the Lord's "steadfast love," his "faithfulness that endures forever," even though he experiences terrible anguish when God might seem to have abandoned him.

God seems remote, seated high in the heavens, but he is mindful of his people, raising up the needy and helpless (Psalm 113) and performing miracles of deliverance like the Passover (Psalm 114). The nations ask, "Where is their God," because the Israelites have no idols. But the idols of the nations are dead, despite their superficial resemblance to the living, and so are those who trust in them (Psalm 115). The Psalmist loves the Lord because he hears the cries of the suffering:

> I love the Lord because he has heard
> my voice and my supplications.
> Because he inclined his ear to me,
> therefore I will call on him as long as I live.
> The snares of death encompassed me;
> the pangs of Sheol laid hold on me;
> I suffered distress and anguish.
> Then I called on the name of the Lord:
> "O Lord, I beseech thee, save my life!"
> [Psalms 116:1–4; see also 118:5–6]

146

The Psalmist is saved, and he will thank the Lord with this sacrificial meal:

> I will lift up the cup of salvation
> and call on the name of the Lord,
> I will pay my vows to the Lord
> in the presence of all his people.
> Precious in the sight of the Lord
> is the death of his saints [i.e., he
> rarely allows them to die]. [Psalms 116:12–15]

The crucifixion was surely a moment when God ignored the cry of his willing servant and abandoned him to a senseless death. But even here, scripture is confirmed. The faithful "shall not die, but . . . shall live and recount the deeds of the Lord" (Psalms 118:17). Sorrow must give way to joy (John 16: 20–24). Jesus' passover, which appears contrary in every way to passover tradition, affirms the true meaning of God's promise to the nations. His human sacrifice, bearing all the superficial features of death, is the true embodiment of God's saving word. The fleshly food of his table has abolished the difference between idolatry and the prohibition of graven images.

The Lion of Judah has conquered in the form of "a Lamb with the marks of slaughter upon him" (Revelation 5:5–6 *NEB*, compare 1 Peter 1:19). Here, above all, the boundaries of the body, physical and social, have been transgressed and broken down:

> Therefore, brethen, since we have confidence to enter the sanctuary by the blood of Jesus, by the new and living way which he opened for us through the curtain, that is, through his flesh and since we have a great priest over the house of God, let us draw near with a true heart in full assurance of faith. [Hebrews 10:19–22]

The Hallel concludes as the suppliant is admitted into the temple with praise and thanksgiving, for "the stone which the builders rejected has become the head of the corner. This is the Lord's doing" (Psalms 118:22–23, quoted in Mathew 21:42, Mark 12:10, Acts 4:11, 1 Peter 2:4–5):

> So then you are no longer strangers and sojourners, but you are fellow citizens with the saints and members of the

household of God, built upon the foundation of the apostles and prophets, Christ Jesus himself being the cornerstone, in whom the whole structure is joined together and grows into a holy temple in the Lord; in whom you also are built into it for a dwelling place of God in the Spirit. [Ephesians 2:19–22]

6

THE FOLLY OF THE GOSPEL

> God has shown me that I should not
> call any man common or unclean.
> Acts 10:28

Jesus sacrificed to confound what Jews traditionally sacrificed to keep from being confounded. Of two separate categories of people, tied tightly to their own kin, he intended to make one new creation in which there were no divisions (Acts 15:9; Romans 3:22, 10:12; 1 Corinthians 12:12–15; 2 Corinthians 5:17; Galatians 6:15) and no favorites (Galatians 2:6; Ephesians 6:9; Colossians 3:25; 1 Peter 1:17):

> Here there cannot be Greek and Jew, circumcised and uncircumcised, barbarian, Scythian, slave, free man, but Christ is all, and in all. [Colossians 3:11]

This was Jesus' hidden purpose, his afikoman, "the mystery hidden for ages and generations but now made manifest to his saints" (Colossians 1:26): that gentiles are "fellow heirs, members of the same body, and partakers of the promise in Christ Jesus through the gospel" that is represented in the Lord's supper (Ephesians 3:6; see also Mark 4:11; Romans 16:25–27; 1 Corinthians 2:6–9; Ephesians 1:9–10; Revelation 2:17). Despite appearances, union, rather than election, is the guarantee of eternal life.

Jesus consistently taught that the "Father, Lord of heaven and earth [has hidden] these things from the wise and understanding and revealed them to babes" [Matthew 11:25; see Luke 10:21]. Yet Jesus' secret was just the opposite of the secret that most children of Israel expected to be revealed at the end of time. It created a variety of theological and practical problems, including one that Leach (1966) might have called "the legitimacy of Jesus." I will conclude by discussing some of the ways in which that problem was solved, for they were ways in which the gospel of eternal life was reworded to apply to the ordinary lives of diverse human believers, the ultimate purpose of midrash.

The Legitimacy of Jesus

It is precisely the legitimacy of Jesus that occupies so many early Christian writers, for how could both Jews and gentiles be "fellow heirs" in the new testament of the Lord if they were not brothers? Only the letters written to the two gentiles in the New Testament, Titus (Galatians 2:3) and Timothy (Acts 16:1–3), try to protest that such genealogical questions are foolish.[1]

> As I urged you when I was going to Macedonia, remain at Ephesus that you may charge certain persons not to teach any different doctrine, nor to occupy themselves with myths and endless genealogies which promote speculations rather than the divine training that is in faith; whereas the aim of our charge is love that issues from a pure heart and a good conscience and sincere faith. Certain persons by swerving from these have wandered away into vain discussion, desiring to be teachers of the law, without understanding either what they are saying or the things about which they make assertions. [1 Timothy 1:3–7; see also 2 Timothy 2:23]

> . . . avoid stupid controversies, genealogies, dissensions, and quarrels over the law, for they are unprofitable and futile. [Titus 3:9]

1. Strictly speaking, Timothy was a Jew, born of a Jewish Christian mother and a gentile father. But he had never been circumcised and was probably regarded as a gentile at Lystra, where he was born and grew up (Harvey 1970: 459). Lystra seems to have had no Jewish community (Luke 14:19). In a sense, he represents the perfect type of the "new creature" to which Paul refers in 2 Corinthians (5:17), neither Jew nor gentile, but Christian. It is therefore interesting that the Jews whom he encountered as a member of the church insisted on his Jewishness and that Paul, contrary to his policy with regard to gentile Christians, as expressed frequently in his letter to the Galatians, deferred to their wishes and circumcised him (Acts 16:3).

The Folly of the Gospel

The evangelists, especially Matthew (1:1–17; 2; 9:27; 21:9) and Luke (1:32–33; 2; 3:23–38; took great pains to provide Jesus with a genealogy relating him to David, thence to Abraham, and to establish his birthplace at Bethlehem, where David was born. (Compare Mark 10:47; John 7:42; Acts 13:23; Romans 1:3; 2 Timothy 2:8; Revelation 5:5, 22:16.) Matthew's genealogy runs from Abraham, father of the Israelites, forward to Joseph. Luke's version runs from Joseph backward to Adam, the progenitor of all mankind. The two genealogies are entirely different, and the many attempts to harmonize them, from Julius Africanus onward, have all failed (see Jeremias 1969:292–97, who sides with Luke).

Early Christian writers also attempted to solve the problem by reinterpreting central symbols in scripture. For example, according to Jewish law, a man could adopt someone simply by calling him "my son" (Harvey 1970:523). Early Christians reversed the ritual and became the children of God by calling "Abba! Father!" as Jesus had (Mark 14:36). In that cry, according to Paul in his letter to the Romans, "it is the Spirit himself bearing witness with our spirit that we are children of God, and if children, then heirs, heirs of God and fellow heirs with Christ, provided that we suffer with him in order that we may also be glorified with him" (Romans 8:16–17; see also Galatians 4:6–7).

They construed kinship with Abraham as a spiritual kinship. Paul emphasizes that God elected Abraham because he had faith in God and therefore was righteous, not because he was peculiarly righteous to begin with (Romans 4:3, 11; Galatians 3:6). Those who have no faith in God are not true sons of Abraham, even though they may be Jews superficially, that is, in the flesh (Romans 2; 4:12, 16; 9:6; Galatians 6:15–16; see also Revelation 2:9, 3:9). This is Jesus' argument in John (8:30–47).

Anyone who has faith in Jesus, "the root and offspring of David" (Revelation 22:16), whether he is a Jew or a gentile, is a true child of God (Mark 3:55; Galatians 3:26), a brother to Christ and therefore a child of Abraham:

There is neither Jew nor Greek, there is neither slave nor free, there is neither male nor female; for you are all one in Christ Jesus. [The *all* is very emphatic, placed twice at the beginning of the phrase in Greek (Harvey 1970:610).] And if you are Christ's, then you are Abraham's offspring, heirs according to promise. [Galatians 3:28–29]

Thus Paul reinterprets the text—"In you [Abraham] shall all the nations be blessed" (Galatians 3:8; see also Genesis 17:5–6, 18:18) —by replacing the usual word, "tribes," by which Jews understood "Jewish tribes," with the Greek word for "nations," *ethnē,* which also meant "gentiles" (Harvey 1970:607).

Another way of solving the problem was to represent Jesus' apostles as the legendary twelve tribes of Israel. The church was the New Israel, to whom God's promises had really been made (Matthew 19:28; Galatians 6:16; James 1:1; 1 Peter 1:1, 2:4–10, 5:13; Revelations 4:10, 7:4–8, 14:3, 22:2).

Teachers like Paul were the fathers, if not the patriarchs, of the communities they served. Paul consistently uses "my true child" in speaking of or to his close gentile companions, describing himself as their "father in Christ Jesus through the gospel" (1 Corinthians 4:14–17; 1 Timothy 1:2; 2 Timothy 1:2; Titus 1:4). Christians also made the Hebrew term for "brother," the most comprehensive term besides "neighbor" and "kinsman" for a member of the Hebrew community of kin (Pedersen 1926, 1:57), the standard appellation for every member of the new Christian community, Jew and gentile alike. As Harvey (1970:100) points out, "brother" is virtually a technical term for "Christian" (e.g., Matthew 5:21–26, 47; 7:3–5; 18:15, 21; Romans 8:29; 1 Corinthians 6:5; 1 Thessalonians 4:9; Hebrews 2:11–18; 1 Peter 1:22).

The outstanding emphasis in Jesus' use of the term "brother" in the gospels and in the use of the term elsewhere in early Christian writing, especially in the letters of Paul and the first letter of John, is on reconciliation. Richardson (1962:82–83) also comments on the remarkable number of *syn*-compounds coined in early Christian writing to express relationships of fellowship: "fellow prisoner," "fellow servant," and so on. He suggests that these compounds, many of which occur for the first time in early Christian writing, indicate "the newness and uniqueness of this Christian fellowship."

These efforts at patching did little more than expose the worn cloak. The inescapable fact was that Jesus persisted in choosing as members of his household "new creatures" (2 Corinthians 5:17) who did not fit into any proper category, no matter how it was renamed or reinterpreted: women, cripples, Samaritans, sinners, publicans, *am ha-arez*, or a combination thereof, minors, half-breeds, and blemished persons who drew attention to the issues of mixture and the ambiguity of kinship by their very nature.

The new creation was nothing less than a tree in which "wild branches" had been grafted "contrary to nature" into the "good," "natural" stock:

> Now I am speaking to you Gentiles. Inasmuch then as I am an apostle to the Gentiles, I magnify my ministry in order to make my fellow Jews jealous, and thus save some of them. . . . if the root is holy, so are the branches. But if some of the branches were broken off, and you, a wild olive shoot, were grafted in their place to share the richness of the olive tree, do not boast over the branches. If you do boast, remember it is not you that support the root, but the root that supports you. You will say, "Branches were broken off so that I might be grafted in." That is true. They were broken off because of their unbelief, but you stand fast only through faith. So do not become proud, but stand in awe. For if God did not spare the natural branches, neither will he spare you. . . . you too will be cut off. And even the others, if they do not persist in their unbelief, will be grafted in, for God has the power to graft them in again. For if you have been cut from what is by nature a wild olive tree, and grafted, contrary to nature, into a cultivated olive tree, how much more will these natural branches be grafted back into their own olive tree. [Romans 11:13–24]

Wine into Water

Christians have become so adept at integrating the image of Christ crucified into everyday life that it is easy to forget that it was a stumbling block to Jews and a joke to gentiles (1 Corinthians 1:23). All the conventional categories of social relations were swamped by the limitless unity advocated by Jesus Christ. The crucifixion was madness from almost any point of view, "sheer folly to those on their way to ruin" (1 Corinthians 1:18).

Paul exalts folly as "spiritual truths in spiritual language" as opposed to "words . . . taught by human wisdom." The "unspiritual" or "natural" person interprets these truths as folly only because he cannot understand them (1 Corinthians 2:13–14). But Paul, perhaps precisely because he had been a Pharisee, recognized that if the church was to grow, folly had to be transformed back into wisdom. Speaking in tongues is nothing without interpretation, as he puts it to the Corinthians. It is necessary to pray, to sing, to bless, to speak with the mind as well as with the spirit (1 Corinthians 14:1–19).

Wine had to be turned back into water; revelation had to be changed into law, and law of the most concrete, everyday sort. The crucifixion was an exceedingly difficult image, involving a variety of complex theological and social issues of which the redefinition of the community was only one. The implications of the crucifixion had to be translated into terms that could be more easily understood by diverse congregations, but without resorting to patchwork compromises in meaning.

Paul was adept at all styles of interpretation, a master of plain speech who was equally conversant in "the secret and hidden wisdom of God" (1 Corinthians 2:7). He was a virtuoso polyglot of custom, who could and would be all things to all people in order to make them understand God's word:

> For though I am free from all men, I have made myself a slave to all, that I might win the more. To the Jews I became as a Jew, in order to win Jews; to those under the law I became as one under the law—though not being myself under the law—that I might win those under the law. To those outside the law I became as one outside the law—not being without law toward God but under the law of Christ—that I might win those outside the law. To the weak I became weak, that I might win the weak. I have become all things to all men, that I might by all means save some. I do it all for the sake of the gospel, that I may share in its blessings. [1 Corinthians 9:19–23]

So he explains to the Corinthians, apparently because they were criticizing him for being too simplistic, that he is feeding them as a mother feeds a baby, because they are not yet capable of understanding more complex ideas:

I, brethren, could not address you as spiritual men, but as men of the flesh, as babes in Christ. I fed you with milk, not solid food; for you were not ready for it; and even yet you are not ready, for you are still of the flesh. For while there is jealousy and strife among you, are you not of the flesh, and behaving like ordinary men? [I Corinthians 3:1–3; see also Hebrews 5:11–14; I Peter 2:1–3]

He had spoken to the Romans in the same way, "in human terms, because of your natural limitations" (6:19), when he presented them with his version of the tree, one of the commonest metaphors of kinship in scripture and a symbol of the law (Psalms 52:8; 128:3; Jeremiah 11:16–17; Zechariah 4:3, 11–12; Sirach 24:12–23). His tree is a hard image, but only a faint echo of the far more terrible and terrifyingly unnatural tree made by Christ on the cross (Deuteronomy 21:22; Acts 5:30, 10:39; 13:29; Galatians 3:13; I Peter 2:24), which totally transformed the laws of separation and devotion to God under Moses.

The last supper was another way of translating the complex imagery of the crucifixion into more manageable terms. But even the last supper could be too simple or too awful, depending on the point of view of the participant. It was too simple, perhaps, to gentiles who did not share a cultural tradition in which God's food was his sacred law: for example, Corinthians who said, "Food is meant for the stomach and the stomach for food" (I Corinthians 6:13). Paul had to warn them not to eat the Lord's supper stupidly, so that they failed to achieve communion (11:17–34). "Do you not know," he asked, "that your body is a temple of the Holy Spirit within you, which you have from God?" (6:19). On the other hand, the meal may have been too awful for Jews, who understood exactly what they ate and could not bear it. Curiously, it is the synoptics, for whom the last supper is unambiguously a passover seder, who convey a "simpler" view; and John, for whom the relationship between the last supper and the passover is more complicated, who conveys the potential horror.

John makes it quite clear that eating blood was anathema, a truly unspeakable act. This is perhaps one reason, although admittedly I am arguing from silence, that early Christian writers say so very little about the consequences of eating blood. But even apart from the restriction on eating it, blood was a highly ambiguous substance in Judaism. Blood was associated with life (Genesis 9:4; Leviticus 17:14; Deuteronomy 12:23), with purity and sanctity (Exodus 29:10–21, Leviticus 8:15, 23–30; Hebrews 9), but also with death and pollution (Exodus 7:14–24; 1 Chronicles 22:8; 28:3; Hosea 9:4; Revelation 8:9; 16:3–4). All of these meanings are present in the passover and in the last supper.

Wine was also viewed with a great deal of ambivalence. On the one hand it was a gift from God, a sign of richness and plenty (Genesis 27:28; Psalms 104:15; Isaiah 55:1; Hosea 2:8–9, 22; Amos 9:13–14; John 2:1–11; 1 Timothy 5:23). On the other hand, there was danger in its abuse (Genesis 9:21–27; Proverbs 23:30–35; Isaiah 28:1–9; Ephesians 5:18; 1 Timothy 3:3, 8; 1 Peter 4:3). Wine represented both God's cup of salvation and his deadly cup of wrath. It was symbolic of the Jews, faithful and faithless, but also of the heathen gentiles; drunkenness was associated with lack of understanding and idolatry (Isaiah 29:9–11; Jeremiah 13:12–14; Hosea 4:11–12, 17–18). Jesus drank wine, but John the Baptist did not. Priests were forbidden to drink wine during their period of service (Leviticus 10:8–9; Ezekiel 44:21). The Mishnah reflects this ambivalance toward wine by requiring at least four cups in the passover, but prohibiting extra cups between the third and fourth so as not to ruin the completion of the Hallel.

Blood and wine were appropriate for a ritual intended ambiguously to "reconcile . . . both [Jews and gentiles] to God in one body through the cross, thereby bringing the hostility to an end" (Ephesians 2:16). But they were too strong and too hard to manage in everyday life. They had to be transformed into substances that were literally more palatable if they were to be taken in, and at the same time more specifically related to the cultural differences in Christian congregations. While gentiles were brought up like babies on mother's milk, "the first principles of God's word" (Hebrews 5:12), Jews like Peter were re-educated in the dietary rules pertaining to solid food.

Peter's Vision

Peter is clearly established in early Christian writing as the antithesis of Paul, a literal-minded doubter who has trouble going from the letter of God's law to its spirit. According to Paul's letter to the Galatians, written about 55 C.E. (May and Metzger 1977:1410), Peter ate with the gentiles to whom he preached when they were all alone, but "drew back and separated himself" from their table when the Jews came for fear of the Jews' anger (Galatians 2:11–12). Paul had to criticize him: "If you, though a Jew, live like a Gentile and not like a Jew, how can you compel the Gentiles to live like Jews" (Galatians 2:14), and Nock (1938:110) doubts that the two were ever reconciled, for had Peter conceded the justice of Paul's position, Paul would have said so.

The evangelists may have been influenced by this tradition, for they describe Peter repeatedly as a man of little faith. Peter, for example, does not understand that "not what goes into the mouth defiles a man, but what comes out of the mouth, this defiles a man" (Matthew 5:11, 15). He fails to recognize that forgiveness cannot be calculated (Matthew 18:21–22). He falls asleep three times while waiting for Jesus to finish praying in the garden of Gethsemane. He is still "taking his ease" when the hour of betrayal comes (Matthew 26:40–46; Mark 14:37–42). And he denies Jesus three times before the night is out, exactly as Jesus predicts he will, despite his protest, "If I must die with you, I will not deny you" (Mark 14:31, 66–72; see also Matthew 26:33–35, 69–75; Luke 22:32–34, 54–61; John 13:28, 18:17–18, 25–27).

For Peter, the meaning of Christ's passover must be spelled out in concrete and unmistakable terms. While he was preaching the gospel in Joppa, he stayed in the house of a tanner (a member of one of the despised trades), where he received a vision:

> Peter went up on the housetop to pray, about the sixth hour [about noon]. And he became hungry and desired something to eat; but while they were preparing it, he fell into a trance and saw the heaven opened, and something descending, like a great sheet, let down by four corners upon the earth. In it were all kinds of animals and reptiles and birds of the air. And there came a voice to him, "Rise, Peter; kill and eat." But Peter said, "No, Lord; for I have never eaten anything that is common or unclean." And the voice came to him again a second time, "What God has cleansed, you must not

call common." This happened three times, and the thing was taken up at once to heaven. [Acts 10:9–16]

"O men of little faith . . . do not seek what you are to eat and what you are to drink, nor be of anxious mind," says Luke's Jesus (Luke 12:29). But Peter is "inwardly perplexed as to what [this] vision . . . might mean" (Acts 10:17). Just then he is called by men from Caesarea. Cornelius, a Roman centurion converted to Judaism, who is stationed in Caesarea, has had a vision of an angel who told him to seek out a man named Peter in Joppa. The Spirit tells Peter to stop doubting and go with the men immediately because he has sent them (19–20). So Peter accompanies the gentiles to Caesarea and finds a crowd waiting for him that includes Cornelius' kinsmen and close friends, presumably also gentile proselytes. He explains his vision to the crowd in terms of the dietary rules. God has ordained a new dietary law for the purpose of establishing a different kind of community:

> You yourselves know how unlawful it is for a Jew to associate with or to visit any one of another nation; but God has shown me that I should not call any man common or unclean. So when I was sent for, I came without objection. I ask then why you sent for me. [Acts 10:28–29]

When Peter learns that Cornelius too has received a vision, he responds: "Truly I perceive that God shows no partiality, but in every nation any one who fears him and does what is right is acceptable to him" (Acts 10:34). In going from Joppa to Caesarea, Peter has made the transition from the literal objects of Jesus' mission, the outcasts of Jewish society, to their allegorical counterparts, the gentiles. He begins to preach Jesus' "good news of peace," beginning with the baptism of John, but he has scarcely finished with the resurrection when the Holy Spirit comes down upon the whole crowd. Peter's Jewish companions are astonished that "the Holy Spirit had been poured out even on the Gentiles" (45). Seeing that they could not forbid water for baptizing people who had already received the Holy Spirit, Peter commands the gentiles to be baptized and accepts their invitation to remain with them for some days (47–48).

The story of Peter's vision is repeated in the next chapter of Acts (11), when Peter is called up by the Jews of Jerusalem to explain why he has been eating with gentiles: "Why did you go to uncircumcised men and eat with them?" (11:3). This time, Peter neither separates himself nor denies. He explains what happened, and they glorify God, saying, "Then to the Gentiles also God has granted repentance unto life" (18).

Peter's vision clearly echoes God's warning to Ezekiel about the unclean food the Israelites would face in the gentile lands to which he would drive them. In this case, however, the experience will be different. Peter must eat because Jews and gentiles are going to associate with one another. The circumstances of Peter's vision confirm it. They reproduce the last supper in a gentile context.

The transformation is announced by the odd time of the meal: Jews ordinarily ate in the early morning and in the afternoon; only gentiles, the Romans, ate at midday (Harvey 1970: 437). It is confirmed by the people and the place. Peter is led to Caesarea, where he reveals the salvation of the gentiles, as the disciples were led to the room where they celebrated the last supper (Luke 22:10–11; see also Matthew 26:18; Mark 14:13–14). But unlike the man with the water jar, Peter's guides are gentiles. Luke emphasizes that Cornelius is not only "a devout man who feared God with all his household, gave alms liberally to the people and prayed constantly to God," but also "well-spoken of by the whole Jewish nation" (Acts 10:2, 22). Nevertheless, he is still a God-fearer. He has not been circumcised and made native-born. Furthermore, like the first gentile proselyte Jesus encountered in the gospels, he is a Roman soldier, a member of the occupying army.

In contrast to Jerusalem, the political and religious center of Judaism, Caesarea was one of the most important gentile communities in Palestine, a center of Roman government and the imperial cult. Herod the Great, who named it after the emperor Caesar Augustus, had transformed it from a small seaside town into the most important port on the coast of Palestine. Unlike Herod's other major city, Sebaste, which was primarily a fortress, Caesarea was "first and foremost a center of Hellenization" (Smallwood 1976:78). It was a model *polis,* laid out on a Roman grid pattern with a theater, amphitheater, and hippodrome. Herod also built a temple to the imperial cult, including two colossal statues of Augustus and Roma, on a hill overlooking the harbor (ibid.:79). When the territory came under direct Roman rule in 6 C.E., the city was made the administrative capital of all Judea and the headquarters of the occupying army. Kee (1977:68) suggests that only the most Hellenized Jews would have lived in Caesarea. Nevertheless, it was the slaughter and expulsion of Jews by gentiles in Caesarea that led to the outbreak of the first Jewish War against the Romans (Smallwood 1976:284–92, 295, 357–58).

Peter's vision, which Luke probably composed between 70 and 90 C.E., is a kind of prayer for an end to the hostility. It came to Peter, while he was praying, in the form of a meal that required nothing less than sacrifice. Everything Paul and the evangelists have told us about Peter makes it clear that he is sacrificing a vital part of himself by giving up the dietary rules in order to achieve union with the gentiles. In breaking the law that hallows him, he is a martyr for the faith exactly as Eleazar or Hannah and her seven sons were to the Maccabees, but in exactly the opposite way and for the opposite reasons.

Peter's vision is another way of stating the sacrifice involved in eating the Lord's supper, suited to a person who could not stomach the blood. It may actually be a version of the prayer that Jesus spoke together with his disciples at the last supper. If Nock (1964:54–55) is right in arguing that the Teaching of the Twelve Apostles, a pseudepigraphic work probably written no later than 100 C.E., contains the earliest known form of that prayer, then it was "no more than an elaboration of the traditional Jewish prayer that God would lift a basket to gather the scattered members of the nation of Israel from the four ends of the earth into their own land" (see Deuteronomy 30:3–4; Psalms 147:2; Isaiah 65:9–10; Jeremiah 23:3, 32:37; Ezekiel 28:5, 34:13, 36:24, 37:21–22).

Jews prayed daily in the synagogue for God to save them in the future as he had in the past by gathering in the scattered members of Israel. It was the tenth of the Eighteen Benedictions (Jeremias 1958:64). Peter's vision states that the ingathering has occurred, exactly as Jesus too predicted it would. God has sent "his angels and gather[ed] his elect from the four winds, from the ends of the earth to the ends of heaven" (Mark 13:27; see also Matthew 8:10–11; Luke 13:29).

In scripture, all the animals belong to the same category. In Ezekiel, for example, it is all God's sheep that he "bring[s] . . . out from the peoples and gather[s] . . . from the countries" to lead home to feed on the fat pastures of Israel (Ezekiel 34:11–16). Wild beasts will be banished from the land by virtue of his covenant:

> [The sheep] shall no more be a prey to the nations, nor shall the beasts of the land devour them; they shall dwell securely, and none shall make them afraid. [Ezekiel 34:25, 28]

The collection in Peter's cosmic sheet is very different, as he discovered by "looking at it closely" (Acts 11:6). The sheet contains "all kinds of animals and reptiles and birds of the air" (10:12), even "beasts of prey" (11:6). The tame beasts are not in the company of wild ones for lack of a shepherd (Ezekiel 34:5, 8), nor are they blind, dumb, and unaware (Isaiah 65:11–12). They are there because God put them there.

Peter's vision brings the world back to the creation that God established after he washed away the first one. Before God singled out Abraham for his faith as the founder of his chosen people, he had taken mercy on Noah because of his faith and spared him from the flood to make him the progenitor of all mankind (Genesis 9:12–17):

> By faith Noah, being warned by God concerning events as yet unseen, took heed and constructed an ark for the saving of his household; by this he condemned the world and became an heir of the righteousness which comes by faith. [Hebrews 11:7; see also Matthew 24:37; Luke 17:26; 1 Peter 3: 20–21; 2 Peter 2:4–5]

In Noah, Jews and gentiles had a common lineage. The text of Genesis clearly states that the diversity of the world is nevertheless established in unity: all the people in the world stem from one man, Noah. And when Paul says that God "made from one every nation of men to live on all the face of the earth . . . that they should seek God" (Acts 17:26–27), the context of his statement indicates that he too is concerned with Noah, not Adam (Daniélou 1965:83).

With Noah, God established an "everlasting covenant" between himself and "every living creature of all flesh that is upon the earth" (Genesis 9:16), with all the descendants of

Noah and with every living creature with him, "the birds, the cattle, and every beast of the earth . . . as many as came out of the ark . . . for all future generations" (9:9–10, 12). Noah, told to admit everything into the ark, the clean and the unclean, to ensure that life would continue on earth (6:19–20; 7:1–3), was also instructed in the words of the covenant to eat all things except blood:

> And God blessed Noah and his sons, and said to them, "Be fruitful and multiply, and fill the earth. The fear of you and the dread of you shall be upon every beast of the earth, and upon every bird of the air, upon every thing that creeps on the ground and all the fish of the sea; into your hand they are delivered. Every moving thing that lives shall be food for you; and as I gave you the green plants, I give you everything. Only you shall not eat flesh with its life, that is, its blood.
> [Genesis 9:1–4]

Jesus' sacrifice rescinds even this last restriction on food. Unfettered feeding does not mean submission to the basest human passions, but submission to the grace of God, as opposed to the exertion of the human will in accordance with the regulations—"Do not handle, do not taste, do not touch" (Colossians 2:21)—with which human beings vainly hope to compel God's grace. As the letter to the Hebrews points out, "it is well that the heart be strengthened by grace, not by foods, which have not benefited their adherents" (13:9; see also 9:10; Romans 16:18; Colossians 2:16–17; Philippians 3:19).

To eat all kinds of animals, clean and unclean indiscriminately, is to fulfill the terms of the new law to love all kinds of human beings equally, Jews and gentiles. The diet that serves union rather than separation must be interpreted flexibly to accommodate a diverse population. As Paul says, turning the Corinthians' evasions to his own end, " 'All things are lawful for me,' but not all things are helpful" (1 Corinthians 6:12):

> Food will not commend us to God. . . . We are no worse off if we do not eat, and no better off if we do. Only take care lest this liberty of yours somehow become a stumbling block to the weak. . . . Therefore, if food is a cause of my brother's falling, I will never eat meat, lest I cause my brother to fall.
> [1 Corinthians 8:8–9, 13; see also Romans 14:13–23]

The Folly of the Gospel

From Caesarea to Antioch

Once Peter's vision is verified, the scene shifts from Caesarea to Antioch, beyond the borders of Judea, Samaria, and Galilee, fully outside Jewish territory, where the disciples are called Christians for the first time (Acts 11:22–26). Antioch had one of the largest populations of Jews in Syria and one of the largest in the diaspora, comparable to the Jewish populations of Alexandria and Rome. Having survived the attacks on it following the revolt of 70 C.E., the community was still flourishing, receiving visits from prominent rabbis both before and after 135 C.E. (Smallwood 1976:508).

Smallwood (1976:508) suggests that the prevalence of gentile proselytes there in the first century may have made the city particularly receptive to Christianity. This is also the opinion of Baron, one of the few scholars to have studied the relationship between Christianity and Judaism during the critical years in which Christianity first started to expand out of Palestine. Baron describes Christianity as "Hellenistic Jewry's new religion" (1952, 2:162–69). He argues that this sect of Judaism was established in the Jewish communities of the diaspora before it came to dominate the empire. Where Jewish groups had made no effort to proselytize or where their efforts had not succeeded, Christianity did not succeed either. Christianity benefited not only from Jewish scripture and other writings, from Jewish methods of interpretation, and from Jewish apologetics, but also from the institutional organization of the synagogues (Gager 1975:126–29, 135–40).

This was not the case in Palestine or Babylonia. If Christians had restricted their redefinition of Israel to the nation, perhaps they might have achieved some sort of accommodation with the Pharisees, who emerged from the wars as the precursors of rabbinic Judaism. I think by insisting on the division of the family, they broke with the Pharisees irrevocably. Even before the first Jewish revolt, the Pharisees had shifted their focus from the temple to the home. The events of the wars, including the destruction of the temple and of monastic communities like the Essenes and guerrilla groups like the Zealots and Sicarii, only strengthened their position.

The subsequent histories of these different kinds of Judaism may be explained in part by the different political and economic possibilities inherent in a monotheism based on kinship and a monotheism based on "love."[2] They were separated officially the year after Constantine became emperor and established Christianity as his state religion. In 325 C.E., he held the Council of Nicaea, and announced that Easter, the holy feast with which Christians celebrated their salvation annually, should be kept "by all and in every place on one and the same day," a different day from Passover according to the calendar of the Jews (Eusebius, *Life of Constantine,* 3:18).

2. See Feeley-Harnik (1980) for an anthropologist's perspective on the relations of hierarchy and authority associated with "love" in the nascent Christian church.

7

CONCLUSION

Good things poured out upon a mouth
that is closed are like offerings of food
placed upon a grave.

Sirach 30:18

I started this essay by asking why Christians of the first century
C.E., then Jewish sectarians, chose to symbolize their beliefs with
a meal in which they ate their master's flesh and blood; why
Christ himself was both exalted and condemned as a glutton and
a drunkard.

The solution, I argued, must be sought in the larger context,
in the dietary rules of Judaic law, recognizing that the law was
not the monolithic creation of archetypical Israelites, but an
ever-changing product of history, subject to bitterly disputed
differences in interpretation. The only constants were the questions the law was intended to answer: what is Judaism, what is
Jewish, who is a Jew?

The evidence suggests that food had long been one of the
most important languages in which Jews expressed the relationships among human beings and God that these questions implied. Food was identified with God's word as the foundation of
the covenant relationship in scripture and in sectarianism. During the inter-Testamental period, as God's word became increasingly identified with the law, food law came to represent the
whole law. Sectarianism was expressed above all through differ-
ing interpretations of the dietary rules. Violation of the dietary
rules became equivalent to apostasy.

Christians of the first century C.E., as observant Jews, used the language of food to establish both the legitimacy of Jesus and the novelty of his interpretation of the law, which required different kinds of relations among human beings and God from those advocated by other sectarians. The last supper, representing Christ's crucifixion and resurrection, was a reinterpretation of many different kinds of covenants in scripture, but it focused primarily on the passover. By conforming closely to the overall pattern of the passover, yet inverting every critical element, it transformed the meaning of the meal and the sacrifice on which it was based. Jesus' passover, like his gluttony, was a rejection of familial and national separatism. His new covenant included all humanity. Peter's vision is one striking example of the way in which early Christians translated their interpretation of the law into still different meals in order to communicate it to every member of their diverse community.

My argument is essentially linguistic. After establishing that food is the language, I attempt to analyze the meaning of the language and some of the ways in which it has been manipulated and transformed in the course of social relations over time. Nevertheless, this is only a partial solution to the problem with which I began. Questions still remain: Just why was food the language? Why did Jews consider this medium to be ideally suited to the messages concerning God and his creation that they wished to convey, while condemning other forms of imagery as idolatry? I would like to conclude by suggesting some areas for further research.

One might focus more closely on the relationships among the media considered to be acceptable representations of God's wisdom: speech, scripture, law, and the language of food into which they might all be translated at different times for different purposes. All of them bridge the gap between God and his creation in different ways. All of them have different properties, and different rules seem to have governed their use.

Food seems to have been regarded as the most accessible, the best way of introducing ordinary mortals to the ineffable wisdom of God, and perhaps also the best way of transcending the babel of tongues in which early Christians found themselves. Not only was it forbidden to utter the divine name, but there were other aspects of God's wisdom that could not be spoken in ordinary language, especially to outsiders. Philo explains the failure of the Jews to repond to Gaius's badgering by saying: "Silence too may in a way serve as a defense, particularly to us who could not answer any of the points which he was investigating and wished to press, because our customs and laws muzzled the tongue and closed and stitched up the mouth" (*Embassy to Gaius,* 360).

Essene texts on separation from outsiders express a similar philosophy: "Let no member of the Community answer their questions concerning any law or ordinance; and let him neither eat nor drink anything of theirs" (Dupont-Sommers 1961:84). Jesus repeatedly emphasizes the difficulty of explaining his gospel in words, and indeed, most of the time his disciples do not understand what he is saying until he finally speaks to them in food. Only Josephus, in the most apologetic of his writings, suggests that "should anyone of our nation be questioned about the laws, he would repeat them all more readily than his own name" (*Against Apion,* 2:178). However his purpose here is to argue that it is precisely because the Jewish legislator "did not leave practical training in morals inarticulate . . . [but] start[ed] from the very beginning with the food of which we partake from infancy and the private life [or diet] of the home" that accounts for "our thorough grounding in the laws from the first dawn of intelligence . . . that we have them, as it were, engraven on our souls" (ibid.: 173, 178).

Food, as opposed to either scripture or graven images, could be eaten. Douglas (1966b) suggests that substances like food, which pass back and forth across the body's boundaries, are well suited to expressing ideas having to do with more abstract boundaries. It is worth remembering, however, that Israel's boundaries were ecological as well as social and political. The desert that surrounded the Promised Land was not only a symbol of desolation and chaos, but a reality, a source of death as well as new life. Rainfall in Palestine was marginal and irregular. There was drought lasting some four months in summer, bordered by periods of a couple of months between April and June and September and November in which either ferocious cyclones or the hot, dry, dusty wind of the *sirocco* blew in from the deserts, destroying vegetation (Baly 1974:43–68). The rains might also fail in winter. Since surface water was scarce, prolonged droughts such as those described in I Kings (17:1) could make whole areas of Palestine almost uninhabitable (ibid.:69–76).

Famine caused by drought is a recurrent theme in scripture (Genesis 12:10, 26:1, 41:54, 43:1; 2 Samuel 21:1, 1 Kings 18:2–5; 2 Kings 4:38, 8:1; Jeremiah 14:2–6, 17:8; Acts 11:28). But famine might also be caused by other natural disasters (Deuteronomy 28:22, 1 Kings 8:37; Joel 1:1–2:27; Amos 4:6–10) and by war (2 Kings 6:24–29, 7:4, 25:2–3; Isaiah 1:7, 3:1; Lamentations 4:8–10). Food was intimately associated with international relations, being one of the primary constituents of trade (1 Kings 5:9–11; Ezra 3:7; Ezekiel 27:17; Acts 12:20). In time of need people traded for food not only their treasures (Lamentations 1:11), but also their sons and daughters (Nehemiah 5:1–5).

All of these ecological and economic aspects of food were tied closely to the theology of Judaism, not only in the sense that natural as well as political disasters were attributed to God's wisdom, but also in the sense that every one of the prophets, including Jesus himself, pleaded for the rights of the literally as well as the spiritually hungry. A complete theory of the dietary rules must ultimately restore the spirit to the flesh.

BIBLIOGRAPHY

Alter, R. 1978. Character in the Bible. *Commentary* 66:58–65.
———. 1979. A new theory of *kashrut. Commentary* 68:46–52.
Andriolo, K. R. 1973. A structural analysis of genealogy and worldview in the Old Testament. *American Anthropologist* 75:1657–69.
Arnott, M. L., ed. 1976. *Gastronomy: The anthropology of food and food habits.* Chicago: Aldine.

Baly, D. 1974. *The geography of the Bible.* Rev. ed. New York: Harper and Row.
Baron, S. W. 1952. *A social and religious history of the Jews.* 2d ed., rev. and enlarged. 16 vols. New York: Columbia University Press.
Barthes, R.; Bovon, F.; Leenhardt, F.-J.; Martin-Achard, R.; and Starobinski, H. 1971. *Analyse structurale et exégèse biblique: Essais d'interpretation.* Neuchâtel: Delachaux and Niestlé.
Bauer, W. 1971. *Orthodoxy and heresy in earliest Christianity.* 2d ed. Philadelphia: Fortress. (Orig. 1934.)
Beidelman, T. O. 1963. A Kaguru version of the sons of Noah: A study in the inculcation of the idea of racial superiority. *Cahiers d'études africaines* 12:474–90.
———. 1974. *William Robertson Smith and the sociological study of religion.* Chicago: University of Chicago Press.
Black, M. 1961. *The Scrolls and Christian origins.* New York: Scribner.
Blackman, P., ed. and trans. 1951–56. *Mishnayoth.* 7 vols. London: Mishnah.
Blau, E. 1974. A new Haggadah will be used by Reform Jews on Passover. *New York Times,* 23 March, p. B1.
Bloch, R. 1955. Écriture et tradition dans le judaïsme—Aperçus sur l'origine du midrash. *Cahiers Sioniens* 8:9–34.
———. 1957. Midrash. *Dictionnaire de la Bible, supplement V,* pp. 1263–81. Paris: Letouzey et Ané.
Bourdillon, M. F. C. 1977. Oracles and politics in ancient Israel. *Man,* n.s. 12:124–40.

Bourdillon, M. F. C., and Fortes M., eds. 1980. *Sacrifice.* New York: Academic.

Bowman, J. 1965. *The Gospel of Mark: The new Christian Jewish Passover Haggadah.* Leiden: Brill.

Box, H., ed. and trans. 1939. *Philonis Alexandrini In Flaccum.* London: Oxford University Press.

Briggs, K. A. 1979. U.S. Reform Jews to challenge Israeli religious policy. *New York Times,* 12 December, p. A5.

Bulmer, R. 1967. Why is the cassowary not a bird? A problem of zoological taxonomy among the Karam of the New Guinea Highlands. *Man,* n.s. 2:5–25.

Bultman, R. 1972. *The history of the synoptic tradition.* Rev. ed. Oxford: Blackwell.

Buttrick, G. A., ed. 1962. *The interpreter's dictionary of the Bible.* 4 vols. New York: Abingdon.

Campenhausen, H. von. 1972. *The formation of the Christian Bible.* Philadelphia: Fortress.

Carroll, M. P. 1977. Leach, Genesis, and structural analysis: A critical evaluation. *American Ethnologist* 4:663–77.

Charles, R. H., ed. 1913. *The Apocrypha and Pseudepigrapha of the Old Testament.* 2 vols. Oxford: Oxford University Press.

Charlesworth, J. H. 1971. Renaissance of pseudepigrapha studies. *Journal for the Study of Judaism* 2:107–14

———, ed. 1972. *John and Qumran.* London: G. Chapman.

———, ed. and trans. 1973. *The Odes of Solomon.* Oxford: Clarendon.

Cleaver, E. 1968. *Soul on ice.* New York: Dell.

Couratin, A. H. 1969. The liturgy. In J. Daniélou, A. H. Couratin, and J. Kent, eds., *The Pelican guide to modern theology, 2: historical theology,* pp. 131–240. Baltimore, Md.: Helicon.

Crossan, J. D. 1976. Empty tomb and absent Lord. In Kelber, 1976b: 135–52.

Danby, H., ed. and trans. 1933. *The Mishnah.* Oxford: Clarendon Press.

Daniel, J. L. 1979. Anti-Semitism in the Hellenistic-Roman period. *Journal of Biblical Literature* 98:45–65.

Daniélou, J. 1965. *In the Beginning . . . Genesis I–III.* Baltimore, Md.: Helicon.

Daube, D. 1971. Pauline contributions to a pluralistic culture: re-creation and beyond. In D. G. Miller and D. Y. Hadidian, eds., *Jesus and man's hope,* 2:223–45. Pittsburgh: Pittsburgh Theological Seminary.

Davies, D. 1977. An interpretation of sacrifice in Leviticus. *Zeitschrift für die Alttestamentlichen Wissenschaft* 89:387–99.

Derrett, J. D. M. 1970. *Law in the New Testament.* London: Darton, Longman and Todd.

————. 1971. Virgin birth in the gospels. *Man,* 6:289–93.

————. 1973. Religious hair. *Man,* n.s. 8:100–103.

————. 1977. *Studies in the New Testament.* Leiden: Brill.

————. 1979. Spirit-possession and the Gerasene demoniac. *Man,* n.s. 14:286–93.

Donahue, J.R. 1976. Introduction: From passion traditions to passion narrative. In Kelber 1976b:pp. 1–20.

Douglas, M. 1957. Animals in Lele religious symbolism. *Africa* 27:46–58.

————. 1966a. The abominations of Leviticus. In *Purity and danger: An analysis of concepts of pollution and taboo,* pp. 41–57.

————. 1966b. *Purity and danger: An analysis of concepts of pollution and taboo.* London: Routledge and Kegan Paul.

————. 1971. Deciphering a meal. In C. Geertz, ed., *Myth, symbol and culture,* pp. 61–81. New York: Norton.

————. 1973. Critique and commentary. In Neusner 1973a:137–42.

Dresner, S. H. 1966. *The Jewish dietary laws: Their meaning for our time.* New York: Burning Bush.

Drury, J. 1977. *Tradition and design in Luke's gospel: A study in early Christian historiography.* Atlanta: John Knox.

Dumont, L. 1970. *Homo hierarchicus: An essay on the caste system.* Chicago: University of Chicago Press.

Dupont-Sommer, A. 1961. *The Essene writings from Qumran.* Oxford: Blackwell.

Ellis, E. E. 1957. *Paul's use of the Old Testament.* Edinburgh: Oliver and Boyd.

Encyclopaedia Judaica. 1972. 16 vol. New York: Macmillan

Epstein, I., ed. and trans. 1935–52. *The Babylonian Talmud.* 18 vols. London: Soncino.

Eusebius Pamphilus, Bishop of Caesarea. 1845. *The life of the blessed Emperor Constantine, in four books, from 306 to 337 A.D.* London: Samuel Bagster and Sons.

Falk, Z. W. 1974. Jewish private law. In Safrai and Stern 1974:504–34.

Feeley-Harnik, G. 1980. Hierarchy and authority in the community of love: The case of the runaway slave. Plenary address, Centennial Meeting of the Society of Biblical Literature. To be published in a collection of the plenary papers by Scholars Press, Chico, California.

Feldman, L. H. 1975. Masada: A critique of recent scholarship. In Neusner 1975, 3:218–48.

Firth, R. 1973. Food symbolism in a pre-industrial society. In *Symbols, public and private,* pp. 243–61. Ithaca: Cornell University Press.

Frazer, J. 1918. *Folk-lore in the Old Testament: Studies in comparative religion, legend and law.* 3 vols. London: Macmillan.

Gager, J. 1974. The gospels and Jesus: Some doubts about method. *Journal of Religion* 54:244–72.

———. 1975. *Kingdom and community: The social world of early Christianity.* Englewood Cliffs, N.J.: Prentice-Hall.

Geertz, C. 1968. *Islam observed: Religious development in Morocco and Indonesia.* New Haven: Yale University Press.

Ginzberg, L. 1909–39. *The legends of the Jews.* 7 vols. Philadelphia: Jewish Publication Society of America.

Glatzer, N. N., ed. 1979. *The Passover Haggadah, with English translation, introduction and commentary.* 3d ed. New York: Schocken.

Goldman, A. D. 1979. Behind the fight of Hasidic sects in Williamsburg. *New York Times,* 30 October, pp. B1, B7.

Goldstein, J. A. 1975. The tales of the Tobiads. In Neusner ed., 1975, 3:85–123.

Goodenough, E. R. 1953–68. *Jewish symbols in the Greco-Roman period.* 13 vols. New York: Pantheon.

Gottwald, N. K. 1979. *The tribes of Yahweh: A sociology of the religion of liberated Israel, 1250–1050 B.C.E.* Maryknoll, N.Y.: Orbis.

Goulder, M. D. 1974. *Midrash and lection in Matthew.* London: SPCK.

Grabar, A. 1968. *Christian iconography: A study of its origins.* London: Routledge and Kegan Paul.

Grant, M. 1973. *The Jews in the Roman world.* New York: Scribner.

Greenewalt, C. H., Jr. 1977. *Ritual dinners in early historic Sardis.* Berkeley: University of California Press.

Hahn, H. F. 1966. *The Old Testament in modern research.* 2d ed. Philadelphia: Fortress.

Harrington, D. J. 1980. Sociological concepts and the early church: A decade of research. *Theological Studies* 41:181–90.

Harris, G. 1978. *Casting out anger.* Cambridge: Cambridge University Press.

Harris, M. 1974a. Pig lovers and pig haters. In *Cows, pigs, wars and witches: The riddles of culture,* pp. 35–57. New York: Random House.

———. 1974b. The secret of the Prince of Peace. In *Cows, pigs, wars and witches: The riddles of culture,* pp. 179–203. New York: Random House.

Harvey, A. E. 1970. *The new English Bible companion to the New Testament.* London: Oxford University Press.

Hengel, M. 1974. *Judaism and Hellenism: Studies in their encounter in Palestine during the early Hellenistic period.* 2 vols. Philadelphia: Fortress.

Hubert, H. and M. Mauss. 1899. Essai sur la nature et la fonction sociale du sacrifice. *L'Année Sociologique* 2:29–138.

Bibliography

Isenberg, S. R. 1975. Power through Temple and Torah in
Greco-Roman Palestine. In Neusner 1975, 2:24–52.
Isenberg, S. R. and Owen, D. E. 1977. Bodies, natural and contrived:
The work of Mary Douglas. *Religious Studies Review* 3:1–17.

Jeremias, J. 1958. *Jesus' promise to the nations.* Naperville, Ill.: A. R.
Allenson.
———. 1963. *The parables of Jesus.* Rev. ed. New York: Scribner.
———. 1966. *The eucharistic words of Jesus*. New York: Scribner.
———. 1969. *Jerusalem in the time of Jesus: An investigation into
economic and social conditions during the New Testament
time.* 3d ed., with author's revisions to 1967. Philadelphia:
Fortress.
Josephus, Flavius. 1926–65. *Josephus.* Translated by H. St. J.
Thackeray and R. Marcus. 9 vols. London: Heinemann.

Kee, H. C. 1977. *Community of the new age: Studies in Mark's gospel.*
Philadelphia: Westminster.
———. 1980. *Christian origins in sociological* perspective.
Philadelphia: Westminster.
Kelber, W. H. 1976a. Conclusion: from passion narrative to gospel. In
The passion in Mark: Studies on Mark 14–16, pp. 153–80.
———, ed. 1976b. *The passion in Mark: Studies on Mark 14–16.*
Philadelphia: Fortress.
Keyser, J. M. B. 1975. Keeping Solomon legitimate. *Archives
Européenes de Sociologie* 16:134–47.
Knox, W. L. 1944. *Some Hellenistic elements in primitive
Christianity.* London: Oxford University Press.
Koch, K. 1972. *The rediscovery of the apocalyptic: A polemical work
on a neglected area of biblical studies and its damaging effects
on theology and philosophy.* London: SCM.
Koester, H. 1971a. One Jesus and four primitive gospels. In Robinson
and Koester 1971:158–204.
———. 1971b. The structure and criteria of early Christian beliefs. In
Robinson and Koester 1971:205–31.
Kraft, J. 1979. Letter from Israel. *The New Yorker,* 12 February, pp.
93–108.
Kraft, R. A. 1970. Jewish Greek scriptures and related topics: Reports
on recent discussions. *New Testament Studies* 16:384–96.
———. 1975. The multiform Jewish heritage of early Christianity. In
Neusner 1975, 3:174–99.
Kümmel, W. G. 1975. *Introduction to the New Testament.* 17th ed.
Nashville: Abingdon.

Leach, E. 1961. Lévi-Strauss in the garden of Eden: An examination
of some recent developments in the analysis of myth.

Transactions of the New York Academy of Sciences, ser. 2, 23:386–96.

———. 1962. Genesis as myth. *Discovery* 23:30–35. Reprinted in Leach 1969:7–23.

———. 1964. Anthropological aspects of language: Animal categories and verbal abuse. In E. H. Lenneberg, ed., *New directions in the study of language,* pp. 23–63. Cambridge, Mass.: M.I.T.

———. 1966. The legitimacy of Solomon. *European Journal of Sociology* 7:58–101. Reprinted in Leach 1969:25–83.

———. 1967. Virgin birth. *Proceedings of the Royal Anthropological Institute for 1966,* pp. 39–49. Reprinted in Leach 1969:85–112.

———. 1969. *Genesis as myth and other essays.* London: J. Cape.

———. 1973a. Solomon's succession. Man, n.s. 8:303–4.

———. 1973b. Melchisedech and the emperor: Icons of subversion and orthodoxy. *Proceedings of the Royal Anthropological Society for 1972:*5–14.

Leaney, A. R. C. 1977. The Roman era (sections 1–6). In J. H. Hayes and J. M. Miller, eds., *Israelite and Judaean history,* pp. 605–63. Philadelphia: Westminster Press.

Lévi-Strauss, C. 1962. *Le totémisme aujourd-hui.* Paris: Presses Universitaires de France.

———. 1964–71. *Mythologiques.* 4 vols. Paris: Plon.

Lieberman, S. 1962. *Hellenism in Jewish Palestine: Studies in the literary transmission, beliefs and manners of Palestine in the first century B.C.E.–fourth century C.E.* 2d ed. New York: Jewish Theological Seminary of America.

Lietzmann, H. 1953–79. *Mass and Lord's Supper: A study in the history of the liturgy.* Leiden: Brill.

Lightstone, J. 1975. Sadducees *versus* Pharisees: The Tannaitic sources. In Neusner 1975, 3:206–17.

Lindars, B. 1961. *New Testament apologetic.* Philadelphia: Westminster.

Loewe, R. 1966. *The position of women in Judaism.* London: SPCK.

MacDonald, E.M. 1931. *The position of women as reflected in semitic codes of law.* Toronto: University of Toronto Press.

McKnight, D. 1973. Sexual symbolism of food among the Wik-Mungkan. *Man*, n.s. 8:194–209.

Malcolm X. 1965. The ballot or the bullet (speech given at Cory Methodist Church, Cleveland, Ohio, 3 April 1964). In G. Breitman, ed., *Malcolm X Speaks,* pp. 23–44. New York: Grove.

Malherbe, A. J. 1977. *Social aspects of early Christianity.* Baton Rouge: Louisiana State University Press.

Marshall, R. C. 1979. Heroes and Hebrews: The priest in the promised land. *American Ethnologist* 6:772–90.

May, H. G., and Metzger, B. M., eds. 1977. *The New Oxford annotated*

Bibliography

Bible with the Apocrypha. Revised Standard Version, containing a second edition of the New Testament and an expanded edition of the Apocrypha. New York: Oxford.

Meeks, W. A. 1972. The man from heaven in Johannine sectarianism. *Journal of Biblical Literature* 91:44–72.

———. 1975a. The social world of early Christianity. *Bulletin of the Council on the Study of Religion* 6:1, 4–5.

———. 1975b. "Am I a Jew?"—Johannine Christianity and Judaism. In J. Neusner, ed., *Christianity, Judaism and other Greco-Roman cults,* 1:163–85. Leiden: Brill.

Meeks, W., and Wilken, R., eds. 1978. *Jews and Christians in Antioch in the first four centuries of the common era.* Missoula, Mont.: Society of Biblical Literature.

Metzger, B. M., ed. 1977. *The Apocrypha.* In May and Metzger 1977:1–340 *Ap.*

Middleton, J. 1961. The comparative study of food habits. Mimeographed document no. 647. London: Tavistock Institute.

Neusner, J. 1971. *The rabbinic traditions about the Pharisees before 70.* 3 vols. Leiden: Brill.

———. 1973a. *The idea of purity in ancient Judaism.* The Haskell Lectures, 1972–73. Leiden: Brill.

———. 1973b. *Invitation to the Talmud: A teaching book.* New York: Harper and Row.

———. 1973c. *From politics to piety: The emergence of pharisaic Judaism.* Englewood Cliffs, N.J.: Prentice-Hall.

———. 1977. Judaism after the destruction of the temple. In J. H. Hayes and J. M. Miller, eds., *Israelite and Judaean history,* pp. 663–77. Philadelphia: Westminster.

———, ed. 1975. *Christianity, Judaism and other Greco-Roman cults: Studies for Morton Smith at sixty.* 4 vols. Leiden: Brill.

The new English Bible with the Apocrypha. 1970. New York: Oxford University Press and Cambridge University Press.

Newman, P. L. 1965. *Knowing the Gururumba.* New York: Holt, Rinehart and Winston.

New York Times. 1970. Jewish men hold "foodless banquet" as Pompidou dines. 3 March, p. 29.

Nock, A. D. 1938. *St. Paul.* New York: Harper and Row.

———. 1964. *Early gentile Christianity and its Hellenistic background.* New York: Harper and Row.

Ortner, S. B. 1978. *Sherpas through their rituals.* Cambridge: Cambridge University Press.

Pamment, M. 1972. The succession of Solomon: A reply to Edmund Leach's essay "The legitimacy of Solomon." *Man,* n.s. 7:635–43.

———. 1973. "Solomon's succession." *Man,* n.s. 8:635–36.

Panoff, E. 1970. Food and faeces: A Melanesian rite. *Man*, n.s. 5:237–52.

Parker, P. 1975. The kinship of John and Acts. In Neusner 1975, 1:187–205.

Pedersen, J. 1926, 1940. *Israel: Its life and culture*. 2 vols. London: G. Cumberlege, Oxford University Press.

Perrin, N. 1969. *What is redaction criticism?* Philadelphia: Fortress.

Philo Judaeus. 1929–62. *Philo*. Translated by F. H. Colson and G. H. Whitaker. 10 vols. London: Heinemann.

Pitt-Rivers, J. A. 1977. The fate of Shechem or the politics of sex. In *The fate of Shechem or the politics of sex: Essays in the anthropology of the Mediterranean*, pp. 126–71. Cambridge: Cambridge University Press.

Pocock, D. F. 1975. North and south in the book of Genesis. In J. Beattie and G. Lienhardt, eds., *Studies in social anthropology*, pp. 273–84. Oxford: Clarendon.

Rayner, J. D. 1968. *Liberal Judaism: Introduction*. London: Liberal Jewish Synagogue.

Richards, A. I. 1932. *Hunger and work in a savage tribe: A functional study of nutrition among the southern Bantu*. London: Routledge.

———. 1939. *Land, labour and diet in Northern Rhodesia: An economic study of the Bemba tribe*. London: Oxford University Press for the International African Institute.

Richardson, A. 1962. *A theological word book of the Bible*. New York: Macmillan.

Robbins, V. K. 1976. Last meal: preparation, betrayal and absence (Mark 14:12–25). In Kelber 1976b:21–40.

Robinson, J. M., and Koester, H., eds. 1971. *Trajectories through early Christianity*. Philadelphia: Fortress.

Rogerson, J. W. 1978. *Anthropology and the Old Testament*. Oxford: Blackwell.

Rost, L. 1976. *Judaism outside the Hebrew canon: An introduction to the documents*. Nashville: Abingdon.

Safrai, S. and Stern, M., in cooperation with D. Flusser and W. C. van Unnik, eds. 1974. *The Jewish people in the first century: Historical geography, political history, social, cultural and religious life and institutions*. 2 vols. Assen: Van Gorcum.

Sandmel, S. 1978. *Judaism and Christian beginnings*. New York: Oxford University Press.

Schäfer, P. 1977. The Hellenistic and Maccabean Periods. In J. H. Hayes and J. M. Miller, eds., *Israelite and Judaean history*, pp. 539–604. Philadelphia: Westminster.

Schapera, I. 1955. The sin of Cain. *Journal of the Royal Anthropological Institute* 85:33–43.

Bibliography

Scroggs, R. 1980. The sociological interpretation of the New Testament: The present state of research. *New Testament Studies* 26:164–79.

Segal, J.B. 1963. *The Hebrew Passover from the earliest times to A.D. 70.* London: Oxford University Press.

Shenker, I. 1979. With them, it's always strictly kosher. *New York Times Magazine,* 15 April, pp. 32–42.

Siegel, S. 1966. *A guide to observance.* In Dresner 1966, pp. 55–68.

Simon, M. 1967. *Jewish sects at the time of Jesus.* Philadelphia: Fortress.

Smallwood, E. M. 1976. *The Jews under Roman rule: From Pompey to Diocletian.* Leiden: Brill.

Smith, C. W. F. 1948. *The Jesus of the parables.* Philadelphia: Fortress.

Smith, J. Z. 1975. The social description of early Christianity. *Religious Studies Review* 1:19–25.

———. 1978a. Too much kingdom, too little community. *Zygon* 13:123–30.

———. 1978b. *Map is not territory: Studies in the history of religions.* Leiden: Brill.

Smith, M. 1961. The Dead Sea sect in relation to ancient Judaism. *New Testament Studies* 7:347–60.

———. 1971a. *Palestinian parties and politics that shaped the Old Testament.* New York: Columbia University Press.

———. 1971b. Zealots and Sicarii, their origins and relation. *Harvard Theological Review* 64:1–19.

Smith, W. R. 1885. *Kinship and marriage in early Arabia.* Cambridge: Cambridge University Press.

———. 1889. *Lectures on the religion of the Semites: First series, the fundamental institutions.* Edinburgh: A. and C. Black.

Soler, J. 1973. Sémiotique de la nourriture dans la Bible. *Annales: Économies, Sociétés, Civilisations* 28:943–55. (A translation, The dietary prohibitions of the Hebrews, appears in R. Forster and O. Ranum, eds., 1979: *Food and drink in history: Selections from the Annales.* Johns Hopkins University Press.)

Stein, S. 1957. The dietary laws in rabbinic and patristic literature. In K. Aland and F. L. Cross, eds., *Studia Patristica,* 2: 141–54. Berlin: Akademie-Verlag.

Stone, M. E. 1973. Judaism at the time of Christ. *Scientific American* 228:80–87.

Talmon, S. 1977. The Samaritans. *Scientific American* 236:100–108.

Tambiah, S. J. 1969. Animals are good to think and good to prohibit. *Ethnology* 8:423–59.

Theissen, G. 1978. *Sociology of early Palestinian Christianity.* Philadelphia: Fortress.

Vecsey, G. 1978. Writings from the time of Jesus sought around world by scholars. *New York Times,* 4 February, p. 6.

Verdier, Y. 1966. Repas Bas-Normands. *L'Homme* 6:92–III.

Vermès, G. 1961. *Scripture and tradition in Judaism: Haggadic studies.* Leiden: Brill.

——. 1975. *The Dead Sea Scrolls in English.* 2d ed. New York: Penguin.

Weber, M. 1952. *Ancient Judaism.* New York: Free Press.

Weeden, T. J., Sr. 1976. The cross as power in weakness (Mark 15:20b–41). In Kelber 1976b: 115–34.

Werblowsky, R. J. Z. 1962. *Joseph Karo: Lawyer and mystic.* Oxford: Oxford University Press.

Widengren, G. 1977. The Persian Period. In J. H. Hayes and J. M. Miller, eds., *Israelite and Judaean history,* pp. 489–538. Philadelphia: Westminster.

Wijeyewardene, G. 1968. Address, abuse, and animal categories in northern Thailand. *Man,* n.s. 3:76–93.

Williamson, H. G. M. 1977. *Israel in the Books of Chronicles.* Cambridge: Cambridge University Press.

Wilson, R. R. 1977. *Genealogy and history in the biblical world.* New Haven: Yale University Press.

——. 1980. *Prophecy and society in ancient Israel.* Philadelphia: Fortress.

Winter, P., 1974. *On the trial of Jesus.* 2d ed., rev. Berlin: W. de Gruyter.

Worgul, G. S., Jr. 1979. Anthropological consciousness and biblical theory. *Biblical Theology Bulletin* 9:3–12.

Yalman, N. 1969. On the meaning of food offerings in Ceylon. In R. F. Spencer, ed., *Forms of symbolic action,* pp. 81–96. Seattle: University of Washington Press.

Young, M. W. 1971. *Fighting with food: Leadership, values, and social control in a Massim society.* Cambridge: Cambridge University Press.

INDEX

abominations of Leviticus. *See* food law

Abraham, 151, 161; and Isaac, 139–41

Acts, 49, 50, 58, 119, 134, 137; quoted, 44–45, 58, 134, 149, 157–58, 159, 161

Additions to Book of Esther, 102–3

afikoman, 123, 130, 149

am ha-arez, 41, 42, 43, 52, 94, 153

Amos, 33; quoted, 77, 78

anthropology: of food, 6–18; of religion, 2–6, 19–20

Apocrypha, 20n, 22, 31, 59n, 96

assimilationists, 35, 40

Baptists, 94

Baruch, 39

Bel and the Dragon, 102

bitter herbs, 122–23, 124, 126, 129, 144

blood, 19, 64–65, 66, 73, 87, 89, 145, 160, 162; ambiguity of, 155–56; of the covenant, 113

bread: in Jesus' passover, 112, 144; at kiddush ceremony, 115; at passover, 63, 82, 83, 121, 122, 124, 125–26, 129, 135; of the Presence, 88, 126. *See also* Jesus, as bread; manna

Bronstein, Herbert, 62–63, 116

calendar: of Christians, 119–20, 164; and sectarianism, 92, 119–20

Caro, Joseph, 84n, 123

Christian iconography, 56, 59

Christianity, 24, 33, 36, 164; calendar of, 119–20, 164; diversity of, 21, 36, 48, 49, 59, 154, 166; and innovation, 18–19, 56–57, 71, 119–20, 166; and language of food, 2, 19, 166 (*see also* last supper); as sect of Judaism, 1, 18, 21, 51, 55, 59, 163, 164, 165. *See also* Jesus

Christians: gluttony of, 19, 107–8; as true Jews, 19, 49, 59

Chronicles, 24, 40–41, 47, 137

clean and unclean food. *See* food law, Jewish

Cleaver, Eldridge, 12–13

cloak, as symbol of cosmos, 58, 132–33

Colossians, letter to, 54; quoted, 44, 85, 144, 149, 162

commensalism, 11–12, 57, 157; and covenant, 85–91, 113; and definition of social groups, 10–12, 86, 87, 89; of Jesus, 57, 69–70, 76, 90; between Jews and gentiles, 43, 44–45, 46, 97–99; and sectarianism, 41, 91–96, 167

Corinthians, 128, 154; letter to, 48, 59, 119, 128–29; quoted, 33n,

Index

genealogy, 40–41, 42, 46, 48, 150–51
Genesis, 9, 161; quoted, 73, 86–87, 140, 161–62
Genesis Apocryphon, 41
gentiles: attitude of, to food law, 18, 99–101, 105–6, 107; in Christian churches, 49, 54, 127–28; common lineage of, with Jews, 150, 151–52, 161; inclusion of, in feeding miracles, 66; involvement of, in crucifixion, 137–38; and Jesus, 46, 50, 67, 68–69, 70, 142; participation of, in new covenant, 109–10, 141–43, 144, 149–53 (*see also* universalism); as proselytes, 45–48, 100, 142, 158, 159, 163; relations of, with Jews, 35–36, 38, 39–54, 87, 94, 95, 97–101, 102–3, 107, 128, 141–43, 147, 156–64; symbolized by wilderness, 45
Gideon, 90
gluttony: of Christians, 19, 107–8; condemned by Moses, 108; of Jesus, 67, 71–72, 165, 166; as symbol of unlawful behavior, 71–72, 107–8
Gnostic codices, 31
Gospel of Thomas, 56–57
gospels, 1–2, 21–22, 48, 63–64, 126, 137, 141, 144, 157, 160; as passion narratives, 129, 133. *See also* John; Luke; Mark; Matthew; synoptic gospels

Habakkuk, 79
haggadah, 61, 62–63, 116, 118–19, 120, 122, 125, 130, 137n. *See also* Jubilees
halakhah, 61
Hallel, 117, 121, 123, 125, 126, 130, 145, 146–47, 156
haroseth, 122, 125, 126, 144
Hasidim, 36, 39. *See also* Judaism, Orthodox
heavenly wedding banquet, 67, 76, 88–89, 108–11, 112, 114, 115, 130
Hebrews, letter to, 113, 114; quoted, 58, 114, 147, 156, 161, 162

Herodians, 32, 35
Hosea, 44; quoted, 81, 139
ḥukkim, 7

Isaac, 86–87, 139–41
Isaiah, 47; quoted, 44, 45, 68, 74, 76, 85, 88–89
Isserles, Moses, 84n

Jeremiah, 34, 47, 48, 77; quoted, 45, 77, 78, 79, 81, 113–14, 135; vision of, 78–79
Jesus: arrest of, 118, 131, 133; as bread, 69, 85, 116–17; burial of, 134; commensalism of, 57, 69–70, 76, 90; covenant of, 19, 51, 54, 65, 66, 68, 108, 113–14, 166; crucifixion of, 63, 71n, 112–13, 118, 129, 130, 131, 132, 133, 137–38, 139, 145, 147, 153, 154, 166; and cups of wine, 77, 80, 112, 113, 126, 129–30, 145–46, 149–53; definition of "neighbor" of, 52; as "drunkard," 67, 71–72, 165; feeding miracles of, 2, 56, 66, 69, 75, 84, 110, 111, 112, 114; and fig tree, 79; and food law, 67, 68, 71; in garden of Gethsemane, 80, 130, 133, 139, 145, 157; genealogy of, 151; and gentiles, 46, 48, 50, 51, 67, 68–69, 70, 141–43, 149–53, 156–64; as "glutton," 67, 71–72, 165, 166; and heavenly wedding banquet, 67; and incomprehension of disciples, 56, 66–67, 84, 167; legitimacy of, 150–53, 166; life of, as midrash on life of Moses, 116, 127; and Moses, 49, 51, 127, 134, 139; passover of, 19, 112–13, 120, 132, 137–38, 141, 144–47, 157, 166; as passover lamb, 114, 116, 118–19, 126, 128, 129, 132, 140; resurrection of, 63, 90, 119, 129, 130, 145, 166; sources for life of, 21–22; and temple, 79; temptation of, 82, 84; trial of, 118; universalism of, 2, 19, 48, 51, 52–53, 67, 133, 137, 144–45, 166. *See also* Christianity; last supper